Mental Health among Taiwanese Americans
Gender, Immigration, and Transnational Struggles

Chien-Juh Gu

D1711718

LFB Scholarly Publishing LLC
New York 2006

Library of Congress Cataloging-in-Publication Data

Gu, Chien-Juh, 1969-
  Mental health among Taiwanese Americans : gender, immigration, and transnational struggles / Chien-Juh Gu.
     p. cm. -- (The new Americans : recent immigration and American society)
  Includes bibliographical references and index.
  ISBN 1-59332-130-9 (alk. paper)
  1. Taiwanese Americans--Mental health. 2. Immigrants--Mental health--United States. 3. Taiwanese Americans--Ethnic identity. 4. Taiwanese Americans--Social conditions. 5. Sex role--United States. 6. United States--Emigration and immigration--Psychological aspects. 7. Taiwan--Emigration and immigration--Psychological aspects. 8. Transnationalism. I. Title. II. Series: New Americans (LFB Scholarly Publishing LLC)
  E184.T35G8 2006
  155.8'4951073--dc22

2006006308

ISBN 1-59332-130-9

Printed on acid-free 250-year-life paper.

Manufactured in the United States of America.

This book is dedicated to my mother,
Chiu-Yueh Lin,
who endured all the roughness, sacrifices, and bitterness of
being a traditional Taiwanese woman throughout her life,
but raised me in a non-traditional way.

TABLE OF CONTENTS

LIST OF TABLES

LIST OF FIGURES

ACKNOWLEDGEMENTS

Like many other things in life, this book would not have been possible if I had not received encouragement, support, and assistance from others. I am grateful to all the Taiwanese Americans interviewed for this study, who generously shared with me their immigration experiences which were filled with both struggles and joy. I will never forget the time I spent in Chicago, losing myself in the stories of my informants' lives. I can only hope that my work conveys the richness and complexity of their social and emotional lives in the United States and Taiwan.

I am indebted to Rita S. Gallin, who invested tremendous amounts of time, energy, and enthusiasm throughout this research. Her critical thinking often pushed and inspired me to sharpen my arguments, and her constant encouragement was always heartening. Without her guidance and mentoring, I would not have been able to materialize this project as presented in this book. My special thanks go to Steve Gold for his insights and support, whose encouragement has facilitated the publication of this book. I am also grateful to Brendan Mullan and Toby Ten Eyck for their valuable comments, encouragement, and support. Mike Lan helped me make field contacts; my publisher, Leo Balk, provided assistance with formatting; and Pauline Acosta made useful editorial suggestions. I thank their help and patience. Russell Stone at American University was so gracious in offering me a visiting position in the sociology department that allowed me to finish this book.

Many colleagues and friends were a constant source of intellectual and personal support: Brook Kelly, Beth Dunford, Tomiko Yamaguchi, Shu-Fen Kao, Heather Dillaway, Teri Swezey, Manashi Ray, Chiai Liang, Patricia Shropshire, Linda Causey, Chuck Spurlock, Emily and Wellington Ow, Wan-Ying Yang, and Wan-Chi Chen.

Several institutions generously funded this project, including the Graduate School at Michigan State University, the Chiang Ching-Kuo Foundation, and the Institute of Sociology at Academia Sinica in Taiwan. I am thankful for their support.

Finally, I thank my husband, Yuan-kang Wang, for his love, understanding, and tolerance. A wonderful husband, father, and scholar, he has enriched my intellectual and personal life. Our sons, Kevin and Johnnie, were born during my writing of the manuscript; they both shared my musings about this book.

CHAPTER 1

INTRODUCTION

WHY STUDY ASIAN AMERICANS' MENTAL HEALTH?

Scholars have found that Asian immigrants to the United States have a lower level of distress than that of the native-born population and refugees from Southeast Asia (Berry, Kim, Minde, and Mok 1987; Meinhardt et al. 1985). They have also found that Asian immigrants tend to under-utilize mental health facilities compared to African Americans, American Indians, Latino Americans, and White Americans (Brown, Huang, and Harris 1973; Kinzie and Tseng 1978; Loo, Tong and True 1989; Matsuoka, Breaux, and Ryujin 1997; Sue and McKinney 1975; Sue and Morishima 1982; Sue, Fujino, Hu, Takeuchi, and Zane 1991). Earlier scholars describe Asian Americans as being mentally healthier than other populations in the U.S., arguing that they are generally well adjusted (Kimmich 1960; Kitano 1962; Yamamoto, James, and Palley 1968). Asian Americans (particularly Chinese and Korean) are, therefore, often regarded as relatively "problem free," just as they are perceived as a "model minority" in U.S. society.

Are Asian Americans really mentally healthier than other populations? Are they really as free from mental problems as represented in their public figure of a "model minority?" Or, do they just sublimate issues related to their emotional life and "disguise" emotional distress? Portes and Rumbaut (1996: 156) point out that migration can produce profound psychological distress, even for those who are the best prepared and most motivated, and even under the most receptive of circumstances. Several studies have found Asian Americans to be in great need of mental health services due to the stress of immigration, minority status, and discrimination (Moritsugu and Sue 1983; Snowden 1982; Wong 1982). Lee, Lei, and Sue (1991) also point out that the prevalence rates of depression, posttraumatic stress, and somatization among Asian Americans are actually as high as those for White Americans (Lee Lei, and Sue 1991). Moreover, data reported by the Centers for Disease Control and Prevention (1999, "Health, United States") indicate that elderly Asian women (more than 65 years old) had the highest suicide rate (8.8%) among female racial groups during 1995-1997. Their suicide rate was four times that of elderly Black women, and about 66 percent higher than that of elderly White women (the Centers for Disease Control and Prevention, 1999). In a study of a Filipino American community, Wolf (1997) argues that while the family is the center of identity for individuals, offering tremendous support and coherence for children of immigrants, it is also a deep source of stress and alienation that may lead to internal struggles and extreme despair. The families of some Filipino girls exercise great control over their bodies, mobility, sexuality, and education, which has led to their depression and suicidal thinking and attempts (Wolf 1997). Obviously, Asian Americans do have psychological problems. However, their low utilization rate of mental health services and cultural differences in perceiving mental problems have prevented sociologists from obtaining in-depth understanding of their psychological suffering.

Many social psychologists, such as Flaskerud and Liu (1990), Sue and Sue (1974), Suan and Tyler (1990), and Uba (1994), have attempted to provide explanations concerning Asian Americans' under-utilization of mental health services from various dimensions. They point out that Asian Americans tend to attach a stigma to mental health problems, have different ways of identifying mental disturbances, tend to choose self-reliance or to rely on the family as a means of dealing with their problems, and many have language difficulties in dealing with health care professionals (Flaskerud and Liu 1990; Sue and Sue 1974; Suan and Tyler 1990; Uba 1994). Asian Americans also tend to distrust mental health services, ignoring available facilities and/or lacking financial resources and living too far away from facilities to use them (Chen 1977; Lum 1985; Van Deusen 1982; Wong 1982). Although these cultural differences and barriers to the use of mental health services have been recognized, little is known about Asian

Americans' mental health, the social context of their emotional life, and cultural variations among sub-groups. Moreover, Asian Americans' coping behavior is seldom discussed. A few studies have documented different mental health status among Asian groups. For instance, in a community study of the prevalence of depression among Asian Americans in Seattle, Kuo (1984) reports that Koreans had the highest mean CES-D[1] score (14.4), Filipinos the second (9.7), followed by Japanese (7.3) and Chinese (6.9). Using the same measurement, Ying (1988) finds that Chinese Americans scored 11.6 on average, among which women had a higher mean score (12.8) than men (10.2). In the population studied by Hurh and Kim (1988), Koreans scored 12.6 on the CES-D scale, but the gender difference was not significant (men/women=12.3/12.9). Another study about elderly Chinese immigrants in Canada reports that women who recently migrated had poorer mental health than men (Bagley 1993).

These comparative studies have provided us with a general picture about mental health status among Asian groups. Unfortunately, systematic analyses concerning what social or cultural factors lead to these differences and how these groups' social lives and contexts differ remain unstudied. Moreover, although these comparative studies, Wolf's research (1997), and the data from CDCP have shown that women are more depressed than men across various Asian groups, the structural and contextual factors that lead to gender differences in experiencing and coping with mental distress remain unexplored.

PURPOSE OF RESEARCH

This study, with a focus on gender, explores Taiwanese Americans' migration backgrounds and social relations, and examines how these factors affect their mental health. More specifically, I investigate (1) how and why Taiwanese American men and women make decisions to migrate to the U.S.; (2) how Taiwanese American men and women experience their social relations in the family and workplace; and (3)

---

[1] CES-D, Center for Epidemiological Studies-Depression measure, is a 20-item scale used to measure depressed mood. It has been broadly used in both national and community samples since the 1970s.

how Taiwanese American men's and women's migration decisions and social relations influence their mental health. Below I discuss the purpose of this research in terms of my empirical and theoretical concerns.

Empirical Concerns: Filling Gaps in the Mental Health Research

Empirically, this study aims to fill gaps in the literature that result primarily from insufficient knowledge about Asian Americans' mental health. To achieve this goal, the focus of this study is three-fold.

First, I highlight the importance of social and cultural contexts. I examine not only the larger societal structure but also the dynamic contexts and cultural meanings within which gendered distress is produced. I also emphasize the power structure that creates unequal statuses and relations, which, in turn, impair individuals' psychological well-being. By integrating a macro analysis of structures and a micro investigation of personal experiences and interactive dynamics, this study adopts a meso approach and culturally sensitive lens to investigate Asian Americans' emotional life and to acquire an in-depth understanding of gendered distress.

Second, I investigate two important elements in Asian Americans' life experiences, migration background and minority status, that have been neglected in mental health research and immigration studies. Today's immigrants are tomorrow's ethnic groups, so a study of Asian Americans cannot ignore informants' migration history and the socio-cultural characteristics of their society of origin. This study therefore provides a more comprehensive understanding about Asian Americans' life experiences than is available in the literature.

Third, following standpoint theory, I highlight various social locations such as generation, class, and ethnicity, to discover if certain groups of Taiwanese Americans have different patterns of migration motives and social relations, and different experiences of mental distress. Most of what we know about Asian Americans comes from research done with very homogeneous populations. This study, in contrast, emphasizes heterogeneity among and within sub-groups of the sample.

Theoretical Concerns: Theorizing Mental Distress from a Structurative Perspective

In addition to the empirical concerns noted above, my theoretical concerns in this study are two-fold. First, I adopt Wolf's (1997) concept of "emotional transnationalism" to highlight the unique experience of distress immigrants and their children encounter in their social lives. By defining emotional transnationalism as "the ambivalent emotion experienced when immigrants and their children attempt to accommodate conflicting values in their search for behavioral guidance and a foundation for moral judgments from cultural norms of both their sending and receiving societies," I provide contextual illustrations concerning how men and women experience different issues of distress within various social and cultural structures.[2]

Second, I attempt to theorize mental health by utilizing Giddens' concept of structuration (1979, 1984) and Foucault's notion of power (1980).[3] I pay attention to the dual and dialectic relations between individuals and structure, underlining the fluid nature of power between the two levels. Accordingly, I consider mental distress "a result of a situation in which the confrontation between structure and individuals produces negative effects on people's psychological well-being," and highlight the effects of socio-cultural structure, power relations, and agency on individuals' experience of distress.

RESEARCH METHODS

I relied on qualitative methods, semi-structured in-depth interviews and limited participant observations, to explore Taiwanese Americans'

---

[2] Although Wolf (1997) coined the term "emotional transnationalism" to describe the emotional struggles second-generation Filipinos went through, she left this notion undefined in her work. I thus provide a definition of emotional transnationalism in this book.

[3] In his structuration theory, Giddens (1984, 1979) argues that the encounters between individuals and structures are on-going and dialectic processes within which agency is exercised. Structure is therefore both enabling and constraining. Moreover, Foucault (1980) insists that power is fluid, and "there are no relations of power without resistances" (Foucault 1980: 142). These notions are central in my conceptual framework (see Chapter Three).

distress experiences. From January to October, 2001, I conducted 54 interviews in the Chicago metropolitan area with 27 women and 27 men. This group of informants was selected in order to maximize variation in generation, age, social class, and occupation. In addition, I also conducted participant observations to enhance my understanding of Taiwanese immigrants' social life. While one-on-one interviewing enabled me to explore Taiwanese Americans' social relations and their effects on mental health, participating in various social activities in the Taiwanese immigrant community helped me to experience and observe the social life of this ethnic group.

PLAN OF BOOK

This book is composed of nine chapters. This first chapter explains the rationale and purpose of this study, outlines my empirical and theoretical concerns, discusses my research methods, and describes the organization of this book. Chapter Two reviews existing bodies of literature on gender and mental health and immigrants' adaptation issues. It also discusses the contributions of and gaps in these substantial literatures that inform and shape this study.

Chapter Three describes my research questions, discusses theoretical perspectives that serve as the foundations of this study, and presents my conceptual and analytical frameworks.[4] There I introduce concepts in the political economy of health, feminist thinking (critiques of mental health research and standpoint theory), and the notion of emotional transnationalism, and discuss how these theoretical insights are used to undergird my study. I also summarize traditional definitions of mental health as well as demonstrate why I use "mental distress' in this book to represent the continuum concept of mental health and illness. Because this is a study of minority mental health, I emphasize the structural (both social and cultural) contexts that result in Taiwanese Americans' disadvantages, differences, and uniqueness in U.S. society that, in turn, cause their mental distress. I insist that unless we situate mental distress in larger social structures and explore its

---

[4] The conceptual framework demonstrates my theoretical concerns, while the analytical framework illustrates my empirical research questions.

cultural meanings, we will not understand the distress Asian Americans encounter, perceive, and manage.

Chapter Four explains the methodological approach of this study, clarifies key terms, describes the research site, and details the methods and processes of collecting and analyzing data. In this chapter I provide a profile of the sample and discuss possible sampling biases and their causes. I also emphasize some ethical issues I confronted during the research and illustrate research difficulties during the recruiting and interviewing processes.

Chapter Five illustrates the push- and pull- factors that lead to Taiwanese immigration to the United States, and introduces the history, politics, and socio-cultural characteristics of Taiwan. In this chapter I also analyze the demographic features of Taiwanese immigrants by using data from the U.S. Immigration and Naturalization Service (INS) and U.S. Bureau of the Census.

In Chapters Six through Eight I present the major findings about three socio-cultural contexts of mental distress facing Taiwanese Americans. Each chapter stands alone in describing a particular context, yet together they create a large picture of Asian Americans' lives and a better understanding of their distress experiences than the existing literature. In these chapters I highlight specific social and cultural factors that produce gendered distress in the Taiwanese American community. I also analyze commonalities among and differences between informants who are in different social locations. By so doing, I highlight the heterogeneity of personal experiences in the sample, as well as the complexity of contextual effects on individuals' social and emotional lives.[5]

Chapter Six reveals Taiwanese Americans' motives for initial emigration and permanent settlement, analyzes who in the family made the decision to migrate, and discusses how this migration decision affects informants' mental health.

Chapter Seven delves into the gendered power structure of Taiwanese American families by exploring the division of domestic labor and family decisions about finances and children's education. It

---

[5] Individuals' social locations shape both their social and emotional lives. In some contexts, the way social life is organized directly affects individuals' mental health, while within others personal distress is engendered by other mechanisms.

also examines if and how familial relations that are built upon gendered and generational power structures generate mental distress. I demonstrate how power relations intertwine with transnationalism in creating emotional struggles, and how individuals in varied social locations exhibit agencies in such struggles.

Chapter Eight explores Taiwanese Americans' experiences of racial and sexual discrimination in the workplace, their relations with co-workers, and how these experiences and relations affect their psychological well-being.

Finally, Chapter Nine provides a summary of my research and conclusions. I summarize my empirical findings and then discuss them from a structurative perspective. Here I highlight the importance of understanding the structural (both social and cultural) context within which mental distress is produced. I conclude by arguing that the psychological struggles facing Taiwanese Americans are not only gendered but also are transnational. Power relations and emotional transnationalism serve as two key mechanisms for producing mental distress. Personal agencies are exerted within the context of such struggles. Following these discussions, I present a model to theorize the process of Taiwanese Americans' experience of distress. In ending, I discuss the limitations of this study as well as suggest directions for future research.

CHAPTER 2

LITERATURE REVIEW

This study aims to enhance sociological understanding of Asian Americans' mental health through a case study of Taiwanese immigrants to the United States. To achieve this goal, in this chapter I review two bodies of literature, the *sociology of mental health* and *immigration studies*, to provide background knowledge and thus contribute to the theoretical foundations of this research.

The sociology of mental health, in which social psychology is the leading approach, has produced abundant empirical findings regarding various aspects of mental health. It also has produced an abundance of sociological knowledge on the subject of gender and mental health, thereby providing a theoretical foundation upon which this project rests. Immigration studies, in contrast, have largely examined the immigrant adaptation process and its psychological outcomes. This literature not only has established important theories of immigrant adaptation, it also has revealed various problems immigrants and their children encounter in the adaptation process. In addition, the ongoing and inseparable relationship between immigration and ethnicity makes it impossible to overlook the migration background of ethnic groups. As Kelly and Schauffler (1996: 31) state, "Today's ethnics are the immigrants of the past and vice versa; present immigrants are already forging tomorrow's ethnic identities." Reviewing the literature of immigration studies therefore helps us to understand the historical backgrounds, social positions, and life situations of ethnics that distinguish them from the general population.

In this chapter, I start by reviewing key notions in the sociology of mental health. I highlight definitional issues concerning mental health, and then synthesize important findings concerning gender differences in mental health. Next, I review the major theories and research reports in the literature of immigration studies that are relevant to this project. I illustrate various perspectives on immigrant adaptation, and then synthesize empirical findings concerning adaptation and mental health. Finally, I briefly summarize key issues derived from the overview of the two areas reviewed in this chapter, and discuss gaps remaining in the literature. Throughout this discussion, I explain why additional concepts are needed to build the conceptual framework that serves as the scaffolding of this project.

SOCIOLOGY OF MENTAL HEALTH

To review key notions in the sociology of mental health that inform my study, I first highlight definitional issues surrounding mental health and illness, then synthesize empirical findings concerning the social determinants of gender differences in mental health status.

Definitional Issues Concerning Mental Health

The definition of "mental health" varies across different periods and contexts, and it has different meanings to different researchers (Horwitz and Scheid 1999). Throughout the 1970s, researchers in the field of mental health used a continuous model, perceiving mental health and illness as two opposite poles of a continuum. From this standpoint, researchers considered most people to fall somewhere in between these two extremes; therefore, the boundary between mental health and illness was fluid and subject to social and environmental influences.

Since the 1980s, however, with the growth of biomedical knowledge, this continuum notion has shifted toward an increased emphasis on a discrete model of mental illness. Mental health and illness are seen as opposites that form a dichotomy. Based on this perspective, people are either mentally well or ill, and the genetic, biological, biochemical, or neurological causes of mental illness have been increasingly regarded as the major bases of mental illness (Michels and Marzuk 1993). For example, most psychiatrists and other mental health professionals consider various forms of mental illness as indicators of disease. They thus use a standardized guidebook, the DSM-IV (Diagnostic and Statistical Manual, Forth Edition), to identify symptoms that constitute mental illness.[6] Influenced by this biomedical model, most contemporary sociologists adopt this discrete perspective and consider "mental health" and "mental illness" antonyms (Aneshensel and Phelan 1999: 3).

Sociologists who adopt the discrete model examine various aspects of mental illness, including stress (Aneshensel, Rutter, and Lachenbruch 1991; Gore 1992; Lennon 1999; Pearlin 1999; Thoits 1999; Turner and Roszell 1994), distress (Eaton and Muntaner 1999; Mirowsky and Ross 1995; Reskin and Corerman 1985), depression (Kandel, Davies, and Raveis 1985; Turner, Wheaton, and Lloyd 1995; Vilhjalmsson 1993), anxiety (Walters 1993; Zuckerman 1989), and substance abuse (Rosenfield 1999). These issues are treated as distinct topics or sub-areas in the sociology of mental health, embracing totally different research foci, conceptual definitions, measurements, and theories. For instance, stress researchers focus mainly on the "stress process" that is made up of stressors, moderators or buffers, and outcomes. Sociologists of stress strive to identify social stressors – usually using a checklist of stressful life events -- and to examine moderators that buffer the psychological effects engendered by stressors. Scholars interested in the stress process also examine group variations in distress --the reaction to stress -- exploring if and why certain groups respond to stress more vulnerably than others. Depression researchers, in contrast, tend to measure the degree of depressive symptoms among individuals – usually using the CES-D scale – and compare various sub-groups in community populations.[7] They also study clinical cases that have been diagnosed as depressed by medical professionals, investigating social factors that produce depression and patients' help-seeking behavior.

While most sociologists examine how and why social factors make various groups more or less likely to develop psychiatric disorders,

---

[6] DSM-IV refers to the "Diagnostic and Statistical Manual of Mental Disorders, Fourth Edition," published by the American Psychiatric Association in 1994. This manual is used by mental health professionals to set forth diagnostic criteria, descriptions, and other information to guide the diagnosis of mental disorders.

[7] CES-D, Center for Epidemiological Studies-Depression measure, is a 20-item scale used to measure depressive symptoms.

others look at the issue of mental illness from a totally different angle: They ask, "How do social factors affect the way people define mental illness?" Scholars who adopt this tradition, so called labeling theorists or social constructionists, argue that definitions of mental disorders are socially labeled or constructed. Thus, they focus on examining this labeling process and revealing the social factors and mechanisms that are involved in it. From this standpoint, mental illness is designated a form of abnormal behavior that deviates from social norms. The label may thus result in negative social consequences such as stigma, social isolation, withdrawal, and low self-esteem in the labeled individual (Phelan and Link 1999). Since every society has behavioral norms, the definitions and perceptions concerning mental disorders can vary by social contexts and cultural values. They also change at different points of time and history. Many cultural anthropologists such as Good (1977), Lutz and White (1986), and Marsella and his colleagues (1985) also share similar ideas and emphasize the importance of culture within which mental illness is perceived, experienced, and expressed. Moreover, some sociologists who adopt the constructionist approach perceive mental illness as a form of social control (e.g., Conrad and Schneider 1992; Friedson 1970; Horwitz 2002). They examine how psychiatrists and other mental health professionals serve to control abnormal or disruptive behavior by virtue of their medical power to define and label mental disorders.

Gender Differences in Mental Health and Their Determinants: The Social Psychological Approach

Gender differences in mental health status have been the subject of scholarly debates. Nevertheless, a great number of studies in social psychological research support the finding that women are more likely than men to be mentally ill (Aneshensel 1992; Caldwell, Pearson, and Chin 1987; Dohrenwend and Dohrenwend 1974; Gove 1972; 1987; Gove and Tudor 1973; Mirowsky and Ross 1986). For example, Gove and Tudor (1973) find that women uniformly have higher rates of psychiatric treatment in mental hospitals, inpatient psychiatric treatment in general hospitals, and outpatient care in psychiatric clinics than do men. Aneshensel (1992) and Mirowsky and Ross (1986) also find that women report higher average levels of depression and anxiety than men. Several studies, (e.g., Bebbington 1996; McGrath, Keita, Strickland, and Russo 1990; Nolen-Hoeksema 1990; Ussher 1991) also identify depression as a problem that particularly afflicts women.

Why do women outnumber men in the population that has mental problems? To investigate this subject, social psychologists mainly adopt two approaches. One examines gender differences in personal characteristics (such as vulnerability, personality traits, self-concepts, and coping strategies), and their effects on mental health. The other stresses the structural factors that produce gender inequality in society, and considers such forces a major cause of one gender's higher rate of mental illness than the other. Family structure, employment status, housework load, multiple roles, social networks, social support, and poverty exemplify these structural factors.

Adopting the first approach, for instance, Newman (1986) and Thoits (1986) attribute the causes of gender differences in mental health to the differential vulnerability and responsiveness of men and women. Both of their studies provide evidence that women are more vulnerable than men to psychological distress and depression. In another study, Zukerman (1989: 442-443) finds that women have less confidence, self-esteem, self-sufficiency, coping ability, public speaking abilities, and leadership than men, which leads to their greater reported symptoms of depression, anxiety, and anger when under stress.

The second approach, the so-called "social causation model," views social structures and social relations as the major determinants of mental health. Family structure (including parenthood and marital status) and employment are two of the most often examined variables in this approach. According to Broman (1991), in general, married people have greater levels of psychological well-being than the non-married, but married women have higher rates of mental illness than married men and single women. In a recent study, Simon (2002) argues that the emotional benefits of marriage apply equally to women and men, but that women and men respond to marital transitions with different emotional problems. In addition, amount of housework and number of children are two major family conditions that have an important negative influence on married women's mental health (Lennon and Rosenfield 1992). Husbands' support and sharing of responsibilities for childcare and housework help reduce married women's risk of mental illness, especially for employed women with multiple roles (Dennerstein 1995). However, sharing domestic work has been found to increase a husband's degree of depressive symptoms (Glass and Fujimoto 1994).

A few studies have discussed the influence of family structure on African Americans' mental distress and the gender differences that emerge as a result of this influence, although the findings remain inconsistent (Ball and Robbins 1986; Reskin and Coverman 1985; Zollar and Williams 1987). Broman (1991) argues that African Americans' family structure is different from that in White families, a factor which is often overlooked in discussions of family stress. In contrast, Asian Americans' familial relations and ideologies have been more frequently studied than their family structure. For instance, several scholars point out that close family ties provide Asian Americans with important support for dealing with psychological problems (Sue and Morishima 1982; Uba 1994). Wolf (1997) finds, however, that the strong family ideology pervading Filipino families encourages the imposition of patriarchal power over young girls and causes serious mental problems.

As for the association between employment and mental health, women's participation in the paid labor force has been found to be an important contributor to their general psychological well-being (Bernard 1984; Dennerstein 1995; Glass and Fujimoto 1994). However, in comparisons of employed women with housewives and men, the reliability of this contention requires reservation because the empirical data have been quite inconsistent. Some studies find that although employed women have lower levels of distress than housewives, both groups of women are more distressed than employed men (Radloff 1975). Others find no difference between employed women and housewives (Cleary and Mechanic 1983; Pearlin 1975). Still others find that employed women do not differ from employed men in levels of distress (Gore and Mangione 1983; Kessler and McRae 1982).

To examine further the conditions under which employment contributes to or constrains women's mental health, some researchers have investigated various control variables that theoretically modify this association. Their findings illustrate that job control, autonomy, and complexity enhance employed women's psychological well-being (Hall 1989; Lennon and Rosenfield 1992; Pugliesi 1992; Rosenfield

1989). Employment also has interaction effects with family structure on women's mental health. Working for pay buffers women's marital stress, whereas parenting has a negative and exacerbating effect on work-related stress (Kandel, Davies, and Raveis 1985). Such interaction effects between women's paid work and unpaid housework are generally addressed in the literature as an issue about how women's multiple roles influence their mental health. Empirical research does provide evidence that certain sets of multiple roles are beneficial for women's psychological well-being (Pugliesi 1992; Thoits 1983). Nevertheless, the consequences of multiple role obligations are not uniformly positive. While women who engage in paid work in most cases still perform the vast majority of domestic work, multiple roles for them could lead to extra burdens and consequently cause higher rates of distress and depression as compared to employed married men and single employed women (Cleary and Mechanic 1983; Pugliesi 1992). Employed married women with young children especially experience higher levels of distress than their childless counterparts or comparable men (Cleary and Mechanic 1983; Thoits 1986).

IMMIGRATION STUDIES

Adapting to the host society is a primary task immigrants carry out in the process of their settlement in a foreign land. It is also one of the key factors that affect immigrants' mental health because adaptation is not always a smooth process, nor does it guarantee successful outcomes. In this section, I first review theories of immigrant adaptation in the literature, then discuss the association between adaptation and mental health.

Adaptation Theories

Studies of immigrant adaptation have a long history, which has fostered continuous refinement of theories in this area. Four approaches synthesize theoretical perspectives on this subject in the literature: (1) assimilation theory, (2) multiculturalism, (3) structuralist perspective, and (4) segmented assimilation theory.

Assimilation Theory

Assimilation theory is a classic perspective of immigrant adaptation. Its main arguments rest on the assumption that diverse immigrant groups will eventually abandon their old ways of life and cultures, and completely melt into the mainstream society. Scholars who adopt this approach, such as Park (1928) and Stonequist (1961), consider assimilation a natural process. They believe that through residential integration and occupational achievement in a sequence of succeeding generations, immigrants will ultimately be integrated into the host society regardless of the "draw-back force" exerted by the culture of their origin (Park 1928). To further elaborate this classical assimilationist theory, Warner and Srole (1945) highlight institutional factors that determine rates of assimilation such as racial and ethnic subsystems, social class, and occupational mobility. They argue that ascribed characteristics (e.g., skin color, native languages, and religion) to a large extent affect the level of acceptance of minorities by the dominant group. These factors in addition to socio-economic status determine the pace of complete assimilation for various groups. In spite of the fact that distinctive ethnic traits are sources of disadvantages that negatively affect assimilation, their effects will be reduced in each succeeding generation.

Gordon (1964) provides a typology to capture the complexity of the assimilation process, which includes cultural, structural, attitude-receptional, behavior-receptional, marital, identificational, and civic assimilation. He argues that "cultural assimilation," or "acculturation," is the first step immigrants take when adapting to the host society. It is also the key of successful adjustment. In Gordon's view, acculturation does not automatically lead to other types of assimilation; it may take place even when no other form of assimilation occurs. In contrast, "structural assimilation" is the "keystone of the arch of assimilation" that will inevitably lead to other forms of assimilation (Gordon, 1964: 81). Gordon believes that most ethnic groups will eventually lose all their distinctive characteristics as they pass through the stages of assimilation.

Regardless of its popularity, classical assimilation theory has encountered challenges since the early 1960s. Instead of convergent assimilation as this perspective predicted, several studies have observed otherwise. For instance, Kao and Tienda (1995), Rumbaut and Ima

(1988), and Landale and Oropesa (1995) all report that length of U.S. residence positively correlates with maladaptive outcomes across immigrant groups, which is a pattern opposite from the conventional assimilation model of adaptation. These scholars observed that rather than diminishing, the disadvantages of immigrants are reproduced in succeeding generations.[8] To explain this phenomenon, Landale and Oropesa (1995) highlight the key factor of acculturation. They argue that even if the parental generation is able to achieve high social positions and incomes, their inability to embrace the dominant culture may greatly subvert their children's access to these gains. Other scholars also enthusiastically defend the classic assimilationism by providing supplementary explanations for the divergent outcomes of assimilation. For instance, Gans (1992b) argues that immigrants' assimilation follows a bumpy-line model; different patterns of assimilation are various bumps in the process of eventually assimilating into nonethnic America. Alba and Nee (1997) also believe that the anomalies assimilation theory fails to explain are adverse effects of unpredictable structural changes, so various outcomes of assimilation are merely differences in the speed of assimilation.

Multiculturalism

In contrast to assimilationists who assume a unified core of American society into which immigrants are expected to assimilate, multiculturalists perceive American society as a heterogeneous collection of racial and ethnic minority groups (Glazer and Moynihan 1970; Handlin 1973). They believe that immigrants are active actors who shape their lives rather than passive victims of Americanizing forces (Conzen 1991). From this viewpoint, pre-migration cultural attributes are not inferior traits that will necessarily be obliterated by the mainstream culture. Rather, these "primitive" characteristics

---

[8] Gans (1992a) uses the term "the second generation decline" to describe the phenomenon that immigrant children from less fortunate socioeconomic families have a much harder time than their middle-class counterparts in succeeding at school and assimilating into middle-class America. He anticipates that these children will exhibit high rates of crime, unemployment, drug use, and other problems associated with poverty, a situation Perlmann and Waldinger (1996) call "the second generation revolt."

persistently interact with the host society to reshape and recreate themselves. Through a process of reconfiguration and recreation, immigrants' original cultural attributes are transformed to ones that characterize an ethnicity which deviates from both homeland and host cultures.

Structuralism

The structuralist perspective focuses on the advantages and disadvantages inherent in social structures that lead to different levels of social adaptation among ethnic groups. From this standpoint, immigrants are constrained by an ethnic and racial hierarchy that systematically limits their access to important social resources such as education, economic opportunities, and housing. These constraints consequently result in ethnic and racial inequalities in social-economic status, educational attainment, and occupational achievement (Portes and Borocz 1989).

Segmented Assimilation Theory

Segmented assimilation theory aims to explain why different patterns of adaptation emerge among immigrant groups, an issue that other approaches have understudied. As Portes and Zhou (1993) argue, assimilation outcomes are segmented. They are a consequence of the interaction between the social context in which children of immigrants grow up (such as family class status, geographic location, and changes in the structure of labor markets) and their acculturation patterns (such as proficiency in English, aspiration and motivation, and educational achievement) (also see Alba and Nee 1997; Gans 1992; Portes and Rumbaut 1996: 247-253). At least three possible directions categorize the divergent destinies of immigrants' adaptation: (1) the upward-mobility pattern (i.e., the acculturation and economic integration into the normative structures of middle-class America) (2) the downward-mobility pattern (i.e., the acculturation and parallel integration into the underclass) and (3) economic integration into middle-class America, with deferred acculturation and intentional preservation of the ethnic group's values and solidarity (Portes and Zhou 1993; Zhou 1997).

In sum, assimilationists examine how immigrants and the generations that succeed them change their ways of life and gradually merge into the receiving society. Multiculturalists recognize the active role of immigrants' pre-migration cultures in reshaping ethnic life. Structuralists focus on the socio-economic structure of the receiving society that affects how immigrants adopt host country ways. Segmented assimilationists aim to explain how and why various forms of adaptation occur among different immigrant groups. Regardless of their varying theoretical stances, the four traditions are all concerned with how immigrants and their children adapt to the host society and with the forces that promote or impede the progress of their assimilation. They also have observed a parallel phenomenon that divergent assimilation does occur among immigrant groups (Zhou 1997). As Rumbaut (1996) correctly points out, segmented adaptations do not take place only among different ethnic groups, but also within the same ethnic group, the same school, the same ethnic neighborhood, and even the same family. While recognizing diverse adaptation patterns among and within ethnic groups, the differences in the forces that improve or impede individuals' psychological well-being in the process of adaptation should also be examined, albeit cautiously.

Generation, Adaptation, and Psychological Well-being

Early sociological studies of subjective immigration experiences center on the themes of "alienation" and "marginality" (Portes and Rumbaut 1996: 155-159). For instance, Thomas and Znaniechi's book, *The Polish Peasant in Europe and America* (1984), explores the struggle for self-esteem by young male immigrants from Russian Poland at the end of the nineteen century and the social disorganization that characterized their community; Handlin's volume, *The Uprooted* (1973), examines the common stress of "uprooting" among immigrants; and Stonequist's book, *The Marginal Man: A Study in Personality and Cultural Conflict* (1961), discusses the double edged marginality of immigrants' social location. "Uprooted" from their society of origin, immigrants inevitably tend to feel alienated, powerless, and marginalized in the receiving country. These feelings become the major source of stress in their experience of migration. Moreover, the cultural conflicts of two worlds in immigrants' minds bring profound transformation in various aspects of individuals' personality (Stonequist 1961). Epidemiological studies and community health research (e.g., Faris and Dunham 1939; Srole, Langner, and Mitchell 1962) also have shown an association between immigration and mental disturbance; higher rates of hospital admissions and incidence of mental disorders were found in immigrant groups than in the general population. Lower-class immigrants in particular were more vulnerable than their middle-class counterparts to the psychological traumas of resettlement and adaptation (Srole, Langner, and Mitchell 1962).

Several comparative studies highlight contemporary sociological research on immigrant mental health: Berry and his colleagues (1987) compare acculturation stress among ethnic minorities in Canada; Kuo (1984) examines the prevalence of depressive symptoms among Asian American groups; Meinhardt and his associates (1985) explore the need for mental health care among Asian immigrants in Silicon Valley; and Ying (1988) and Bagley (1993) investigate gender differences in mental health status among Chinese immigrants. These studies have drawn fairly parallel conclusions, based on what Portes and Rumbaut (1996: 168) call "contexts of exit." They found high rates of mental disturbances in the lower-class, refugees (compared to voluntary immigrants), women, the elderly, the un-employed, the less-educated, those who lack English proficiency, and those who lack co-ethnic social support (Bagley 1993; Berry et al. 1987; Meinhardt et al. 1985; Kuo 1984; Rumbaut 1999b; Ying 1988). These results are also analogous to the findings for the general population. People who occupy disadvantaged positions in society tend to have a poorer mental health status than their counterparts (Portes and Rumbaut 1996: 155-191). Nevertheless, time affects immigrants' mental health status because contexts of exit, as noted above, gradually lose their significance when "contexts of reception" gain salience (Portes and Rumbaut 1996; Rumbaut 1989). For both refugees and voluntary immigrants of various social classes, time attenuates the severity of depressive symptoms that are engendered by settlement and adaptation.

In contrast, the impact of acculturation on immigrants' psychological well-being has been under debate. While earlier assimilation scholars commonly believed that acculturation benefits both economic achievement and psychological well-being, several contemporary studies have challenged this assumption. For instance,

Burnam and her colleagues (1987), Kaplan and Marks (1990), and Vega and his associates (1984) all found a high prevalence of mental distress in highly acculturated immigrants. Schnittker (2000) also reports that participating in Chinese cultural activities decreases Chinese immigrants' depression to a significant extent. Several studies of immigrant physical health also show supportive evidence that, when compared to their U.S.-born counterparts, immigrants not only tend to practice less risky behaviors, their infants also tend to have superior health outcomes and better pre-pregnancy nutrition than the general population (Portes and Rumbaut 1996; Rumbaut 1999a). By underlining these ironies and paradoxes that classic assimilation theory fails to explain, Rumbaut (1999a) reminds sociologists to carefully examine various effects of assimilation and acculturation on immigrant groups. Why does the acculturation progress not necessarily lead to positive mental health outcomes? Portes and Rumbaut (1996) argue that acculturated immigrants may hold more realistic perceptions about American society than newcomers and thus, become more critical concerning its shortcomings such as racial discrimination. They also believe that acculturation may itself be a traumatic process rather than a simple solution to the traumas of immigration.

Sociological studies concerning the adaptation process of "the new second generation" (children of post-1965 immigrants) have mushroomed since the 1990s. This literature focuses mainly on issues of education attainment, bilingualism, and ethnic and racial identity. While these subjects all relate to psychological well-being in one way or another, only a few studies directly investigate the theme of mental health. In a study of high-school youth in southern California and South Florida, Rumbaut (1996) examines second-generation immigrants' psychological adaptation in terms of ethnic identities and self-esteem. He concludes that gender, parental nationality, family context, perceptions of discrimination, and residential location are all determinant factors that affect the self identifications and mental health of second-generation immigrants. In his study, parent-child conflict, followed by gender, is the most significant factor that correlates with respondents' low self-esteem and high depressive symptoms. Other factors such as economic stress and perceived discrimination are also somewhat associated with both low self-esteem and high depressive symptoms. English-language proficiency and educational achievement are positively related to self-esteem but not significantly in relation to depression. Moreover, recentness of arrival and perceived discrimination lead to high depression scores but do not lower self-esteem (Rumbaut 1996).

A recent study of Portes and Rumbaut (2001: 192-232) confirms most findings in the research noted above. Among all factors in the exploratory model developed by Portes and Rumbaut, gender and family contexts continue to be the most significant, affecting both the self-esteem and depressive symptoms of the second-generation. Women and people whose families indicate "dissonant" acculturation tend to show a high level of depressive symptoms.[9] In another study of Filipino youth, Wolf (1997) shows that second-generation girls suffer psychological despair as a result of the strict control imposed by their parents. A recent study of Portes and Zady (2002) also documents women's high level of depression across various Spanish-speaking groups of second-generation immigrants, confirming again the significance of gender in this subject of inquiry. Gender and family contexts, therefore, are two noteworthy factors for investigating the psychological well-being of the new second generation.

Family support and ethnic networks have been found to benefit immigrants' mental health and adaptation process. In an earlier study, for example, Lin and his associates (1979) report that group membership decreases distress among Chinese Americans. Portes and Rumbaut (1996) also point out that having close coethnic friends reduces immigrants' experience of stress. In another study, Kuo and Tsai (1986) state that immigrants' social ties to both the immigrant community and the host society help ease immigrants' cultural adaptation. By identifying parent-child conflict as one of the key factors that obstruct psychological adaptation of immigrants and their children, Rumbaut (1996) highlights the importance of family ties and support for enhancing both generations' mental health. In a study

---

[9] According to Portes and Rumbaut (1996:241), generational dissonance occurs when the parental generation lacks adequate education or is insufficiently integrated into the host society to guide their children in the acculturation progress. This situation will lead to role reversal between parents and children as the first generation depends on their children for helping them cope with the outside environment.

regarding Mexican and Central-American immigrants, Padilla and her associates (1988) report that social support derived from ethnic networks serves as an effective mechanism for overcoming various difficulties in adapting to American society. Moreover, O'Connor (1990) found that Mexican immigrant women create female-centered networks in order to adapt to the new and foreign environment of the work place. In a study regarding Greek and Filipino immigrants in Australia, Niles (1999) argues that a strong sense of cultural identity, support from family, and association with members of their ethnic community are all important factors for helping immigrants to deal with racism and discrimination. Zhou (2003) also shows that participating in ethnic institutions not only nurtures ethnic identity of second-generation Chinese, it also provides them with cultural resources for coping with familial conflicts. Close family relations and connections with the ethnic community, therefore, play important roles in enhancing immigrants' psychological well-being.

SUMMARY AND DISCUSSION

The two bodies of literature reviewed in this chapter, the sociology of mental health and immigration studies, provide fundamental knowledge that informs and shapes this study. Summarizing from the literature review, gender is a significant variable in mental health research. Abundant evidence in both bodies of literature has repeatedly shown the vulnerability of women's psychological well-being, highlighting the importance of investigating the subject of gender and mental health. Family contexts are another noteworthy factor. The sociology of mental health has examined various family factors -- such as family structure, marital status, and the division of domestic labor – and their effects on mental health by gender. Immigration studies, on the other hand, focus more on parent-child conflicts, acculturation discrepancies between parents and children, and the impact of these factors on mental health. The sociology of mental health also has explored how work (e.g., employment status, work autonomy, and multiple roles) affect women's and men's psychological wellbeing, but the connection between these phenomena has rarely been discussed in the literature about immigration and immigrants' mental health.

Inadequacy in the Literature: What Don't We Know about Asian Americans' Mental Health?

As noted above, empirical research has established abundant sociological knowledge about gender and mental health. Nevertheless, some gaps remain in the literature.

First, the discrete model of mental health that is prevalent in contemporary sociology presumes a universal presentation of mental disorders but ignores cultural variations in which mental problems are perceived, experienced, and presented. Sociologists who adopt the discrete approach often use symptom-check lists, large-scale surveys, or clinical data in their studies because these measurements can identify individuals who show specific psychological disturbances. These methods, that are highly influenced by modern biomedical ideology, however, risk the possibility of losing validity when they are administered to ethnic or cultural groups that perceive mental illness otherwise than the researchers or mental health professionals. As Fabrega (1990) insists, contemporary mental health paradigms lack cultural sensitivity that is suitable for studying Hispanic groups. I observed this problem in mental health studies of Asian Americans as well. In particular, a great number of studies have reported that Asian Americans tend to underutilize mental health services (Brown, Huang, and Harris 1973; Sue and Morishima 1982; Sue et al. 1991; Matsuoka, Breaux, and Ryujin 1997) and tend to attach cultural values to mental illness different from the White population (Lum 1985; Sue and Sue 1974; Uba 1994; Wong 1982), but only a few studies have considered the issue of cultural appropriateness in adopting research strategies. I suggest that the continuum model, in this case, allows more flexibility and space for developing sociological explanations that are culturally sensitive.

Second, in general, sociological studies of mental health are based on the social experiences of the White middle-class. When race is discussed, it is often Blacks rather than other racial or ethnic groups that provide a reference point for the White population. Little is known about Asian Americans, except their low utilization rate of mental health services. Moreover, when Asian Americans are included in discussions of mental health, they tend to be homogenized. As Sue and his colleagues (1994: 61) correctly point out, "substantial individual differences exist between different Asian American groups and within each group." Unfortunately, the unique social characteristics of individual Asian groups remain overlooked. This neglect exists not only in the general discussion of mental health, but also across various sub-topics in the literature.

In contrast, immigration studies have dealt with many issues concerning immigrants' psychological adaptation. By highlighting adjustment difficulties and consequent psychological effects among immigrants and their children, immigration studies to some extent correct the deficiencies found in the sociology of mental health. Nevertheless, problems associated with immigration do not constitute a complete picture of the mental health issues confronting Asian Americans. Many social factors that are important in mental health research such as family structure, spousal relationships, and the division of domestic labor, have not yet been well explored in the field of immigration studies of psychological well-being. While migration background demonstrates Asian Americans' historical and cultural origins, minority status illustrates their position in American society. The former significantly shapes Asian Americans' social practices and values, where the latter to a large extent determines the ethnic and racial relations in which migrants are embedded. These two structural factors are inseparable; they interweave with each other in shaping Asian Americans' social life. I therefore suggest that both migration background and minority status need to be addressed in order to acquire a more comprehensive understanding than currently exists of the structural contexts that situate Asian Americans' life.

Third, social contexts have been ignored to a large extent in social psychological studies of mental health (Hall 1989). Mental health studies tend to be empirical examinations of specific variables. This tendency often overlooks the social contexts and the larger societal structure within which the social experience of mental distress is produced. Although a few sociologists have attempted to consider social context and structure in mental health research (e.g., Broman 1991; Wolf 1997), the dynamic social context of emotional life remains ignored in the literature. The major research method of the sociology of mental health -- large-scale surveys -- might make this goal difficult because quantitative approaches are not designed for capturing dynamic contexts surrounding the inquiry. In her study of Filipino families, Wolf (1997) provides some evidence that a qualitative approach can help contexualize the social dynamics of emotional life, which are what quantitative measurements fail to reveal. She thus advocates more in-depth qualitative investigations of immigrant mental health.

The omission of social contexts within immigration studies is apparent as well. For instance, several studies have reported the significance of gender differences in mental health status both among immigrants and among the second generation (e.g., Bagley 1993; Portes and Rumbaut 2001; Portes and Zady 2002; Rumbaut 1996). Nevertheless, *why* women show more distressed or depressed states than men in these cases is rarely explored. Nor is it well examined *if* and *how* the social contexts that cause gender differences in mental health vary across immigrant groups. From the findings of previous studies, we obtain a picture that women are generally more distressed than men across Hispanic and Asian groups, but we do not know if the social factors and contexts that cause these gender differences differ in various groups and how. Are Hispanic and Asian women more depressed than their male counterparts because of the same reasons? If yes, what are these common factors? If not, what is responsible for their dissimilarities and why? What are the similarities and differences within Hispanic or between Asian groups? Do gender relations, ideologies, family structure and values differ between Hispanics and Asians? Do they differ among these two ethnic groups? How and why? To answer these questions, I argue that in-depth qualitative investigations, as Wolf (1997) and Agbayani-Siewert, Takeuchi, and Pangan (1999) advocate, are needed for contextualizing individuals' emotional life.

The sociology of mental health and immigration studies have greatly contributed to the establishment of sociological knowledge concerning Asian Americans' mental health. As the literature reviewed in this chapter shows, empirical studies in the sociology of mental health provide a valuable empirical foundation for investigating key determinants that lead to gender differences in mental health status. Immigration studies, on the other hand, highlight important adaptation issues confronting immigrants and their children. These two bodies of literature, however, leave gaps that demand to be filled.

Despite the rich discussions on gender differences in mental health, Asian Americans' life experiences and social contexts have been overlooked. This neglect is due, in part, to the fact that current research definitions and measurements are not culturally sensitive to the study of ethnic groups. It is therefore necessary to redefine mental health and develop research strategies that are different from those adopted in the conventional approach. Moreover, immigration studies have pointed out various adaptation difficulties that confront Asian immigrants and their children, but more in-depth qualitative research is needed to further contextualize factors surrounding their psychological adaptation. Investigations also need to be expanded in order to go beyond the migration-related problems that are documented in the current literature of immigration studies. These gaps are the focus of my study of Taiwanese Americans' mental health. To pursue this goal, I suggest that incorporating concepts from the political economy of health, feminist thinking, and the emerging field of transnational studies can help fill these gaps. In the next chapter, I discuss how these perspectives, along with the two bodies of literature reviewed in this chapter, contribute to the conceptual and analytical frameworks of this project.

CHAPTER 3

THEORETICAL FOUNDATIONS AND CONCEPTUAL FRAMEWORK

In Chapter Two, I synthesized major empirical findings concerning gender and mental health, and summarized the results of studies about adaptation difficulties confronting Asian Americans. I also discussed the contributions of and gaps within these bodies of literature, and suggested that we can learn a lot about Asian Americans' mental health by incorporating concepts from the political economy of health, feminist thinking, and transnational approaches. In this chapter, I discuss my research questions, lay out the theoretical foundations that ground this book, and present the conceptual and analytical frameworks used in my analysis. While my review of the substantive literature on mental health in Chapter Two informs and shapes this study, my discussion of the theoretical perspectives and frameworks in Chapter Three creates the scaffolding of this book. Despite the different purposes of these two chapters, both represent necessary foundations for this project.

Every researcher has her or his own position, which is often presented in academic projects. While my research questions emerge from the literature reviewed in Chapter Two, the theoretical perspectives I present in this chapter structure both my conceptual and analytical frameworks that guide the design of this project and analysis they develop, and reveal my stance in this study of gender and mental health. In other words, this chapter demonstrates why I build a conceptual framework to approach mental health that is different from previous scholars, ask research questions in certain ways, and analyze specific aspects of gender and mental health.

CORE RESEARCH QUESTIONS

The goal of this project is to conduct a sociological study that reveals Asian Americans' emotional life more in-depth and more comprehensively than has been done in the past. By "more in-depth," I mean a study that is able to contextualize mental distress issues, one of the major omissions in sociological studies of mental health; by "more comprehensively," I refer to a study that takes into account both migration background and minority status in mental health, thereby expanding the range of previous investigations in immigration studies. I therefore frame my research questions to mirror the types of research findings and gaps that were reviewed and discussed in Chapter Two. My core research questions are:

A. *How and why do Taiwanese Americans make decisions to migrate to the United States?*

B. *How do Taiwanese Americans experience their social relations in the family and workplace in the U.S.?*

C. *How do Taiwanese Americans' migration decisions and social relations influence their mental health?*

D. *How do men and women differ in their life experiences?*

Acknowledging the significant influence of migration background on Taiwanese Americans' social life, my research questions concern how the decision to migrate was made by women as well as by men, and how this decision affects their mental health in a new homeland. In contrast to conventional immigration studies that mainly focus on family conflicts, this project extends its range of investigation to the arena of work -- a consideration that meets feminists' demands not to limit comparisons of gendered conflict solely to the family. To avoid the omissions existing in traditional sociological studies of mental health, this study emphasizes informants' subjective experiences and the social contexts in which distress is produced.

As demonstrated in Chapter Two, we know very little about Asian Americans' emotional life, especially the social contexts that produce their mental distress. Because my research questions aim to fill this gap, I need to draw on other bodies of literature that provide insights into the social contexts of distress. In the next section, I discuss concepts in the political economy of health, feminist thinking, and transnational approaches, to illustrate why notions within all three contribute to the theoretical underpinnings of this project. I explain what concepts I take from these perspectives and how they correct omissions left by pervious studies.

INSIGHTS FROM OTHER PERSPECTIVES

The political economy approach to health emphasizes structural factors and power relations that produce inequalities in well-being, two phenomena that have been overlooked in social psychological studies of mental health. Feminist thinking, both critiques of mental health research and standpoint theory, call for a production of knowledge that is women-centered and power sensitive. They highlight the power issues and contextual factors that underlie gendered distress, consider women as agents of knowledge, underscore the heterogeneity of women, and encourage a feminist imagination in the study of gender and mental health. Transnational approaches highlight the unique socio-cultural characteristics of immigrant communities, and underline the importance of culture for understanding and contexualizing distress in ethnic groups. These perspectives all bring insights to this study.

Political Economy of Health

The political economy approach has been used by many feminists (e.g., Doyal 1979, 1995; Fee 1982; Shiva 1994) to examine the interlocking social, political, and economic factors that impair women's health. Drawing on Marxist perspectives, the political economy approach argues that the social production and distribution of health and illness cannot be separated from larger social, economic, and medical systems. Under the operation of capitalism, not everyone is affected equally by the illness-producing process. For instance, we can find class differences in morbidity and mortality, differential health risks of specific occupations, and unequal health status in developed and under-developed societies. Even medical organizations and practice, whose goal is supposed to produce health, often work in the interests of capital (Doyal 1979).

The notion of *power* is central to the political economy approach to health. According to Doyal (1995), the contemporary crisis in medicine is deeply rooted in the nature of capitalism, as both an economic and social system. As an economic system, medical institutions often function according to the logic of capitalism, frequently benefiting the medical profession and industry rather than patients. Furthermore, as a social system dominated by men and medical/scientific knowledge, the medical setting is an arena within which power relationships are omnipresent. In other words, economic power dominates the operation of the medical industry, while social and professional power determines the definitions of health and illness that are used in medicine. In a similar vein, in the larger society, various forms of power determine the distribution of resources, leading to unequal social and health statuses. The political economy of health approach, therefore, aims to investigate the power structure that is shaped by interlocking economic, social, political, and cultural forces.[10]

Feminists who adopt the political economy of health approach emphasize the importance of social contexts and their impact on women's health. For example, Becker and Nachtigall (1992), Fee (1982), Hubbard (1995), and Lowis and McCaffery (2004) all argue that women's health has been over-medicalized, a phenomenon that entraps women's bodies within a male-dominant medical gaze and control. Women's "problems," especially reproductive health issues such as pregnancy, childbirth, and menopause, all have been medicalized. Women as a group thus tend to be defined by their biological sex and reproductive potential in medicine.

---

[10] In a broad sense, culture also can be considered a social force. Here I distinguish these two terms to highlight the difference between structural contexts (i.e., systems, organizations, etc.) and cultural forms (i.e., values, symbols, meanings, etc.), i.e., social and cultural forces, respectively.

In addition to medical power, how larger structural factors affect women's health has also been widely discussed in the political economy approach of health. For instance, ecological feminists Shiva (1994) demonstrates how capitalism, imperialism, and colonialism can damage the environment and consequently endanger women's survival and health in the Third World. Following Weber's concept of social closure, Thomas (1994) argues that poverty, an indicator of economic inequality, constrains women's life chances and places them at great risk for many stress-related illnesses. She therefore advocates that sociologists examine social hierarchies, social relations, and power structures that prevent women and other minorities from equal access to health care.

Moreover, Krieger and Fee (1996) maintain that the way gender, as a social reality, intrudes into the body and transforms our biology is usually ignored by sociologists. They illuminate this statement by referring to a widely acknowledged discrepancy: in childhood, boys and girls receive different (gendered) expectations about exercise and, thereby, develop different body builds. The biological category "female," as a result, actually carries and is shaped by cultural norms of gender that are differentially experienced according to ethnicity and social class. Krieger and Fee therefore argue that patterns of health and disease are highly related to how people live in the world, and thus they insist that women's lives and the social contexts (the intersection of gender, social class, and ethnicity) within which women live should be carefully examined (ibid.). In other words, from the perspective of political economy of health, macroeconomic structure, class, race, ethnicity, and paid and unpaid work are all considered important contextual dimensions that affect women's health and lives (Bartley, Popay, and Plewis 1992, Gallin 1989, Graham 1990, Kynaston 1996, Messias et al. 1997).

Although social psychology has been a leading approach in studying mental health in the past four decades, it has been criticized for overlooking social contexts and macro structures (Hall 1989). I believe that the political economy approach can serve as a complementary perspective to situate social psychological studies of mental health in a larger structure. In my view, mental health research is, to some extent, the study of the oppressed because mental illness is frequently found in disadvantaged populations (e.g., women, minorities, the elderly, the uneducated, the unemployed, and the poor). In other words, the interlocking social, political, economic, and cultural factors that cause social inequalities are often the same ones that engender mental distress.

Specifically, the political economy of health brings insights to this study in at least two ways. First, structural factors such as migration background, historical and cultural origin, and minority status need to be considered in the explanatory model because they illustrate Taiwanese Americans' unique ethnic characteristics and social position in U.S. society. Second, power structure and relations in the family and workplace need to be examined because they lead to unequal distribution of resources that can have varying effects on individuals' psychological well-being.

Feminist Thinking

Mental health is gendered. As in the literature I reviewed in Chapter Two, one of the most consistent findings in the study of mental health is that women have higher rates of depression and psychological treatment than men do. A great number of sociologists, therefore, have devoted themselves to investigating the associations between gender and mental illness. In addition to the extensive scholarly interest on this topic, many feminists (e.g., Astbury 1996; Broverman et al. 1981; Davar 1999; Gitlin and Pasnau 1989; Hall 1989; Rosewater 1985; Showalter 1985; Stoppard 2000) have focused on the examination of the epistemology of mental health research, highlighting important omissions in the literature and advocating a gender-sensitive lens. Their critical commentaries shape my stance as a feminist sociologist of mental health, a researcher with a "feminist gaze," in Hune's (2000) term, and impel me to exercise what Garey and Hansen (1998) call a "feminist sociological imagination." [11] Below I synthesize these

---

[11] Hune (2000) utilizes the term "doing gender with a feminist gaze" to describe her effort to reconstruct Asian American history by reconsidering women's gendered lives. According to her, researchers who engender history with a feminist gaze offer a comprehensive and systematic reassessment of the lives of both women and men. Garey and Hansen (1998) follow Mills' notion of "sociological imagination" and use the term "feminist sociological

feminist critiques of mental health research, introduce the feminist standpoint theory that serves as the major theoretical foundation of these critiques, and then discuss how these two feminist perspectives undergird this study conceptually and analytically.

Feminist Critiques of Mental Health Research

Since the 1980s, feminists have critically scrutinized the role of gender in science, challenging what is perceived to be a problem worthy of scientific inquiry and the unequal relationship between the researcher and the researched (see Bleier 1986; Harding 1986, 1991). This reflective point of view also has penetrated the sociology of mental health, a field that has been dominated by "scientific" knowledge of mental health and illness.[12] In sum, feminist critiques of mental health research focus mainly on three issues: gender biased perceptions of researchers and medical professionals; the othering of women; and the neglect of women's subjective experiences.

First, gender stereotypes exist among mental health professionals and researchers. In an early study, Broverman and her associates (1981) point out that mental health professionals convey gender stereotypes in their clinical judgment. These scholars illustrate that clinicians' views of a "healthy adult" are similar to their conception of a "healthy male" and that an "unhealthy adult" is most similar to a "healthy female." In another study, Rosewater (1985) found that according to the diagnostic criteria in DSM III, women suffering from abuse may be mistakenly labeled as mentally ill.[13] Moreover, because men comprise the majority

---

imagination" to illustrate their analyses of the differing relationships of women and men to work, privilege, and power within and outside families. These scholars all encourage feminist perspectives in conducting research about gender and gender relations.

[12] The development and growth of biomedical knowledge since the 1980s to a large extent shapes the dominant perspective in mental health research. Clinical diagnoses and standards of mental disorders have been widely adopted in sociology.

[13] "DSM III" refers to the "Diagnostic and Statistical Manual of Mental Disorders, Third Edition," published by the American Psychiatric Association in 1980. This manual was used by mental health professionals to set forth

of mental health professionals and researchers, their measurements create more men's than women's perceptions of mental health (Rosewater 1985). Showalter (1985) also argues that professional conceptions of mental health and insanity are fundamentally gendered. She points out that madness is a female malady, not only because women are statistically more likely to have psychiatric disorders, but also because insanity is an essentially feminine malady. In short, feminist scholars highlight the gender bias of mental health professionals in labeling mental disorder, that is, their tendency to presume that women are emotional, irrational, hysterical, and even "abnormal," and to attribute this abnormality to women's reproductive organs and hormones (Astbury 1996; Gitlin and Pasnau 1989; Showalter 1985).

Similar bias can also be found in empirical work. For instance, in a study about women patients who received psychiatric treatment for neurotic disorders, Miles (1988) argues that women are unable to distinguish their own emotional disturbance from mental illness. In her view, the anxiety and depression women report at clinics are not "real" mental illness, but problems they can themselves avoid. Miles' statement implicitly suggests women's inability to distinguish their "emotional problems" from "mental illness." This viewpoint devalues women's competence, implying their "irrational" predisposition; it also reinforces the perception that bio-medical knowledge comprises the "orthodox" judgments of mental illness, a perception that overlooks individuals' subjective experiences of distress in social life.

As mentioned earlier, women receive higher rates of psychological treatment than do men (Gove and Tudor 1973). Compared to their male counterparts, women are more likely to report depressive symptoms because of, on the one hand, their lack of confidence and self-coping ability and, on the other, their lower self-esteem (Zukerman 1989). This tendency might lead to the high frequencies with which women seek professional help. Nevertheless, sociologists also find that women suffer more psychological distress than men (Aneshensel 1992, Caldwell, Pearson, and Chin 1987, Dohrenwend and Dohrenwend 1974, Gove 1972, 1987, Gove and Tudor 1973, Mirowsky and Ross 1986).

---

diagnostic criteria, descriptions, and other information to guide the diagnosis of mental disorders.

Miles' concluding remarks that women's depressive and anxious "symptoms" need no "real" clinical attention convey a bias in her judging of women's emotional problems. By perceiving women's help-seeking behavior as a "wrong conduct," Miles' statement shows a "blame-the-victim" attitude. This viewpoint not only reinforces gender stereotypes; it also tends to normalize women's psychological sufferings and leaves the socio-structural roots of their "problems" unexamined. As Miller (1976: 126) notes, "Women are not creating conflict; they are exposing the fact that conflict exists." The social contexts of gendered mental distress therefore should be central to the sociological study of gender and mental health.

Second, women are often treated as "the other" in studies of gender and mental health. As Hall (1989) points out, most social psychological studies of mental problems were done about men, and women subjects tended to be regarded only as a reference group for them. In other words, men are often perceived "the standard" while women are judged on the basis of this "norm." This tendency is particularly obvious in the study of occupational stress. Whenever women are studied as an independent group, it is often women's family conditions rather than their occupation that are investigated. Women are frequently analyzed in terms of their "place" in society – the family. Furthermore, women's mental health as a subject is mostly subsumed within the general issue of gender differences but is not treated as an independent matter in the literature. The neglect of women per se not only courts the danger of over-generalizing gender differences in mental health, but it also homogenizes women and ignores their diversity. Women of various ethnicities, classes, sexualities, nationalities, and cultures have different life experiences and perceptions of mental health. They may use different terms to describe their mental problems, adopt different coping strategies in reaction to them, and practice different styles of help-seeking behavior. While studies of gender differences of mental health have recognized that in most cases women are more vulnerable than men to mental problems, it is necessary to investigate how women from different standpoints differ in their perception and experience of mental health.

Third, women's subjective experiences of mental health are often overlooked. In *Understanding Depression*, Stoppard (2000) points out that the meaning of depression to a large extent depends on the social context in which the term is used and who uses it. She argues that researchers' notions of depression, primarily based on positivist perspectives, do not necessarily reflect subjects' depressive experiences. Stoppard therefore has developed different meanings for terms, distinguishing between depressive disorder (a disorder defined by mental health professionals and researchers), depressive symptoms (a person's responses on a questionnaire designed by clinical researchers to assess depression), and depressive experiences (people's subjective experiences in everyday life that are described by themselves as depression). She criticizes mental health researchers for their tendency to adopt positivist perspectives and measurements, thereby neglecting women's experiences as perceived from their own standpoint (Stoppard 2000).

Feminist critiques, as demonstrated above, challenge the extant scholarship on gender and mental health. They underline women's disadvantaged position not only in terms of their mental health status but also in scholarly work. By drawing attention to gendered social contexts as well as the gendered nature of distress experiences, these feminist perspectives contribute to the improvement of women's psychological well-being in practice. Similar to the political economy approach to health, feminists emphasize the importance of structural factors and power relations that have been neglected in the literature on mental health. Even more, they highlight individuals' agency for defining life situations and for resisting structural constraints or the imposition of power.

Feminist Standpoint Theory

Feminist critiques of mental health research, as well as feminist critiques of science in general, represent and extend the central concerns of feminist standpoint theory, one of the prominent feminist thoughts since the 1980s. In her influential book, *Money, Sex, and Power*, Hartsock (1983a) asserts that women's unique standpoint in society provides the justification for the truth claims of feminism. It also provides feminism with a method with which to analyze reality. According to Hartsock, the everyday world in its experiential reality and the structures that limit, shape, organize, and penetrate it are different for people in different social locations, and that "women's lives make available a particular and privileged vantage point on male supremacy" (Hartsock 1983b: 284). Largely adopting Marx's views on social class, Hartsock underlines women's oppressed voices and positions both in society and in the industry of knowledge production (both in the natural and social sciences). She insists that knowledge must be produced from a woman's as well as a man's point of view, so that women's experiences and perspectives should be central, not invisible or marginal, to knowledge, culture, and politics (Hartsock 1983a, 1983b). Hartsock argues that the feminist standpoint allows us to "go beneath the surface of appearances to reveal the real but concealed social relations (ibid.: 304). It also "expresses female experiences at a particular time and place, located within a particular set of social relations" (ibid.: 303).

Hartsock's standpoint theory is a critique of mainstream science and social science, a methodology for feminist research, and an analysis of the power that lies in producing knowledge. It extends important influences to later development, elaboration, and refinement of feminist thought. For instance, Smith (1987a, 1987b) develops a sociological method from the standpoint of women. Criticizing the discipline because women's lives are absent from the domain of sociology, Smith wishes to establish a sociology for women that is anchored in the everyday world that women actually experience. She argues that the sociological method must be rooted in the life world of women's standpoints, a material and local experience that is always situated, relational, and engaged (ibid.). Also influenced by Hartsock's theory, Collins (1986, 1990) articulates a black feminist standpoint that underlines the common experiences of black women yet also recognizes the differences among them.

In her well-known book on science and feminism Harding (1986, 1991) marks feminist standpoint theory as one of the three feminist epistemologies, along with feminist empiricism and feminist postmodernism. She points out that the situations of women are too diverse to claim just one feminist standpoint, and considers women's lives as the place where research should begin (1991: 134-42). As Harding states, "Starting research in women's lives leads to socially constructed claims that are less false – less partial and distorted – than are the (also socially constructed) claims that result if one starts from the lives of men in the dominant groups" (ibid.: 185).

While highlighting the importance of grounding social research onto women's standpoints, these scholars also acknowledge the variation of women's standpoints and life experiences as there is no single standpoint that women occupy. Various social locations can produce very diverse life experiences, and ethnicity and class are just as significant as gender in shaping these differences. While recognizing the multiple realities, however, as Hekman (1997) critically points out, standpoint theorists inescapably face the difficulty of dealing with the endless multiplicity of standpoints and of acquiring convincing accounts of the world. "How can we talk about accounts of the world at all if the multiplicity of standpoints is, quite literally, endless?" asks Hekman (1997: 358). She therefore proposes a paradigm that adopts Weber's methodology of the ideal type to solve this problem, thereby achieving a credible feminist analysis. Hekman argues that by creating an ideal type of women's standpoints will enable feminist standpoint theorists to avoid the problem of "absolute relativism" in seeking systematic understanding about the seem-to-be endless segments of women's experiences at different social locations. Following Weber, Hekman believes that what feminists can offer are persuasive arguments in defense of their values and the politics these values entail. In the process of advancing both persuasive and unpersuasive arguments, feminists are able to change the norms of what constitutes an argument (Hekman 1997).

To achieve a "feminist objectivity" as Hekman does, Haraway (1988, 1991) introduces the insightful concept of "situated knowledges." Sharing standpoint theorists' notion that knowledge is situated, located, and shaped by individual perspectives, Haraway (1988, 1991: 183-201) argues that feminist paradigmatic models of scientific knowledge – what she also calls "rational knowledge" -- should be a "power-sensitive conversation" that provides a common ground for conversation, rationality, and objectivity. For Haraway, "Feminism is about a critical vision consequent upon a critical positioning in inhomogeneous gendered social space" (1991: 195), and that "feminist embodiment resists fixation and is insatiably curious about the webs of differential positioning" (196). She states that "situated knowledges are about communities, not about isolated individuals," and "the only way to find larger vision is to be somewhere in particular" (1988). Treating feminist objectivity as "positioned rationality," Haraway (1988, 1991) advocates a production of rational knowledge that is in nature a process of ongoing critical interpretation among fields of interpreters and decoders. Feminist standpoint theory brings insights into this study in two ways. First, it highlights the importance of analyzing how social locations affect individuals' life experiences. Second, it encourages researchers to engage in a power-sensitive conversation when interpreting data. Both are carried out in my analyses.

Gender, Power Relations, and Agency

The notion of "power" is central in feminist thought. Issues that contain the power question, such as women's disadvantageous position in society, oppressed voices and life experiences, heterogeneities, embodiment and empowerment, and the unequal status between the researcher and the researched, have been drawing great attention and discussions from feminists (e.g., Bleier 1986; Broverman et al. 1981; Doyal 1995; Hall 1989; Harding 1986, 1991; Hartsock 1983a, 1983b; Showalter 1985). Feminist critiques of mental health and standpoint theory, as reviewed above, also represent a common concern about power, bringing important insights into this study epistemologically, conceptually, and analytically

First, in this study I treat both Taiwanese American men and women as agents of knowledge. Feminists ask important epistemological questions such as: Who can be an agent of knowledge? Can women? How is knowledge legitimated? Whose experiences and observations are valid? What counts as knowledge? Do subjective "truths" count? As noted in Chapter Two, the inadequacy and insufficiency of existing sociological understanding about Asian Americans' mental health reveals the fact that Asian Americans, including Taiwanese, have not yet become agents of knowledge in the sociology of mental health. Their experiences of distress lack a systematic investigation and in-depth understanding. This study, therefore, fills this gap by examining the social and emotional lives of both Taiwanese American women and men.

Second, I treat informants as social actors, highlighting their agencies. Considering the theme of power, many feminists (e.g., Davis 1997; Parker 1995; Wolf 1992a; Yeoh, Teo, and Huang 2002)

emphasize the importance of individual agency in confronting structural constraints. The term "agency" is used to demonstrate women's resistance against structural domination and their empowerment. Following the discussions of Giddens (1979, 1984), these feminists consider individuals' agency to be conditioned by outside forces and structured within the context of their collectives. In other words, individuals are not completely free; they are constrained by structures. Agency, therefore, is the reaction to such structural constraints, and takes various forms including passivity, withdrawal, accommodation, defiance, and resistance (Wolf 1992a). As Haraway (1991: 198) states, "situated knowledges require that the object of knowledge be pictured as an actor and agent." In this study I take the informants' reactions to distress as a form of exercising individual agencies in their confrontations with structural power (see next section). Both men and women are considered competent agents who are capable of defining their life situations and transforming or adapting to structural constraints.

Third, I investigate the informants' social and emotional lives from their standpoints, underlining not only their heterogeneities shaped by different combinations of social locations and cultures but also their commonalities as a social group. Sharing standpoint theorists' perspective that "knowledge is situated," I interrogate the informants' "local knowledge" (Geertz 1983) of social and emotional lives at different sites of their "standpoints" (e.g., as Taiwanese Americans, Asian Americans, men, women, *waishengren*, *benshengren*, middle class, and lower class), in varied contexts (e.g., when considering emigration and settlement, their relationships and interaction with children, mothers-in-laws, relatives, and co-workers), and within different social institutions (e.g., in the family and at the workplace). When investigating these situated, stratified, and contextual experiences, I also frequently "zoom out" my lens of analysis to look at the informants as a whole (as Taiwanese Americans) or as two groups -- women and men – to compare gender differences. By so doing, I avoid the danger of losing "feminist objectivity" to endless analytical segments of individual standpoints, thereby acquiring what Haraway (1988, 1991) calls "rational knowledge" about the informants.[14]

Fourth, like many other feminist works, power is the central theme of this study. I examine how varied forms of power relations (e.g., gender, spousal, generational, familial, cultural, ethnic, racial, and class) shape the informants' social life, their impacts on mental distress, the mechanisms of these impacts, and individual agencies exerted to reproduce or transform these power relations.

Transnational Approaches

Since the 1990s, a new notion, "transnationalism," has come into wide use among cultural anthropologists and sociologists. Anthropologists Glick Schiller, Basch and Blanc-Szanton (1992, 1999) first introduced the concept of transnationalism as a novel analytical approach to understanding contemporary migration. They define transnationalism as "the processes by which immigrants build social fields that link together their country of origin and their country of settlement" (Glick Schiller, Basch and Blanc-Szanton 1999: 26). In contrast to early immigrants who were "uprooted" from their home countries in the late nineteenth and early twentieth centuries, contemporary immigrants are "composed of those whose networks, activities and patterns of life encompass both their host and home societies. Their lives cut across national boundaries and bring two societies into a single social field" (Glick Schiller, Basch and Blanc-Szanton 1999: 26). According to Glick Schiller and her colleagues, this qualitative difference characterizes today's immigrants as "transmigrants," who build social fields that connect both receiving and sending societies.

Portes' advocacy of the use of the transnational perspective in analyzing new immigrant communities (1996, 1998, Portes, Guarnizo, and Landolt 1999) to a large extent has contributed to the popularity of this concept in sociology. Seeking to offer a middle-range theory of transnationalism that is able to shape a research agenda, Portes, Guarnizo, and Landolt (1999) carefully examine the necessity of

---

[14] According to Haraway (1991: 196), "Situated knowledges are about communities, not about isolated individuals. The only way to find a larger vision is to be somewhere in particular."

creating this new concept of transnationalism, and further refine and delimit its broad definition, as provided by Glick Schiller and her associates. Portes and his colleagues argue that only the activities that involve continuity of social relationships across national borders over time can be described by the term transnationalism. They also suggest that the units of analysis for transnational research should be individuals and families. In contrast to Glick Schiller, Basch, and Blanc-Szanton who view transnationalism in a broader sense, Portes and his colleagues (1999) question the need of using the term "transmigrants" because it does not extend the meaning that the old notion of "immigrants" contended conceptually.

Portes, Guarnizo, and Landolt (1999) further distinguish three different forms of transnationalism: economic, political, and social-cultural. Economic transnationalism involves entrepreneurs whose network of capital, markets, and suppliers crosses nation-state borders. Political transnationalism refers to the political activities of governmental functionaries, party officials, or community leaders whose primary goals are to achieve political power and influence in the sending or receiving countries. Socio-cultural transnationalism involves activities that are oriented to reinforce national identity abroad or the collective gratification of cultural goods and events.

Faist (2000a) recasts the term "social fields" in Glick Schiller and her colleagues' theory by speaking about "transnational social spaces." He attempts to construct a transnational paradigm of immigration that transcends the push-pull model and the centre-periphery model. Faist's idea of transnational spaces treats the migratory system as a process in which two or more nation-states are penetrated by and become a part of a singular new social space. This transnational social space model includes not only the migration of people, but also the circulation of symbols, ideas, and material culture (Faist 2000a: 13, 2000b).

Despite continuing theoretical debates and refinements, many sociologists have adopted the concept of transnationalism to investigate various transnational activities in immigrant communities. For instance, Levitt (2001) studied how Dominican immigrants maintain familial, religious, and political connections between Boston and Miraflores in the Dominican Republic; Goldring (1996) examined how Mexican immigrants construct a transnational community in the immigration process; Gold (1997) investigated Israeli immigrants' vocabularies of immigration motivation; Al-Ali (2002) explored the limitation of transnationalism through empirical studies of Bosnian and Eritrean refugees in Europe; Louie (2000, 2004) examined how Chinese American youth construct their cultural identities and transnational connections with China; Ong (1996, 1999) discussed the meaning of citizenship in a transnational era; and Chee (2005) explored Taiwanese American women's role and life experiences in sustaining transnational families. Conceptual discussions and empirical studies of transnationalism have mushroomed in contemporary anthropology and sociology.[15]

Although several scholars (e.g., Faist 2000a, 2000b; Gold 1997, 2002; Kivisto 2001; Portes, Guarnizo, and Landolt 1999) have explored the connection between transnationalism and adaptation, very few have discussed how mental health is related to transnationalism. One noteworthy exception is Wolf's study (1997, 2002b) of second-generation Filipino. In her article, "Family Secrets: Transnational Struggles among Children of Filipino Immigrants," Wolf (1997) uses the term "emotional transnationalism" to describe the mental distress second-generation Filipino youth experience when confronting conflicting cultural codes and ideologies from the Philippines and the U.S. Despite her failure to offer a clear definition of emotional transnationalism, Wolf vividly depicts the struggles, conflicts, and feelings of ambivalence immigrant children encounter in their emotional life.

Because of their parents' migration background and their cultural heritage, immigrant children's values and behavior are inevitably influenced by social norms in both sending and receiving countries. To use a social psychological term, cultural norms in a given society create a "cognitive schema" that directs individuals' thoughts and behavior, distinguishing "appropriate" and "inappropriate" values and conducts. In other words, this "schema" serves as a behavioral guide or a foundation upon which individuals make judgments in their social life. Being nurtured by two cultures, immigrants and their children seek

---

[15] For more recent works on the conceptionalization and studies of transnationalism, see also Brettell and Hollifield (2000), Foner, Rumbaut, and Gold (2000), Morawska (2003), Olwig (2003), Pessar and Mahler (2003), Portes (2003), and Waldinger and Fitzgerald (2004).

such sources of value and behavioral norms from two worlds – both from the receiving and sending societies – that are not absolutely separate in the mind. For them, the process of constructing a "cognitive schema" is fluid. It is a dynamic progression that goes across national borders, a flowing process that goes back and forth between two cultures. This "transnational field" that connects two cultures not only provides sources of behavioral guidance and value judgment, it also produces meanings that support and legitimate individuals' actions. Nevertheless, the search for behavioral guidance in a "transnational cognitive schema" is not always smooth, especially when two cultures attach contradictory meanings to the same behavior.

For instance, Filipino youth place a special emphasis on family cohesion and closeness – a value that derives from traditional Filipino culture. But at the same time, they also suffer from the restraints imposed by derivative family practice that, from their perspectives, are a form of authoritarian control – a view that emerges as they reflect upon or awaken to the emphasis on individualism and independence or autonomy in American culture. It is not difficult to imagine that conflicts may occur when they attempt to accommodate such disparate and contradicting values. These conflicts also may cause mental distress or, what Wolf (1997, 2002b) calls, "emotional transnationalism."

In my view, Faist (2000a, 2000b) and Wolf (1997, 2002b) transcend previous scholarly discussions about the socio-cultural dimension of transnationalism. In contrast to Portes and his colleagues (1999), who limit socio-cultural transnationalism to material cultural goods and collective cultural events, Faist (2000a, 2000b) and Wolf (1997) both highlight the existence and importance of transnational symbols, values, and norms, and their influence on individuals. In other words, socio-cultural representation of transnationalism does not occur only in a material form as Portes and his colleague suggest. Rather, it takes place in individuals' everyday life and in various forms. Other than material goods and collective events that represent "visible" ethnic culture, immigrants and their children are themselves "carriers of culture," whose social practices, beliefs, and values are to some extent shaped by the cultural norms of both their sending and receiving societies. They are also "actors" who make their own culture in addition to serving as the carriers (or instruments) of culture.

As noted above, Wolf (1997, 2002b) has powerfully illustrated how Filipino youth face conflicting cultural codes and ideologies between traditional Filipino values, which they learn from their parents, and American culture by which they are acculturated into the larger society. Similar emotional contradictions also face first-generation immigrants because they are directly governed by two different cultures. In other words, both first- and second-generation immigrants experience a certain degree of "emotional transnationalism" because their "social spaces" of cultural codes, values, and meanings are transnational. Following Louie (2004: 19-23) who demonstrates how the cultural identities of Chinese American youth are produced, contested, and negotiated in various contexts, I argue that experiences of emotional transnationalism are also fluid and situated. Emotional transnationalism is experienced differently in diverse settings, within shifting contexts, and in response to varied structural constraints.

Transnational viewpoints, particularly the concept of emotional transnationalism, bring insights to this study in a significant way. They highlight the unique life situations and cultural contests facing immigrants and their children -- factors that are important for understanding mental health issues in this community, and for investigating the contexts in which these issues are produced. For the purpose of this book, then, I define emotional transnationalism as "the ambivalent emotion experienced when immigrants and their children attempt to accommodate conflicting values in their search for behavioral guidance and a foundation for moral judgments, from cultural norms of both their sending and receiving societies."

APPROACHING MENTAL DISTRESS FROM A STRUCTURATIVE PERSPECTIVE

Considering both the insights of the perspectives discussed in this chapter and the review of relevant empirical literature in Chapter Two, I construct my conceptual and analytical frameworks differently from previous studies of mental health. [16] Empirically, in addition to

---

[16] I demonstrate my theoretical concerns in the conceptual framework (Figure 3-1), and illustrate my empirical concerns in the analytical framework (Figure 3-2).

examining traditionally important independent variables in mental health research such as family and work, I also explore the impact of the decision to migrate on mental distress. I stress power relations at different levels of analysis, as well as situate my investigation in the larger social structure and culture. In other words, conceptually, this project is a study of gender and mental health that highlights structural (both social and cultural) contexts. To demonstrate my conceptual framework and analytical model, I first explain how mental health is defined in this study, and then discuss the importance of socio-cultural contexts in mental health.

Defining "Mental Health," "Mental Illness," and "Mental Distress"

The continuum viewpoint of the 1970s and the discrete model after the 1980s demonstrate the change in dominant perspectives on mental health in sociology. As described in Chapter Two, definitions of mental health and illness vary at different times, in different cultures, and among different researchers. Clarifying basic concepts and the approach employed in a study is therefore necessary to illustrate the researcher's standpoint. In this project, I believe that using the continuum notion of mental health and illness is more appropriate than the discrete model because (1) perceptions of mental health and mental illness differ across cultures; and (2) the purpose of this study is not to measure or assess a specific mental problem, but to address the general issue of psychological well-being.

As many anthropologists have observed, each society has distinct beliefs about normal and abnormal behavior, and the concepts of emotion, self and body, and general illness differ significantly in different cultures (Good 1977; Lutz and White 1986; Marsella et al. 1985). Culture is therefore critical in understanding how mental disorder is perceived, experienced, and expressed in everyday life (Kleinmen 1988: 3). In other words, concepts of mental illness are not fixed, but are specific to a culture at a given time in its history (Foucault 1965).

Many studies have discussed how Chinese culture and Asian culture in general shape people's views of mental illness. For example, Abgayani-Siewert, Takeuchi, and Pangan (1999) point out that the notion of collectivism in Asian culture prevents people from seeking professional help for their mental problems, because mental illness is a stigma and admission of it would make them "lose face" in front of others. Lin and Cheung (1999) argue that, because Asian traditions view the body and mind as unitary rather than dualistic, people tend to focus more on physical discomfort than emotional symptoms. The overrepresentation of somatic complaints and neurasthenia, a phenomenon called somatization of mental distress, also has been found in Chinese societies (Kleinman 1988; Kuo and Kavanagh 1994; Parker, Gladstone, and Tsee-Chee 2001). Chinese views of the harmony between nature and the universe, as well as the balance of yin and yang forces in health, also have been discussed in explorations of cultural differences in the perceptions of mental illness (Kuo and Kavanagh 1994; Leung 1998).

Language is the carrier of cultural meanings (Bernal, Bonilla, and Bellido 1995). As Arthur Kleinman and Joan Kleinman (1997: 14) argue, because the experience of suffering is expressed in lay terms, it is important to understand how mental health and illness are perceived and described in a given culture. In fact, the language used in Chinese societies to express psychological problems is different from that in western societies. For instance, a commonly used adjective in the U.S., "depressed," is seldom spoken in Chinese societies. Instead, people usually say *fan-nao* (worried), *yu-chu* (unhappy), *chuo-tse* or *ju-san* (frustrated), *hsin-ku* (experiencing hardships), *di-chao* (in low spirits) much more often than "depressed" (*yo-yu*). The Chinese word *ya-li* refers not only to "stress," but also to "stressed" and "distress." These terms are often interchangeable in lay conversations, and their use is dependent on the context and meaning of the narrative. Accordingly, developing distinct conceptual definitions and measurements of sub-topics in mental health and illness that are culturally appropriate in Chinese societies requires considerable experiential research and conceptual refinement. The existing techniques and theories derived from western societies need to be empirically tested and revised in order to conform to appropriate cultural meanings, and thus achieve methodological and theoretical validity. Yet, this is by no means a task this project aims to accomplish.

In reality, Taiwanese Americans may not act exactly in accordance with traditional Chinese culture; [17] rather, they possibly may also integrate American culture into their worldview and behavior. [18] Moreover, even when sharing the same culture, individuals can adopt views, narratives, and practices relative to mental health and illness that vary to a large extent, and this possibility suggests the importance of subjects' interpretations of their experiences (Wong and Tsang 2004). The continuum model of mental health and illness, a perspective that does not presume rigid distinctions of specific social psychological notions, allows me to explore the perceptions and narratives informants use to express their psychological problems.

Conceptually, I use the term, mental distress, in my framework and throughout this book to illustrate the continuum notion. The concept of "mental distress" was first suggested by Davar (1999) to replace "mental illness" in mental health studies. Using India as an example, Davar (1999) examined discourses in mental health research, theories, clinical practice, and policies regarding women's mental health. She realized that mental health scholars used varying and inconsistent terms that present positivist bio-medical views, overlooking the standpoints of the subjects themselves. Davar therefore advocates the usage of "mental distress," emphasizing the subjective perceptions and experiences of psychological suffering and the social contexts of these experiences. This idea supports the goal of this project -- to conduct a sociological study of mental health that prioritizes subjects' standpoints

---

[17] As I explain in Chapter Five, the usage of "Chinese" and "Taiwanese" involves a complex of identity and political issues because of the historical background of Taiwan and Taiwan-China relations. Culturally, however, people who are of Chinese origin, including those of Chinese nationality (*zhong guo ren*), people in Taiwan, and overseas Chinese *(hua qiao)* and Taiwanese, are all influenced by traditional Chinese culture that is based on Confucian teaching to some degree. This is what Tu (1994) defines as "cultural China." While calling all people in Taiwan (including *benshengren* and *waishengren*) "Taiwanese," I utilize the term "Chinese culture" in this book to refer to the culture shared by all *hua ren*, people who are of Chinese origin.

[18] As Faist (2000b) argues, immigrant culture is not a "baggage" or "container" that implies fixity and locality. Rather, it ought to be considered as a general human "software" or "tool kit" that suggests fluidity and spatiality.

and social contexts. I therefore follow Davar's argument, adopting her perspective on mental distress and considering it as a notion that embraces various psychological indicators (e.g., anxiety, frustrations, unhappiness, and hardships) that deviate from a perfect state of mental health. In other words, the concept of mental distress signifies my position in this study, which emphasizes the social contexts of emotional life, highlights informants' perceptions and experiences, and addresses the general issue of "mental health" or "psychological well-being" rather than a specific "mental disorder."

Theoretical Concerns and Conceptual Framework

In *Mental Health of Indian Women: A Feminist Agenda*, Davar (1999: 87) examines existing research on women's mental health and synthesizes a bio-psycho-social model. Rejecting the reductionism of any single dimension of this model, Davar calls for a sophisticated understanding of women's mental distress that takes into account complex contextual factors, especially psycho-social causes (ibid.: 74-89). In my view, this insightful argument fails to see an important element – that is, the role culture plays in the context of mental distress. As mentioned above, many anthropologists have stressed the importance of culture in understanding mental health issues (Fabrega 1990, 1992; Good 1977; Kleinmen 1988; Lutz and White 1986; Marsella et al. 1985). Sociologists (e.g., Agbayani-Siewert, Takeuchi, and Pangan 1999; Brown et al. 1999; Lefley 1999, Takeuchi, Uehara, and Maramba 1999) also have stressed the importance of culture in mental health research. Studies have shown how individuals' social relations and psychological well-being can be impacted by specific ethnic cultures, such as the egalitarianism of African American couples (Broman 1991) and the close family ties among Asian American groups (Sue and Morishima 1982; Uba 1994; Wolf 1997), shaping their mental health experiences in a way that is significantly distinctive from the Euro-American population.

As Chakraborty (1992: 2) states, "Nothing human can be taken out of culture and studied in isolation." Takeuchi, Uehara, and Maramba (1999: 565) also stress that "cultural factors are critical to understand access to mental health services, the proper screening and diagnoses that lead to treatment, and the actual effectiveness of treatment." While the psycho-social dimension of distress has been broadly explored in the sociology of mental health, cultural aspects of this issue are relatively neglected (Agbayani-Siewert, Takeuchi, and Pangan 1999; Brown et al. 1999; Fabrega 1992; Lefley 1999, Takeuchi, Uehara, and Maramba 1999; Triandis 1993). As Lefley (1999: 584) argues, culture can profoundly affect not only the experience of mental illness and health, but also its course. Triandis (1993) also insists that psychological well-being is associated with individuals' cultural values and beliefs. Following these scholars, who acknowledge the importance of culture in mental health studies, I modify Davar's model and create one that is diamond-shaped and includes biomedical (including both biochemical and neurological factors) as well as psychological, social, and cultural factors of mental distress (See Figure 3-1). I argue that the lower half of this diamond model, the social-cultural-psycho triangle, ought to be the major focus of mental health research in social science. Although something "cultural" can be considered "social" in a broad sense, I differentiate these two factors to highlight the difference between structural contexts (e.g., systems, organizations, systems of stratification, social positions and relations) and cultural norms (e.g., symbols, meanings, values) represented by social and cultural forces, respectively.

Figure 3-1: Conceptual Framework of Mental Distress from a Structurative Perspective

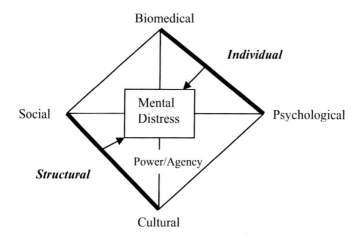

In this framework I distinguish two dimensions of factors that affect mental health, *the structural aspect* that includes social and cultural causes and *the individual aspect* that contains psychological and biomedical factors (see Figure 3-1). While the structural characteristics of *the social* are more self-evident, treating *the cultural* as something "structural" avoids reducing culture to "mere" thought – something soft, infinitely malleable, subjective, private, and "immaterial" – and acknowledges its material existence. I agree with anthropologist Douglas (1975) that culture is "the" structure ordering social life. As Hays states (1994: 65), culture is and "must be understood as a social structure." It is not only the product of human interaction but also the producer of human interaction. I also agree with Hays that, structure has two central interconnected components: systems of social relations and systems of meaning. The former consists of patterns of roles, relationships, and forms of domination (e.g., class, gender, ethnicity), and the latter refers to what is usually known as culture (e.g., beliefs, values, language, rituals, interactional practice). I utilize "the social" and "the cultural" to refer to what Hays labels "the systems of social relations" and "systems of meanings" respectively – two major factors in my investigation of this project. While presenting the social and the cultural as conceptually distinct in this framework, I argue that these two elements of structure interlock with each other and the form of their interconnections varies within different contexts.

I take mental distress to be a result of the confrontations between structure and individuals, producing negative effects on individuals' psychological well-being (see Figure 3-1). Following Giddens (1979, 1984), I consider the relations between structures and individuals dialectic, rather than tacit or uni-directional. Mental distress is engendered, although not always, when the individual confronts power imposition from the structure, either socially or culturally. Individuals, however, are not merely passive "victims" of structure. Rather, they are competent actors who are able to exert their agency in defining situations, negotiating meanings and identities, resisting structural power (in various forms), and empowering themselves.[19] As Giddens (1979: 69) states in his structuration theory, "structure is both enabling and constraining." I take this "structurative perspective" as the base of my conceptual framework, which considers the encounter between individuals and structures as on-going and dialectic processes that create the (dynamic) contexts within which distress is engendered and personal agency is exercised.

Adopting this structurative viewpoint, therefore, I take power in a Foucaudian sense, perceiving it (as well as resistance to power) as fluid (Foucault 1980). As Gallin (2002: 74) argues, "power involves the ability to see social spaces that can be taken advantage of, and the skill to dominate as large a part of a situation as possible." Those labeled powerful therefore never absolutely take control of specific circumstances, nor are those considered powerless completely passive victims (Gallin 2002). Moreover, "there are no relations of power without resistances" (Foucault 1980: 142). Power involves struggle, negotiation, and compromise. Resistance, as a counter force of power,

---

[19] In this sense, power relations are two-way and fluid. However subordinate an actor may be in a social relationship, his or her involvement in that relationship gives him/her a certain amount of power over the other (Giddens 1979: 6).

is also multiple and fluid. Individual agencies, while taking diverse forms, are exerted through such resistance.

The notions of structure, power, resistance, and agency are frequently discussed together because of their mutual presupposition and conceptual inseparability (Barbalet 1985; Foucault 1980; Fuchs 2001; Giddens 1979, 1984; Hays 1994; Sewell 1992). Although focusing on different subjects of discussion, these theorists along with feminist scholars, such as Gallin (2002), Yeoh, Teo and Huang (2002), Villarreal (1992), and Wolf (1992a), all agree that manifestations of structure, power, resistance, and agency are multi-level and fluid. Taking these concepts to my conceptual framework, therefore, I intend to understand distress experiences by revealing the causes, connections, and consequences of the dynamic contexts that involve power processes in the everyday lives of the actors. Next I incorporate these notions with my empirical concerns and frame an analytical model of this project.

Empirical Concerns and Analytical Framework

As noted above, my project asks four core research questions:

A. How and why do Taiwanese Americans make decisions to migrate to the U.S.?

B. How do Taiwanese Americans experience their social relations in the family and workplace in the U.S.?

C. How do Taiwanese Americans' migration experience and social relations influence their mental health?

D. How do men and women differ in their life experiences?

These questions represent my empirical concerns, and they mirror the types of research findings and gaps that were reviewed and discussed in Chapter Two. As demonstrated earlier in my conceptual framework, I approach this study from a structurative perspective that highlights mental distress as the negative psychological result of the dialectic relations between (social and cultural) structures and individuals within which personal agency confronts power domination. To do this job, as I call it "to contextualize mental distress" -- or to put it in a simpler way, "to situate my investigation in socio-cultural contexts" -- I elaborated and re-framed these core questions in three ways in my analytical framework.[20]

    First, I add a macro-level analysis about Taiwanese Americans' migration background and socio-cultural characteristics. This examination introduces structural factors that lead to Taiwanese immigration to the U.S. as well as the demographic and socio-cultural characteristics of Taiwan and Taiwanese immigrants (see Chapter Five). Not only does this examination enhance sociological understanding of the contexts from which Taiwanese immigrants originated, it also refines the core research questions into a more comprehensive analytical framework that links together macro, meso, and micro factors.[21] The elaborated research questions that frame my analysis in this book can be illustrated as follows:[22]

---

[20] In this chapter, I use the term "conceptual framework" to demonstrate my theoretical concerns of constructing a structurative approach; and "analytical framework" to illustrate my empirical concerns that derive primarily from my review of the literature, but also incorporate my conceptual ideas. This analytical framework serves to guide the design of my study, the analysis it develops, and the organization of this book.

[21] I follow Faist (2000a) and Gold (1997) to develop my research design and analytical framework at the meso or intermediate level. According to Fiast (2000a: 33-35), an investigation at the meso level is a relational analysis that focuses on the form and content of the relationship. It establishes firm links to both micro- and macro-level analyses. Gold (1997) states that immigration motives as a form of transnational practice address concerns of both macro and micro perspectives.

[22] I examine the macro level by synthesizing relevant literature and analyzing both census and INS data (see Chapter Five), and investigate the meso and micro levels by analyzing my interview data with Taiwanese Americans (see Chapters Six, Seven, and Eight).

1. At the macro level:
   (a) *What major structural (political, economic, social, cultural) factors lead to Taiwanese immigration to the United States?*
   (b) *What are the demographic and socio-cultural characteristics of Taiwanese immigrants in the U.S.?*

2. At the meso or intermediate level:
   (a) *How and why do Taiwanese American men and women make decisions to migrate to the U.S.?*
   (b) *How do Taiwanese American men and women experience their social relations in the family and workplace?*

3. At the micro level:
   How do Taiwanese American men's and women's migration decisions and social relations influence their mental health?

Second, I identify important variables for investigation from my review of the literature. I primarily analyze the impact of three structural factors -- immigration, family, and work – on mental distress. Drawing insights from previously reviewed literature and various perspectives, I pay special attention to power relations at each level of analysis. As Villarreal (1992: 258) points out, power takes place in different forms and at different (structural) levels. This nature of power makes it difficult to measure but "conspicuous enough to describe." For instance, decision-making, the gender division of domestic labor, and discrimination are all different manifestations of power relations: The power to make important decisions for the family, the power to determine the domestic division of labor, and the power to discriminate against others (or to put it another way, the powerlessness of being discriminated against), all reveal unequal statuses and relations that could possibly impair individuals' psychological well-being. Highlighting power also shows the interactive relations between individuals and structures, illustrating how individuals respond to structural constraints and demonstrate agency. In my analytical framework, therefore, "being a decision-maker for migration or not" and "the decision to migrate" are examined at the immigration level and how they relate to mental health. At the family level, I analyze two variables, "gender division of domestic labor" and "family decision-making about "finances" and "children's education," and how they relate to mental distress. At the work level, I explore how experiences of "racial discrimination" and "sexist treatment" affect mental health. These concepts and my analytical framework are illustrated in the following model (Figure 3-2).

Figure 3-2: Analytical Framework

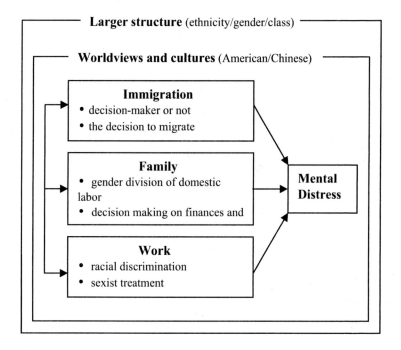

Third, I situate my analysis within the larger structure of the intersection of ethnicity/gender/class and of cultures. I believe that a good sociological inquiry should not be carried out in a contextual vacuum. While the major goal of this project is to explore how Taiwanese American men and women differ in their social relations and experience of distress, I also examine how these gender differences interact with the larger structure and culture (see Figure 3-2). In other words, I attempt to investigate (1) if gendered patterns of social relations reflect the larger structure of racism/sexism/classism in U.S. society, and how this hegemonic structure interacts with the structure of ethnicism/sexism/classism brought by these immigrants from their home country, Taiwan; (2) How the interlocking political, economic, social, and cultural factors of the migration process influence these two interacting societal structures in shaping Taiwanese Americans' gendered social relations; (3) How social contexts and structural characteristics (e.g., gender, race/ethnicity, or class) interact and influence gendered experiences of mental distress; and (4) How the worldviews derived from American and Chinese cultures play a role in shaping these experiences.

SUMMARY AND CONCLUSION

"Gender is about the relationship between women and men and that relationship is about power" (Vannoy 2001: 2). I believe, therefore, that a study of gender and mental health has to examine the power relations between women and men, the socio-cultural contexts within which this inequality is produced, and their consequent effects on individuals' psychological well-being. It is also important to extend this investigation of power relations to other aspects of social structures such as race, ethnicity, and class as well as to their impact on mental health. The political economy of health and feminist thinking both provide insights for exploring power issues and contextual factors that undergird this study of gender and mental health. The concept of emotional transnationalism, on the other hand, illustrates one of the most significant and unique psychological states immigrants and their children experience in their search for cultural meanings of behavior and values. These perspectives direct the construction of both my conceptual and analytical frameworks, what I call a "structurative approach," in a way that is different from those used in previous studies of mental health. This study of gender and mental health, in short, highlights the importance of social and cultural contexts, stresses the influence of migration background on the social life of ethnic groups, highlights the connection between power and social relations, and considers mental distress as the negative psychological impact of individuals' confrontations with (social and cultural) structures.

Viewing the concept of mental health and illness from a continuum perspective, I use the term "mental distress" in this book to describe negative psychological reactions. I investigate three major contexts – immigration, family, and work – and their impact on mental distress. At the immigration level, I examine two indicators, "being the decision-maker or not" and "the decision to migrate." At the family level, I explore informants' "gender division of domestic labor" and "decision-making on important family issues," including family finances and children's education. At the work level, I question closely subjects' perceived experiences of "racial discrimination" and "sexist treatment." Most importantly, I situate my study in larger social and cultural structures, highlighting the contextual factors that produce gender differences in the experience of distress.

CHAPTER 4

METHODOLOGY AND DATA

To answer the questions posed in Chapter Three, I turn in this chapter to the methodology applied in this study and the nature of the collected data. First, I explain why I adopted a qualitative approach of extended case study in this project. Next, I clarify two key terms in this book, Taiwanese Americans and culture, and then describe the research site. Following this description, I illustrate the range of methods employed in data collection, sampling categories, procedures of recruiting respondents, and relevant ethical issues. I also provide the demographic characteristics of the sample and discuss sampling biases. In the final section, I illustrate the way data were analyzed, and discuss the analysis units used to investigate different subjects.

METHODOLOGICAL APPROACH

Each study has its own methodological approach, demonstrating the characteristics of the research and the principles of how the findings are produced. This project was an exploratory study because it investigated a neglected population, Taiwanese Americans, in the sociology of mental health. Because of the scarce academic inquiry, sociological understanding concerning this ethnic group was limited, making this project an exploratory and primary inquiry. In addition, some of the variables I chose to investigate were not yet fully explored in traditional sociological studies of mental health (e.g., immigration decisions, family decision-making, and co-worker relations). These pioneer attempts also added an exploratory trait to this study.

This project was also a case study, aimed to explore a particular problem in rich detail in a specific site. Broadly speaking, "every study is a case study because it is an analysis of social phenomena specific to time and place" (Ragin 1992: 2). To further conceptualize the meaning of cases in this study, I found Ragin's definitions useful. In *What is a Case?*(1992), Ragin distinguishes four types of case studies according to two key dichotomies in how cases are conceived: (1) whether cases are viewed as involving empirical units or theoretical constructs; and (2) whether cases are understood as general or specific. Similar to most qualitative research, this project can be categorized as that of "cases are found," using Ragin's term, -- a study in which cases were "empirically real and bounded, but specific" (ibid.: 9). Harper (1992) uses his research of a homeless community to exemplify this type of case study. He argues that the "community" of homeless was found through interviewing and interacting with members of this community, and the researcher thus established understanding of this community through the study of these "real" and "specific" cases. Similarly, my project aimed to comprehend a community of Taiwanese Americans through interviewing individuals and participating in social activities among members.

I adopted a qualitative approach to undertake this project. As Jayaratne and Stewart (1991: 102) state, qualitative methods are more appropriate than quantitative methods when "the research goal is descriptive of individual lives and designed to promote understanding." Earlier studies that adopted large-scale quantitative surveys have failed to reveal Asian Americans' mental health problems, so scholars such as Agbayani-Siewert, Takeuchi, and Pangan (1999), Uba (1994), and Wolf (1997) have advocated the importance of in-depth qualitative research to fill this gap (also see Chapter Two). I therefore employed a qualitative approach to contextualize mental distress issues, so as to improve sociological understanding of Asian Americans' emotional life. As McCracken (1988) points out, generalizability is not the motivating issue of qualitative cases. The purpose of this project is not to generalize its findings to other Taiwanese Americans or other Asian groups, but rather, to provide a primary analysis of this specific case with an endeavor to supplement sociological understanding regarding Asian American's mental health issues. I believe that "the extended case study" explicated by Burawoy (1991) best describes the nature of this project. According to Burawoy (1991), the method of extended case study is the reconstruction of existing theories, taking into account the particularities of each situation. It aims to improve and reconstruct existing theories, but not to reject or disprove them. Although various social antecedents and consequences of mental distress have been examined in the sociology of mental health, it is unclear if the existing knowledge of mental health is applicable to Asian Americans' experiences, or, if the social context within which Asian Americans live produce unique situations that provide fresh implications for mental health research. This study sought to fill this gap, thereby improving sociological understanding of mental health.

DEFINITIONS AND OPERATIONALIZATION OF KEY TERMS

"Taiwanese Americans," "mental distress," and "culture" are key terms in this study, but they are also three terms that can be controversial. The usage of "Taiwanese Americans" has not yet become popular in academia, so I provide a definition and explanation regarding what I mean by "Taiwanese Americans." In Chapter Three, I highlighted the importance of culture in mental health research and provided a conceptual definition.[23] I also explained why I used the term "mental distress" and demonstrated its conceptual definition (see Chapter Three).[24] Here, I also describe how I operationalized mental distress and culture in my project.

Defining Taiwanese Americans

The ethnic-Chinese American community is composed of three sub-groups that migrate from China, Hong Kong, and Taiwan. These three groups share a traditional Chinese culture, but they have distinct historical, economic, social, and political backgrounds that are implicated in their different motives for migration, life situations and experiences, and worldviews. While Hong Kong was a colony of the UK until 1997, studies regarding Hong-Kongnese were seldom

---

[23] Following Hays (1994), I take culture as "systems of meanings," underlining symbols, meanings, and values in the informants' social and emotional life.

[24] Following Davar (1999), I take "mental distress" as a notion that embraces various psychological indicators (e.g., anxiety, frustrations, unhappiness, and hardships) that deviate from a perfect state of mental health.

considered together with those about Chinese before that time. In the literature, however, immigrants from Taiwan and their children are often treated the same as those from Mainland China, or simply overlooked. At least two factors lead to this phenomenon -- the categorization in census data and the complex historical and political relations between Taiwan and China.

In U.S. census data, information about the Taiwan-born population was not listed until 1982. Before 1982, Taiwanese immigrants were included in the category of China-born population. Even after the distinction between these two groups was made after 1982, inconsistent usage has remained. In some tables, Taiwanese are included as Chinese while they are separate in others. "Chinese except Taiwanese" and "Taiwanese" are both reported under the category of "Chinese." The case of Taiwanese is also separated from the major summary of census data and included in a "special report." Moreover, the population in the category of "last permanent residence is Taiwan" differs from that of "region and country of birth is Taiwan," because the latter excludes *waishengren* who were born in China and then retreated to Taiwan with the KMT government. These inconsistencies make it difficult to conduct a complete investigation of the population and social characteristics of Taiwanese Americans. In addition, some immigrants from Taiwan identify themselves as Chinese (see below and Chapter Five). As a result, the number of immigrants "whose last residence" is Taiwan, as reported in some census data, would be more accurate than self-reported ethnicity for approximating this population. Yet, an estimation based on last residence remains limited to first-generation immigrants and thus overlooks second and later generation Taiwanese Americans. Because of these limitations in census techniques, an accurate estimation of the number of Taiwanese Americans is not yet achievable.

In addition, Taiwan and China are involved in close but complex relations. Despite the fact that Taiwan was an integral part of China for hundreds of years, Taiwan and China have been two separate political entities since 1949, when the Koumintang (KMT) government retreated to and took control of Taiwan after losing the civil war to the Chinese

Communists.[25] The KMT regime also brought many officials, soldiers, and supporters to the island, creating a clear ethnic distinction between Mainlanders or *waishengren* (post-1945 Chinese immigrants who are primarily Mandarin speakers) and Taiwanese or *benshengren* (pre-1945 Chinese immigrants who speak Hokkien and Hakka) (see Chapter Five).[26] During the KMT rule, 1949-2000, the government had been preparing to conquer the Chinese Communists and return to the Mainland. Many people in Taiwan, especially *waishengren*, thus perceive the island as a temporary retreat and the Mainland as their motherland. As a result, national identity has been an ambivalent and contested issue on the island. Despite the fact that China and Taiwan are two separate political entities, many people on the island identify and claim themselves as Chinese. Most *benshengren*, however, view the KMT government as a colonizer and the *waishengren* as the privileged and oppressors. They advocate Taiwanese identity and national independence. Questions such as "What does Taiwanese mean?" "Who are the real Taiwanese?" "Are we Chinese or Taiwanese? Or both?" therefore have been controversial issues not only in the political arena but also in people's social life. This subject has been even more complicated since the aborigines began to openly strive for their rights and social status after the 1980s.[27]

---

[25] Taiwan was incorporated into the Chinese empire during the Tang dynasty (618-907), but it had not always been an integral part of China. Taiwan was occupied by the Dutch (1624-61) and Japanese (1895-1945). After Japan's defeat in World War II and the Chinese Communists' triumph in the civil war, the KMT government retreated to Taiwan in 1949 and governed this island for fifty-one years. The de facto K.M.T rule was ended in 2000 when the leader of the opposition Democratic Development Party (D.P.P.), Chen Shiu-bien, won the presidency (Gu and Gallin 2004).

[26] To avoid confusion, I use the terms "*waishengren*" and "*benshengren*" to refer to post-1945 (Mainlanders) and pre-1945 (Taiwanese) immigrants, respectively, and "Taiwanese" to refer to both.

[27] The aborigines in Taiwan, who are of Austronesian descent, were the original inhabitants of the island. They were forced to retreat to the mountain areas when *benshengren*, mainly from the Fujian and Guangtong provinces of China, migrated to Taiwan beginning in the sixteenth century (see Chapter Five).

The above two factors contribute to the difficulty of defining Taiwanese Americans. In the literature, studies of Chinatown had long been regarded as representative of the overseas Chinese community, and the Taiwanese had not been widely perceived as an ethnic group that is different from the Chinese. It was not until 1992 that an anthropologist from Taiwan, Chen, first challenged this homogeneous perception of Chinese communities. In his book, *Chinatown No More*, Chen (1992) portrays the distinct socio-cultural life of the Taiwanese-immigrant community in Flushing, New York, and corrects the misleading perspective of conceiving Chinatown as the only Chinese community in the U.S. As a result, later scholars began to notice the diversity of ethnic Chinese communities. For example, Tseng's study (1995) of "Little Taipei" in Los Angeles supports Chen's observation of the unique community life of Taiwanese immigrants. Historian Ng's book (1998), *The Taiwanese Americans*, signifies Taiwanese immigrants and their children as one of the "new Americans."[28] It is therefore important to follow this academic trend and treat Taiwanese Americans as an ethnic group that differs from Chinese Americans. Studying Taiwanese Americans also enriches sociological understanding of this newly recognized ethnic group.

Regardless of its recognition in academia, the usage of the term "Taiwanese Americans" remains a sensitive matter in research. During my fieldwork, several informants questioned my use of "Taiwanese Americans" in the informed consent letter because they did not acknowledge its existence. In contrast, others became disturbed if I used the term "Chinese" under any circumstances. Not only did this phenomenon remind me of the complexity of identity for people from Taiwan, but it also kept me alert in using the two terms, Chinese and Taiwanese, in my research. I therefore allowed myself some flexibility and ambiguity when using these terms in fieldwork and interviews, depending on the conversational context and informants' preference in order to retain rapport with the subjects, although I believe that it is

---

[28] The Greenwood Press (Westport, Connecticut) has published and continues to publish the New Americans series that portrays various groups of the post-1965 immigrants in the U.S. *The Taiwanese Americans* (Ng 1998) is one of the series.

necessary to maintain preciseness and clarification of the terms and concepts used in academic writings.

Following Ng (1998: 1-3), I define Taiwanese Americans as "immigrants from Taiwan and their descendants who are U.S. citizens." The subjects of this study therefore included those who were of *waishengren* (post-1945 Chinese immigrants, so-called Mainlanders) and *benshengren* (pre-1945 Chinese immigrants, so-called Taiwanese) descent, regardless of their national identity. In addition, in order to prevent confusion, I use the term "Taiwanese" to refer to all people who are Taiwan (R.O.C.) citizens, which include *waishengren*, *benshengren*, and aborigines; the term "Chinese" to refer to people who are citizens of China (P.R.C.); and *"waishengren"* and *"benshengren"* to refer to "Mainlanders" and "Taiwanese" respectively. The usage of *waishengren* and *benshengren*, instead of Mainlanders and Taiwanese, especially helps to prevent the misconception of viewing Mainlanders as "non-Taiwanese."

Operationalizing Mental Distress

In Chapter Three, I demonstrated the reason why I adopted the term, "mental distress," in this book and provided its conceptual definition. When conducting interviews, the terms I used to express the meaning of mental distress were fairly diverse and flexible. As I had explained in Chapter Three, Mandarin and Taiwanese have very different ways than does English to express psychological states such as "stressed," "distressed," and "depressed." To explore how the informants expressed their psychological problems in lay language, I used rather loose words such as *"yo-ya-li"* (stressed), *"fan-nao"* (worried), *"yu-chu"* (unhappy), *"chou-tse"* (frustrated), *"hsin-ku"* (experiencing hardships), *"di-chao"* (in low spirits) in my interviews with first-generation subjects (who mostly spoke Mandarin or Taiwanese). With second-generation informants who mainly spoke English, I said "stressed," "depressed," or "frustrated," assuming that they were more familiar with the meanings of these English terms than those in the parental generation.

In each interview, I allowed and encouraged informants to freely express their emotion and feelings in their own words. Particularly, my use of relatively neutral lay terms, such as "frustration," hardships," difficulties," social pressure," "stress," "worries, "bother" and "unhappiness," avoided cultural stigma of mental illness and abandoned "scientific" terminology developed in western academia. In other words, the way I solicited various expressions of distress experiences in the interviews gave me the flexibility and opportunities to "walk in the informants' shoes" in perceiving mental health.

Interpreting Cultural Factors

In Chapter Three, I emphasized the importance of culture and featured this project as a study of gender and mental health that highlights socio-cultural context. I have to admit that, despite its importance, culture is a term and analytical factor that is difficult to clearly and precisely define and to operationalize. The meaning of culture is exceptionally broad. It can refer to "a whole way of life" (Chakraborty 1992: 1), "a system of symbolic meanings" (Jayasuriya 1992: 37), or "the beliefs, values, symbolic meanings, and normative behavioral practices of a specific human group" (Lefley 1999: 566). In a global era in which culture penetrates national borders, it is especially difficult to accurately identify what "American culture" is or what "Taiwanese culture" is. Identification is particularly difficult when ethnic groups are exposed to two or even multiple cultures. As Brown and his colleagues (1999) point out, culture has multiple-level influences on both aggregate groups and individuals. In fact, it can have both general and specific influences on any given individual – the so-called "unboundedness" of culture (Swindler 1986). For instance, Taiwanese Americans are exposed to the general American culture, while simultaneously nurturing Taiwanese culture.

Given the difficulties and complex issues that are involved in conceptualizing culture, Agbayani-Siewert and her colleagues (1999) suggest the use of "specific cultural constructs" in mental health research. From their viewpoint, a culturally specific construct refers to a characteristic that is a distinctive feature of a given culture, such as "individualism," "collectivism," and "loss of face." By using specific cultural constructs, as Agbayani-Siewert and her colleagues argue, the broad definitional range of culture can be turned into operationalizable concepts. By so doing, researchers are able to directly assess the multiple facets of culture. While this effort to conceptualize culture is praiseworthy, it also produces some problems.

First, using cultural constructs may limit scholarly investigations to certain aspects of culture but overlook others. For example, variables such as individualism and collectivism are commonly used as cultural constructs, especially to compare western and non-western populations. This collectivism-individualism model well illustrates people's concepts of self and self's relations with others in a general way, but it fails to portray other dimensions of cultural beliefs, attitudes, norms, and values that might be more or as significant in interpreting the subject under investigation. For instance, Taiwanese people value the maintenance of cordial relationships among in-laws. To explain this cultural standard in a general sense, one can argue that Taiwanese, like other Asians, are collectivism-oriented. They have high regard for kinship relationships and, thus, go to great lengths in the pursuit of harmony. Underneath this cultural presentation, however, it is often women rather than men who, in practice, are going to these lengths. In Chinese culture, married women are expected to subordinate themselves to their husbands and to their husbands' families. The women's obedience constructs the foremost element in the development of satisfying in-law relationships. The patriarchal ideology and the gender roles that serve to sustain harmony among in-laws, therefore, might be based on cultural explanations alternative to those of collectivism.

The second weakness in using specific cultural constructs results from its limitation as noted above. That is, such usage encourages the tendency of reductionism in analytical explanations, and thus represses the complexity, diversity, and abounding features of culture in research. In contrast to social structures such as class, gender, and ethnicity that have particular compositions, representations and meanings, the meaning of culture is rather fluid, changeable, situational, and sometimes abstract. [29] Rather than pre-selecting certain cultural constructs or operationalizable cultural variables, I believe that attentive contextual observations and careful narrative analyses can reveal more vibrant cultural elements in contexts that are related to mental health issues. As Rogler (1989) suggests, conducting culturally

---

[29] Here I follow Faist (2000b), Geertz (1973), and Swidler (1986), emphasizing the fluidity, spatiality, and interpretations of cultural meanings.

sensitive research in mental health requires a continuing, incessant, and open-ended series of substantive and methodological insertions and adaptations in the process of inquiry. In this book, therefore, although I introduce the general socio-cultural characteristics of Taiwan (see Chapter Five), I did not presume which aspects of Chinese culture to associate with the subjects' psychological well-being in this project. My discussion of the relationship of culture and mental health is embedded in the interpretation and analysis of the informants' discourses concerning their situations. Specific cultural constructs are emphasized when they surface from the data, complemented with contextual explanations and discussion.

RESEARCH SITE

This study was conducted from January to August, 2001, in the Chicago metropolitan area. In this section, I first introduce the geographic distribution and ethnic characteristics of other Asian Americans in the greater Chicago region, then I provide a portrait of the Taiwanese American community.

Other Asian Americans in Chicago

Chicago is an immigrant city. A variety of ethnic backgrounds and cultures, (e.g., Irish, German, Swedish, Polish, Italian, Greek, Asian, African, and Hispanic) compose the kaleidoscope of this city's people and modern life. Each ethnic group has its own history of immigration and development. Different populations also hold distinct occupations and dwell in separate geographic areas in the greater Chicago area. Compared with other ethnic groups, Asian Americans are the latest to settle in Chicago (Holli and Jones 1995: 6-12). Among subgroups of Asian Americans, Japanese are the most integrated and assimilated into the dominant White society. Koreans, like their co-ethnics elsewhere, have been active in Chicago's retail market. Many of them are self-employed entrepreneurs, and their businesses are concentrated primarily in two areas: Koreatown in the north part of Chicago around Albany Park; and the south and southwest side in the African American neighborhood (Park 1997: 56-58). Two clusters of Asian Indians can be found on the metropolitan map of Chicago: earlier immigrants, among whom are a predominately highly educated professional elite of doctors, engineers, scientists, and college professors, who reside throughout the suburbs; a second cluster, mostly newcomers, is made up of the traditional Indian poor. They concentrate around the so-called "Indian street," Devon Avenue, on Chicago's north side, where Indian shops and restaurants have proliferated since the 1970s (Holli and Jones 1995: 12).

The Chinese began migrating to the United States in the early 1850s, but mainly settled on the west coast, particularly in California. As a result of rising anti-Chinese feelings and the consequent passage of exclusion laws in the late nineteenth century, they began migrating eastward. [30] Large cities, such as New York, Boston, and Chicago, became the major destinations of their journey from the west of the U.S. In Chicago, the first Chinese community, Chinatown, was founded in the 1880s. The Chinese population grew substantially thereafter.[31]

Chicago's Chinatown, located south of downtown and north of the African American district, has expanded its area since it was first established, although it has remained in the same region. Similar to their co-ethnics in other cities, the Chinese in Chicago's Chinatown are primarily Cantonese-speakers who migrated from the southeastern part of China. They worked in shops and restaurants in this Chinese community, and established their homes there. Almost a century after the original Chinatown was founded, a new Chinese business community was formed in the uptown area of Chicago, when the fall of Saigon in 1975 brought a group of Chinese immigrants from Vietnam. Many of these Southeast Asian Chinese speak both Cantonese and

---

[30] The economic recession of the late 1870s gave rise to an anti-Chinese movement. The Chinese were blamed for the decline of economic conditions, and rising "white America" sentiments led to the exclusion laws targeted particularly at the Chinese. The Exclusion Act of 1882 prohibited the entry of Chinese laborers into the U.S., and Chinese already in the U.S. were denied American citizenship. Moreover, the 1924 Immigration Act excluded aliens who were ineligible for U.S. citizenship, and the Chinese population gradually declined thereafter, until 1943 when it began to rise again.

[31] The Chinese population in Chicago in 1890 was only 567, but doubled to 1,209 by 1900 (Moy 1995). According to the 2000 census data, 31,280 Chinese live in the inner city of Chicago.

Mandarin, and they had operated businesses in Vietnam. Hence, a great number of Vietnamese restaurants and shops also are features in this new ethnic Chinese community, which is very different from Chinatown.

The Taiwanese American Community in Chicago

According to census data, the Taiwanese American population in Illinois is 3,427, the largest among Midwest states. The Chicago metropolitan area (see Map 4-1) contains nearly 80 percent of this population (2,676, about 78.1%).[32] In other words, the greater Chicago vicinity is an important geographic area of the Taiwanese American community in the Midwest region. In contrast to other Chinese populations living in the region, Taiwanese Americans are scattered throughout the Chicago metropolitan area.[33]

Since most Taiwanese Americans are white-collar professionals (see Chapter Five), they tend to live in suburbs as do other middle-class families. Several large companies in suburban Chicago, such as Abbott, Lucent, Motorola, also attract Taiwanese employees to nearby neighborhoods. Taiwanese Americans who are employees of the University of Chicago or its hospital reside close to their workplace, Hyde Park, in the south side of the city. Second-generation Taiwanese Americans who already are working or have established their own families tend to live in the downtown area. Because of their wide distribution across the area, there is no particular community landscape with which they are identified, such as Chinatown, which highlights the presence of the Chinese as a social group on the map of Chicago. Nevertheless, several Taiwanese churches, stores, and restaurants in the north (Lake County) and west (DuPage County) suburbs do suggest that these areas are home to substantial numbers of Taiwanese Americans.

---

[32] Source: Census Bureau, Census 2000 Summary File. Table QT-P7.

[33] According to the 2000 Census Data, of the 2,676 Taiwanese Americans living in the greater Chicago area, 1,455 (54.4%) reside in Cook County, 996 (37.2%) in DuPage County, and 225 (8.4%) in Lake County.

Map 4-1: The Chicago Metropolitan Area

Source: Census Bureau Maps.
* Cook, Lake, and Dupage are the three counties within the metropolitan area.

In contrast to "Little Taipei" in Los Angeles, Taiwanese-owned businesses in Chicago do not congregate in a certain district, but are spread throughout the metropolitan area. Moreover, no single industry is a prominent feature of this community, as the types of businesses operated by Taiwanese Americans are very heterogeneous. A variety of enterprises are randomly scattered throughout the metropolitan area, such as eat-in and take-out Chinese restaurants, laundries, Baskin and Robin stores, gift shops, bookstores, import companies, computer companies, clinics, and hotels. These Taiwanese-owned businesses do not necessarily indicate their ethnicity, as many of them hire non-Asian workers and do not have Chinese or Taiwanese logos.

Some of the few places that "look Taiwanese" at first glance are a supermarket DIHO and the shops next-door to it within the International Plaza. This plaza is located in Westmont, a small town in the west suburb of Chicago (see photos 4-1, 4-2, and 4-3). "DIHO" is a Taiwanese-chain supermarket in Taiwan, but it has nothing to do with the DIHO in Chicago. By using this popular name, DIHO attracts clients from Taiwan and tries to make them feel as if they are shopping at home.[34] All kinds of ads, newspapers, and activity fliers written in Chinese can be seen inside this supermarket, which has become an information center for the Taiwanese and Chinese community. The International Plaza is a two-story marketplace. A small food court featuring booths selling Taiwanese snacks and Chinese food is on the first floor, and several stores, offices, and clinics occupy the second story. Two TV sets showing satellite programs from Taiwan and China hang on the two sides of the food court.

---

[34] "DIHO" has become a popular name for supermarkets in the overseas Taiwanese community. For instance, a DIHO supermarket is in "Little Taipei" in L.A., but it has nothing to do with either the one in Chicago or those in Taiwan.

Photo 4-1: The International Plaza in Westmont (west suburban Chicago)

Photo 4-2: DIHO Supermarket in Westmont

Photo 4-3: The International Market in Westmont

Photo 4-4: Taiwanese Church

Churches also serve as markers of Taiwanese ethnicity in the greater metropolitan area. More than ten Taiwanese churches have been established in the greater Chicago area, and noticeable signs that demonstrate their ethnic backgrounds are displayed outside the church buildings (see photo 4-4). These Taiwanese churches usually conduct their sermons and fellowship programs bilingually (Taiwanese and English), to meet the needs of both first-generation and second-generation Taiwanese. Mandarin is also used in some churches during sermons when members communicate with church personnel. A few Taiwanese Christian groups that do not have their own churches rent Anglo-owned chapels, conference rooms in hotels, or classrooms in schools to worship and hold gatherings.

In addition to these markers of identity, other places in the metropolitan area serve as magnets for Taiwanese Americans. For instance, several large American corporations located right outside the city, such as Abbott Pharmaceutical Company and its laboratories, Motorola Technology, and Lucent Technology, bring a great number of Taiwanese professionals and their families to suburban Chicago. They live in middle-class White neighborhoods, and many own luxurious houses and cars. This group, primarily made up of members of the "brain drain," predominates among Taiwanese Americans. They are highly educated, have high income and social status, and many work for high-tech companies, practice medicine, or hold academic jobs.

The Chinese Culture Center of the Taipei Economic and Cultural Office in Chicago, located in Westmont (in west suburban Chicago), is also an important gathering place for the Taiwanese community. As a branch of the Taiwan government, whose goal is to serve overseas Taiwanese, this center provides various services and activities. A range of courses, such as English, computer skills, immigration consultation, and swing dancing, are regularly offered by this center to help immigrants adapt to American society. The library inside this center has a wide collection of Chinese books, newspapers, and videotapes that help people maintain a connection with Taiwan. The Chinese Cultural Center also supplies teaching materials for Chinese schools, and lends meeting rooms to Taiwanese organizations for their social activities. This Center does not exist solely to meet the needs of Taiwanese Americans, but also serves as a tourist and information center for other U.S. citizens who are interested in learning about Taiwanese culture and society.

Chinese schools are another important place that draw members of the Taiwanese American community (see Photo 4-5). Due to their desire for their children to learn Mandarin, Taiwanese parents establish schools, and many of them share administrative and educational responsibilities. They usually rent rooms from a high school in the neighborhood, and hold classes of various levels during weekends. Parents find teachers from their own community, often the students' mothers or those who had teaching experiences while in Taiwan. Class materials can be purchased from the Chinese Cultural Center, but some schools create their own textbooks or import other resources directly from Taiwan.[35] By 2001, more than ten Chinese schools had been founded in the greater Chicago area.

Photo 4-5: Chinese School

---

[35] The Chinese Cultural Center also provides relevant teaching information and services for Chinese schools, such as teaching workshops, curriculum competitions, and various extracurricular activities.

Taiwanese American organizations are numerous in Chicago's Taiwanese American community, and these associations serve diverse political, social, professional, cultural, and religious purposes. They enrich the everyday lives of the Taiwanese Americans, especially for first-generation immigrants, helping them adapt to the host society, maintain connections with Taiwanese society, form national or transnational identities, and establish social networks. Since this community does not have an evident landscape or a distinct location such as Chinatown, organizational activities become exceptionally important for understanding Taiwanese Americans' social lives, adaptations, and community identity.

METHODS OF COLLECTING DATA

Pilot Investigations

Prior to initiating this project, I conducted pilot investigations during several trips to Chicago in the summer of 2000, which helped me to obtain access to the Taiwanese American community, elaborate my research proposal, and develop interview questions. First, I visited the Center for Multicultural and Multilingual Mental Health Services and consulted with the director regarding mental health issues confronting Asian Americans in general, and ethnic-Chinese immigrants specifically. The information I acquired from this visit indicated that extremely few Taiwanese Americans employed the Multicultural Mental Health Services, confirming the public impression that the Taiwanese, like many other Asians, may adjust well in the host society. Alternatively, this non-use may reflect the fact, as some social psychologists (e.g., Flaskerud and Liu 1990; Suan and Tyler 1990; Sue and Sue 1974; Uba 1994) have revealed, that Asian Americans, including Taiwanese, tend to under-utilize mental health services simply because of their cultural differences in perceiving and coping with mental health problems. Regardless of reason, I realized that exploring mental health issues facing Taiwanese Americans might not be feasible by gathering information from mental health services, confirming one of my research rationales to conduct this project by in-depth interviewing "ordinary" people rather than a clinical population.

Second, I visited several social welfare organizations in Chinatown, and collected information regarding ethnic-Chinese immigrants' difficulties when adapting to the host society. The social workers in these welfare organizations had adequate knowledge concerning and good connections with those who were in need of help in the Chicago area. Again, however, I obtained the message that very few Taiwanese sought help from these non-profit organizations. Among the few Taiwanese families who kept in touch with these organizations (mainly lower-class families), financial difficulties, loneliness, isolation, and language barriers were the major problems they encountered in everyday life. Despite these few cases, the social welfare people stressed repeatedly that most immigrants from Taiwan resided in suburban Chicago and were pretty well-off. This information led me to foresee the difficulties of locating lower-class Taiwanese due to the imbalanced class composition of this population.

Finally, I contacted several Taiwanese immigrants through personal referrals to solicit opinions on my project and their willingness to be interviewed. These personal contacts ensured the possibility of executing this project as well as providing sources of potential informants. I also attained information through these contacts regarding the locations where Taiwanese Americans most often gather, and visited these places to enhance my knowledge of this community. I realized that the number of Taiwanese Americans in Chicago seemed to be much larger than I imagined, based on the informants' description and my observation. Coming from a college town where immigrant communities were rather small and homogeneous, I realized that my knowledge of Taiwanese Americans was pretty limited before entering their community in Chicago -- a community that is large, diverse, and full of various social activities. Compared to "Little Taipei" in Los Angles within which small enterprises constitute the majority, Taiwanese Americans in the Chicago area feature a typical "brain drain" population primarily made up of professionals in high-tech industries, academia, and medicine. Some, especially women, work as administrators in public libraries or private corporations; some are businesspeople such as hotel and restaurant owners, while only a few hold blue-collar occupations such as waiters or waitresses, and factory workers. Political, social, religious, and cultural activities are frequently held, reflecting the vitality of this community.

Research Methods and Sources of Data

My main data were developed by semi-structured in-depth interviews (see Appendix A for the schedule of interview questions) and limited participant observations. I also collected relevant documents to improve my understanding of the local ethnic-Chinese community. My sources of data therefore included: (1) Fifty-four individual interviews; (2) a fieldwork journal of brief notes that I took during my interviewing phase and participation in community activities; and (3) documental archives, including Chinese newspapers, activity fliers, and magazines, that helped me to understand the Taiwanese American community. The first source, personal interviews, produced the major data set for this project, while the other two were an aid that deepened my understanding of this community and interpretation of findings.

Individual In-depth Interviews

Individual in-depth interviews constituted the main data in my analysis. I conducted 54 personal interviews, each lasting from one to four hours with an average length of two hours. These interviews took place in the setting of the informants' choice, such as their home, workplace, or a coffee shop (see next section for the details of my interview procedures).

Participant Observations

In addition to personal interviews, I also was a participant observer at various activities (e.g., social gatherings, association meetings, speeches, concerts, religious activities) in the Taiwanese immigrant community. I observed how Taiwanese immigrants organized their social life, how men and women interacted with each other, and how second-generation children mingled in this community. The observable settings in the field, however, to a large extent centered around first-generation immigrants' social life. Second-generation Taiwanese seldom appeared at the activities I attended, except for church events. Even at churches where more Taiwanese youth were visible, they tended to congregate with those who were their own age. Compared to their parental generation who frequently met in person at various social occasions, second-generation Taiwanese tended to form their community and maintain contacts through the internet and e-mail.

Observing and participating in these activities not only deepened my understanding of this ethnic group, but also helped me to recruit informants. Moreover, I approached Taiwanese immigrants who worked in ethnic stores and talked to them about their migration motives, family lives, work situations, and distress. These informal talks helped to bring me closer to the real life of the subjects I studied. They also provided information and research ideas that I might not have been able to obtain through individual interviews. For instance, I heard stories regarding how Taiwanese youth indulged themselves in luxury goods, how a well-behaved teenager died of drug overdose, how happily-married couples got divorced because of the difficulties in adapting to their new life after immigration, how people of different political stances fought with each other, and how some rich Taiwanese men gambled away their businesses.[36] These "stories on the street" revealed the possible "downside" of immigrant life and indicated potential directions for investigation and future studies. Unfortunately, I was unable to interview the people in these stories after several contact attempts.

I tried to write some notes in my research journal immediately after I returned home from an interview or a social event. These notes recorded what I observed, thought, and felt during the interviews or in the field. They also documented the recruitment difficulties I encountered (e.g., difficulties with gaining access to working-class subjects), interview circumstances that I struggled with (e.g., the usage of "Chinese" or "Taiwanese"), memos for future interviews (e.g., better conversational flow to start talking about work with men, but to begin with family issues with women), and possible or interesting topics for future research. I also attempted to keep track of themes or patterns I was finding across interviews and observations. Although most of these notes did not directly become the text in my analysis, they played an important role in this project by offering a venue for my thoughts that were beneficial while interpreting data and refining analytical conclusions. In other words, being a participant observer in the field enriched my knowledge of this community in a dynamic and

---

[36] During my fieldwork, I twice witnessed Taiwanese immigrants who took different political stances fiercely quarrel with each other in public.

comprehensive way; it also equipped me to think and sense the life world from the informants' standpoints.

Chinese Documentary Materials

During my fieldwork, I also collected relevant archival and documentary materials, such as Chinese newspapers and activity fliers, to broaden my understanding of this ethnic group. These materials helped to locate organizational activities, to understand what types of social events interested the members, and to get acquainted with ongoing issues that concerned this community.

Recruiting and Sampling Procedure

In this section, I first introduce how I operationalized sampling categories that were listed in my stratification plan. Following this introduction, I explain how I recruited informants, carried out the consent procedures, and dealt with ethical issues. Lastly, I illustrate my interview schedule.

Conceptualization and Operationalization of Sampling Categories

I used a stratification plan to recruit respondents, which was based on the informants' gender, generation, social class, and ethnicity of origin (*benshengren* and *waishengren*). While gender is self-evident, I explain below how I conceptualized and operationalized other sampling categories I used in this study.[37]

First, "generation" is frequently used in immigration studies to describe immigrants and their children. The term "first generation" refers to immigrants who leave their society of origin and settle in another country, while "second generation" refers to native-born children of immigrant parents. Some first-generation immigrants may already have had young children at the time they migrated, and scholars

---

[37] "Conceptualization" and "operationalization" deal with different research issues. While "conceptual" definitions demonstrate the theoretical base for each sampling category, "operational" definitions illustrate how a researcher puts these categories into practice in a study.

use the term "one-point-five generation" to refer to these immigrant children who were born abroad and came to the host country at a very early age. Usually, both the second generation and the 1.5 generation are included in the category of "children of immigrants" (Portes 1996b: ix-x).

In scholarly work, the second generation often includes the 1.5 generation, unless the latter is treated as a comparison to the former or when it is regarded as an individual group for study. Since comparing these two groups of children of immigrants was not the concern of this project, I adopted the broad definition of the second generation that also included the so-called 1.5 generation in my operationalization of sampling categories. As for the first generation, the broad definition of "immigrants" include those who temporarily migrate to another country for study or work, those who are in the process of acquiring citizenship, those who have already obtained citizenship, refugees, and those who are undocumented immigrants. I studied only those Taiwanese immigrants who have become U.S. citizens.

Second, "social class" is a major structural inequality, a ranking in a stratification system that is based on economic resources (Eitzen and Baca Zinn 2000: 43). Social class can be categorized in many ways and very meticulously (e.g., capitalists, upper-middle class, middle class, lower middle-class, working class). In this study, I focused only on two groups, "middle class" and "lower class." Conceptually, the middle-class include those who held high prestige jobs that require considerable formal education and have a high degree of autonomy and responsibility; it also includes those who work in minor jobs in bureaucracies. The lower-class, in contrast, have little autonomy in their jobs. They are closely supervised by other people and have little control over other workers or their own work. Working-class individuals usually have no more than a high school diploma, and are thus blocked from significant upward mobility (Eitzen and Baca Zinn 2000). Examples of the middle-class include professionals, business people and executives, secretaries, police officers, and teachers, while instances of the lower-class include workers in factories, stores, offices, or restaurants.

According to Eitzen and Baca Zinn (2000), work autonomy, authority, and control (over other workers or the job) is the major distinction between the middle-class and the lower-class. I therefore operationalized the term "social class" by the informants' job authority and autonomy. When informants had little control on their job or over other workers, they were listed as "lower class," while others who had job autonomy and authority were designated as "middle class"

Third, "ethnicity" refers to "the condition of being culturally rather than physically distinctive," and "ethnic peoples are bound together by virtue of a common ancestry and a common cultural background" (Eitzen and Baca Zinn 2000: 232). As mentioned earlier in this chapter, although immigrants from Taiwan may identify themselves differently in terms of ethnicity (as Chinese or Taiwanese Americans), I call this group of immigrants who migrated from Taiwan and their descendants "Taiwanese Americans" to signify their common origin and culture. In this sense, all the informants' ethnicity in the U.S. was Taiwanese Americans because they were all Americans who were of Taiwanese heritage. Their ethnicity in Taiwan, however, could be *waishengren* or *benshenren*. To distinguish informants' ethnicity in the U.S. and Taiwan, I adopted the term "ethnicity of origin" to refer to the latter and used it as a variable to compare sub-groups in my analyses. Conceptually, "ethnicity of origin" means the informants' ethnicity in their society of origin, Taiwan. In this study, I concentrated on two ethnic groups of origin, "*waishengren*" and "*benshengren*" (see earlier in this chapter for their historical relations and term explanations). To operationalize these two terms, I adopted the informants' subjective identity regarding who they were. In other words, I asked the question, "Are you *benshengren* or *waishengren*?" and recorded the informants' ethnicity of origin based on their answers. [38] Second-generation subjects' ethnicity of origin was recorded based on their parents' ethnic background. Those whose parents were both *benshengren* (including Hakka) were regarded as *benshengren*, and those whose parents were both *waishengren* as *waishengren*. If one parent was *benshengren* while the other *waishengren*, then the informant was recorded

---

[38] All informants responded this question without hesitation or confusion. They all told me immediately and clearly if they were *waishengren*, *benshengren*, or Hakka. Hakka was recorded as *benshengren* because I used the traditional distinction of *waishengren* and *benshengren* in this study (see earlier in this chapter).

"interethnic."[39] By so doing, I intended to avoid the conventional gender-biased categorization that only took fathers' background into account when defining individuals' ethnicity. Family ethnicity was recorded in a similar way. *Waishengren* families referred to those families within which both (first-generation) husbands and wives were *waishengren*. *Benshengren* families indicated those in which both husbands and wives were *benshengren*. Interethnic families were recorded when the husbands and wives belonged to different ethnic groups.

Recruiting Procedures

My sample was developed through purposive sampling procedures. Informants were recruited through multiple methods, including my personal networks, snowball sample referrals, e-mail ads on organizational list-servers, and through various ethnic-Chinese organizations.[40] Among these recruiting methods, snowball sample referrals were the most efficient, especially in finding first-generation and lower-class subjects. This phenomenon was consistent with what Tsai (1998) discovered in her research of middle-class Taiwanese. Coming from a society that emphasizes inter-personal relations, Taiwanese immigrants usually accepted my invitation to be interviewed easily when we knew someone in common but refused otherwise. In contrast, children of immigrants responded to my invitations much

---

[39] Nevertheless, none of the second-generation informants were interethnic in this study (see Appendix D). Their parents were all of the same ethnicity of origin.

[40] These ethnic-Chinese organizations include three major types: (1) Taiwanese immigrant associations, such as Taiwanese Association of America Greater Chicago Chapter, Taiwanese American Fund, Taiwanese American Student Club, Taiwanese Hakka Association of USA, Chinese Academic and Professional Association in Mid-America; (2) social service organizations, such as Chinese Mutual Aid Association, Chinese American Service League, Chinese Culture Center of the Taipei Economic and Cultural Office in Chicago; (3) religious organizations, such as Tzu-Chi Foundation, Dharma Drum Mountain Buddhist Association, Taiwanese Community Church, and Evangelical Taiwan Church.

more voluntarily. Several of them volunteered to be interviewed when they saw my ads on e-mail list-servers, and others agreed to be interviewed immediately when I approached them at social events without any personal referrals. This dissimilarity may indicate that the two different generations of Taiwanese maintain a different degree of *guanxi* from their society of origin.[41]

Moreover, my "standpoint" – being female, young, and from Taiwan – brought advantages to my research proceedings. Taiwan is a society in which gender and age are two important stratification markers in social relations (also see Chapter Five). First-generation informants were positioned higher than me in this stratification. This asymmetric relation corresponded to our role plays in interviews – they as speakers and myself as a listener. Therefore, first-generation informants were quite willing to tell me almost about everything, in a way of showing generosity and knowledge that marked their senior status. My ability to speak both Mandarin and Taiwanese also helped to minimize my distance from both *waishengren* and *benshengren* who are different language speakers (see Chapter Five). In contrast, while interacting with second-generation subjects, my shared ethnic and cultural background with them surely facilitated our conversations (in English). Feeling that I truly understood what they were talking about, second-generation informants expressed themselves freely. Some even found our interviews "therapeutic," using an informant's word. As a result, I acquired much in-depth information concerning the subjects' social and emotional lives.

I experienced a little emotional struggle while interviewing informants through referrals of social service organizations. These informants were lower-class and lived in the Chinatown area, so most of them encountered financial difficulties or family conflicts because of their economic burden. They agreed to be interviewed without hesitation, but expected for my substantial future assistance. Being viewed as a social worker (no matter how I tried to explain my research

---

[41] *Guan-Xi*, interpersonal relations that involve reciprocity, is a significant characteristic of Chinese culture. Doing favors, treating meals, knowing common friends, and presenting gifts or money, are all the ways to establish *guan-xi*. Reciprocity is expected once *guan-xi* is established between two persons (also see Chapter Five).

purpose and status in lay language) who will provide help, I felt a little awkward. This feeling of unease was particularly strong while leaving the subjects' house, after I learned about their unfortunate lives. Questions such as "Should I bring some gifts to them?" "Should I offer some money as remuneration for the interview?" "Should I help them in a substantial way?" "How should I play the role as a researcher in these encounters?" often occupied my mind. Despite my inner battle with sympathy, I finally decided not to offer material rewards. Rather, I provided these lower-class informants information about available welfare resources in their neighborhood, and informed social workers in welfare organizations about these informants' need for aid.

Consent Procedures

Before every individual interview, I provided the informant a brief introduction to my project, and obtained his or her verbal informed consent. I used a verbal but not written consent form in this study because of the way the Taiwanese community perceives a formal written document that requires the respondent's signature. In Taiwanese culture, asking an informant to sign a formal document can arouse serious fears and doubts because people are afraid of leaving any written "evidence" that might cause them trouble in the future. Usually, Taiwanese people are willing to be interviewed when they trust the interviewer or researcher, or when they feel they have something to say about the topic under study. Personal connections and friends' referrals, therefore, are important to earn people's trust and willingness to participate in research, and verbal consent is more appropriate than a written form based on the subjects' culture. I informed the respondents verbally before every interview that their participation was totally voluntary, and that they were free to refuse to answer any questions in the interview or to stop the interview at any time. Interviewees' verbal consent was taped before the interview.

The language used in my interviews (Mandarin, Taiwanese, or English) was totally up to respondents' preference. Interviews took place in the setting of the informants' choice (e.g., their home, their workplace, or a coffee shop). All interviews were tape-recorded unless the respondent refused to do so, and were translated into and transcribed in English.[42] Among the 54 subjects, six refused to be taped (all first-generation informants, including three middle-class men and three lower-class women), and one middle-class woman asked me to stop recording when talking about racial discrimination at her workplace. In these cases, I wrote down as much as I could during the interviews, and then re-organized my notes and supplemented what I remembered immediately after returning home while my memory of the interviews was still fresh.

Informants' privacy was protected by guaranteeing each person interviewed anonymity in this study. In addition to including a confidentiality statement in my verbal consent, I signed a confidentiality form for each individual interviewee to support my guarantee to protect the subjects' privacy. Furthermore, because this is a study of mental health, the informants might have needed consultation or shelter services if they were encountering physical or psychological abuse. I therefore prepared information regarding mental health and social welfare services in the Chicago area, in anticipation that some interviewees might be in need of professional help. As a researcher of mental health, I am responsible to my respondents for informing them about available resources.[43]

After the interviews, I assigned each informant a number and removed names from the transcripts. Then, I assigned pseudonyms to each numbered subject and used only these pseudonyms in analyses and in this book. No significant life stories or anything that might identify individuals (e.g., the names of meeting places or personal characteristics) were and will be reported in any written papers,

---

[42] Interviews conducted in Mandarin or Taiwanese were transcribed in Chinese first, then translated into English. Both versions were kept and referenced to each other frequently when conducting coding and memoing. I adopted the English version when using NUDIST to analyze the entire data, but also referred to the Chinese version to double-check codes and memos (see next section on data analysis).

[43] A second-generation female informant mentioned that she had suffered serious physical abuse from her mother during her childhood and adolescence. I provided information about available mental health services, but she refused to accept the materials because she, in her own words, "had managed it well."

published or unpublished. I also maintained the security of all files, notes and tapes in a locked area in my home, to which only I had access.

The Interview Schedule

In addition to acquiring demographic background from the informants, my interview questions were organized based on the three levels of analysis in my research framework that is described in Chapter Three: the association between immigration decisions and mental distress, between familial relations and mental distress, and between work relations and distress (see Figure 3-2 in Chapter Three). At the immigration level, I asked questions concerning how and why the informants made decisions to migrate to and settle in the U.S., as well as if and how the decision to migrate affected their mental health. At the family level, I asked questions regarding family decision-making (including financial decisions and children's education), and the gender division of domestic labor. At the work level, I asked questions about racial and gender discrimination and relationships with co-workers. At each level, I asked questions concerning frustration, worries, difficulties in adaptation, and methods of coping with distress (see Appendix A).

In other words, I used a semi-structured format to design my interview schedule -- what Merton, Fiske, and Kendall (1990) call "the focused interview." My questions were topical, centering around my analytical framework and serving as interview guidelines. My interviews were also conversationally-oriented, as I initiated open-ended questions and followed up the informants' responses. By so doing, I allowed considerable flexibility and latitude for the informants to respond to the questions, and for them to talk about relevant subjects that even went beyond my prepared guidelines. The order of topics that I went through on this interview schedule was sometimes changeable, depending on the conversational context and the informants' interest. For instance, I found that it was an efficient strategy to form flowing and pleasant conversational interviews by starting with work-related subjects with men while beginning with family issues with women. This style of qualitative interview meets what Rubin and Rubin (1995: 42-64) describe as "keeping on target while hanging loose."

THE SAMPLE

Since individual in-depth interviews constitute the major data in my analysis, information about the sample is important to understand the findings and limitations of this study. In this section, I first describe the demographic characteristics of my sample, then discuss some sampling biases and their causes.

Demographic Information

In total, I interviewed 54 Taiwanese Americans, including 27 (50%) men and 27 (50%) women. Their ages ranged from 18 to 82. Almost all (87%) were between 21 and 60 years of ages (see Appendix B). Of the 54 informants, 34 (63%) were first-generation, while 20 (37%) were second-generation Taiwanese. The majority of the respondents were *benshengren* (39 individudals, 72%), and only 15 (38%) identified themselves as *waishengren*. The class distribution of the sample was very skewed, as most informants (48 individuals, 89%) were middle-class and only six (11%) were lower-class (see Appendix B).

About half of the Taiwanese Americans I interviewed (28 individuals, 52%) were currently married and lived with their spouses. All but one of them were in their first marriage. Among these 28 married respondents, two women were married to Caucasians, while the others had spouses who were either first- or second-generation Taiwanese. Of the 54 informants, 21 (39%) were never married at the time of our interviews, two women (4%) were divorced, and three (5%) were widowed (see Appendix B).[44]

Biases in the Sample and Their Causes

Before initiating the sampling procedure, I devised a stratification plan that aimed to recruit equal numbers of men and women, equal numbers of first- and second-generation, and two-thirds of middle-class and one-

---

[44] One of the divorced women was previously married to a Taiwanese immigrant, while the other's ex-husband was from Hong Kong. All three widowed women's late husbands were Taiwanese immigrants.

third of lower-class informants.[45] Besides this stratification schema framed by gender, generation, ethnicity, and class, I also sought to obtain variation in age, marital status, and occupations while recruiting informants in order not to make my sample too homogenous. Nevertheless, I achieved only the goal of equal gender distribution but failed the planned recruitment of generation and class proportions, which made my sample biased in some ways. The degrees of these sample biases were different – some reflected the population features of this ethnic group, while others were caused by the difficulties in actual recruitment.

First, I interviewed more first- than second-generation informants mainly because of the difficulties of eliciting the latter for the following reasons. (A) Very few children of Taiwanese immigrants attended organizational activities in this community. Those who were involved in ethnic organizations, either were church members or college students (mostly members of Taiwanese or Chinese American associations).[46] My participation and personal contacts in community activities therefore only led to access of limited and rather homogenous individuals. (B) Most of the adult children of first-generation informants I knew lived in other states where they were studying or working, making it difficult to recruit them for interviews through personal referrals. (C) Several second-generation Taiwanese who were middle-class professionals, such as computer programmers, doctors, or

---

[45] I planned to recruit more middle-class than lower-class subjects, rather than equal numbers, because the information from Tseng (1995), Portes and Rumbaut (1996), and my pre-research investigation all indicated that Taiwanese immigrants were primarily composed of professionals. In addition, Tsai (1998) reported that locating lower-class Taiwanese immigrants were very difficult in practice. Nevertheless, recruiting 18 informants (one-third of the sample) who were lower-class remained a too-optimistic goal.

[46] A great number of second-generation Taiwanese were actively involved in ethnic organizations that were nation-wide, such as Taiwanese American Foundation (TAF), the Society of Taiwanese Americans (SOTA), and the Intercollegiate Taiwanese American Students Association (ITASA). They held a variety of occupations, and many were accessible via e-mail. Nevertheless, it was difficult to arrange personal interviews because they resided throughout the U.S.

engineers, refused to be interviewed because of their busy schedules. Consequently, the number of second-generation respondents in this study was less than that of the first-generation.

Second, the imbalanced proportions of middle- and lower-class informants in this study were caused primarily by recruiting difficulties, but they also reflected the demographic characteristics of Taiwanese Americans. I was only able to successfully interview six (11%) informants who were lower-class.[47] These six respondents were all first-generation immigrants, including two men and four women. Two factors led to my failure to elicit more lower-class subjects. (A) Very few Taiwanese Americans lived in the Chinatown vicinity. Some who worked in ethnic stores or small-business owners in this area resided in the suburbs, and were actually from middle-class families. (B) Several potential informants refused to be interviewed because, they reported, they were too busy surviving everyday life.

Third, more *benshengren* (72%) than *waishengren* (28%) were included in this study, but this sample bias may not be a serious problem. If we compare it with Taiwan's ethnic structure within which *waishengren* compose only 14 percent of the entire population (Lin and Lin 1993), the ethnic background in this study may actually closely resemble that of Taiwan.

ANALYSIS OF DATA

As mentioned earlier in this chapter, this project was essentially an exploratory study. While I devised an analytical framework and topical sets of interview questions based on the literature and theoretical perspectives, these open-ended questions and my strategy of conversational interview purposefully were broad and flexible enough to elicit a variety of responses, including the responses that went beyond my analytical framework. For example, one of the major

---

[47] Actually, I recruited eight subjects of lower-class. Two of them, however, did not respond to my questions appropriately. Most of their answers were unrelated to my interview questions, so I had to discard these two interviews in my analysis. In addition, I also discarded a middle-class informant's interview because he spent more than two hours talking about Taiwan's politics rather than answering my questions.

associations I hoped to find, according to my analytical framework (see Figure 3-2 in Chapter Three), was how social relations at the workplace affect mental distress. I used two indicators, experiences of racial discrimination and sexist treatment, as the independent variables in my measurement. In actual analysis, however, it is possible to find these two indicators unrelated or remotely related to informants' distress but another variable, such as social exclusion or racial segregation (or, what I call "racial othering," see Chapter Eight), "popped out" of the data as a significant factor in the association between work and mental health. I therefore adopted a two-sided analytic strategy – one followed the analytical framework while the other inductively looked for patterns and themes emerging from the data. As Rubin and Rubin (1995: 237-238) state, we examine the interviews for "confirming and disconfirming evidence to ensure that the linkages are grounded in the data." Throughout the coding and analyzing processes, I remained as close to the data as possible in my typologies and characterizations of the informants' experiences.

Rigidly speaking, this project was not a grounded theory case as put forth by Strauss (1987) because it did not utilize a complete inductive approach. Rather, it followed a guiding framework and sought specific themes in the data. But some techniques used in grounded theory, such as coding and memoing, were valuable for drawing thematic categories and patterns from the interviews. In addition, while compiling data, I was learning a software program for qualitative data, NUDIST. Since I was not yet familiar with NUDIST in the beginning, I coded and analyzed my interview data mainly by traditional methods of cutting and pasting from interview transcripts. With the increase of my familiarity with NUDIST toward the end of my coding process, I tried to code data in NUDIST in the same way as I did manually and used this software to do comparisons on groups of informants. This software therefore also facilitated my data organization and analysis. Below, I explain the analysis units used in this project and then describe the logistics of coding and analyzing interview data.

Analysis Units

I used two forms of analysis units, individuals and social groups, in my analyses. Analyses related to personal demographic information, such as individual generation, ethnicity of origin, working experiences, distress experiences, and data from the census bureau, used individuals as the analysis unit. On the other hand, groups (such as families, ethnicities, generations, and genders) were used as the analysis unit when the analyses were related to group comparisons. Particularly, in the analyses of family-related issues (mostly in Chapter Seven, partly in Chapter Six regarding migration decisions), conjugal units constituted the so-called "family" in this study. In other words, I investigated how the husband and wife (first-generation immigrants) in a family divided domestic labor and made family decisions.

Coding and Analyzing Interview Data

I coded my data through multiple processes, in which primary analysis was produced. First, I re-organized interview transcripts based on the major themes I chose to examine: (1) immigration and mental health, (2) family and mental health, and (3) work and mental health. By copying and pasting excerpts from the interviews that were representative of these major themes, I created three separate Microsoft Word documents that represent different analytical topics. Second, in each thematic document, I color-highlighted, coded, and categorized passages that illustrated the subthemes such as "gender division of domestic labor," "family decision-making," or "family-related distress." These categorized excerpts were then placed in separate files. Some subthemes contained several issues, so I added one more procedure of categorizing and coding in these cases. Third, I carefully went through interview conversations under each subtheme or each issue of the subthemes, and coded them with key phrases such as "family reunion," "job opportunity," or "children's education." These small sets of codes were also placed in separate files, which made it easier to draw relevant quotes and compare informants' background information. Appendix C illustrates the final configuration of my coding schemes that shaped my finding chapters.

Comparing Groups of Informants

Rubin and Rubin (1995: 226-256) suggest that finding the similarities in how people who are in different social locations interpret their world is one of the important ways of analyzing qualitative interviews. I believe that it is also important to discover differences in how people who are in same social locations experience their lives. As my coding schemes showed (see Appendix C), I compared different groups of informants by their gender, class, ethnicity of origin, immigration period, or generation under each issue or subtheme in order to highlight commonalities and dissimilarities. These comparisons were mainly done by the NUDIST software, although I did double-check the analysis manually and hand-calculated the numbers when I needed to present different result categories by percentages. When linking codes ("nodes" in NUDIST) or subthemes across interview transcripts, NUDIST can create a separate file showing these respondents' demographic background such as their gender, age, class, and ethnicity of origin. This file then can be used to analyze how diverse the respondents were under the same code or the same subtheme (exploring "node attributes" in NUDIST). It helped to highlight differences and commonalities among the informants. It also facilitated the analytic process to look for patterns and themes in distress experiences.

SUMMARY

In this chapter, I illustrated the methodological approach of this study, clarified key terms, described the research site, and detailed the methods and processes of collecting data. I provided a profile of the sample, discussed sampling biases, and explained how I analyzed data. I also emphasized some of the important ethical issues and research difficulties during the recruiting and interviewing processes. Throughout this chapter and those that follow, I attempt to stay as close to the distress experiences of the informants I interviewed. I also endeavored to disclose the socio-cultural context of these experiences.

CHAPTER 5

TAIWANESE IMMIGRATION TO THE UNITED STATES

Today's ethnic groups are yesterday's immigrants. Therefore, a study of Taiwanese Americans has to be situated in the historical background of immigration from Taiwan in order to comprehend the socio-cultural origins and characteristics of this ethnic group. Moreover, comparisons of Taiwanese immigrants with other immigrant groups from East Asia will help to show the unique characteristics of the Taiwanese American community. In the existing literature, particularly, studies of Chinatown have long been regarded as representative of overseas Chinese communities, including immigrants from Taiwan. A few studies, such as Chen (1992) and Tseng (1995), have challenged this misleading perspective and shown the distinctive socio-cultural life of the Taiwanese immigrant community. Highlighting the attributes of Taiwanese, which are discrete from those of Chinese, therefore, is particularly important in elucidating the differences between these two communities.

This chapter, therefore, begins with the historical context and causes of Taiwanese immigration to the United States. This background is followed by an analysis of demographic and social characteristics of immigrants from Taiwan. Comparisons with Chinese, Korean, and Japanese immigrants are juxtaposed with this analysis in order to illuminate the uniqueness of Taiwanese Americans. In the final section, I introduce some social norms and cultural values in Taiwanese society in order to highlight the socio-cultural characteristics of the people of this study.

HISTORICAL BACKGROUND OF TAIWAN AND THE TAIWANESE

Taiwanese have been in the United States in relatively large numbers for at least five decades or since the end of World War II.[48] Yet, it was not until the late 1990s that the term "Taiwanese American" was used in public arenas and academic works. This phenomenon, to a large extent, reflects the complex historical and political relations between Taiwan and China.

Taiwan, an island sometimes called Formosa, is located in the Western Pacific, approximately 100 miles east of Mainland China and 250 miles north of Luzon, the main island of the Philippines. The Dutch occupied Taiwan during 1624-61 as part of their East Indian Empire. When Japan conquered China in the Sino-Japanese War in 1895, Taiwan became a colony under Japanese rule for fifty years, until Japan was defeated in World War II in 1945. The Kuomingtang (KMT) government then took over Taiwan. In 1949, the KMT government lost the civil war to the Chinese Communist Party. Its leader and supporters retreated to Taiwan. Since then, Taiwan and China have been separate "entities" with two different political regimes and societies. Communists claim a People's Republic of China (PRC) on the mainland whereas the Kuomintang (until 2000) governed Taiwan in the name of the Republic of China (ROC). The orthodoxy of "one China" has been a debatable issue and a point of political contention between the two parties.[49]

When they retreated to Taiwan, the KMT government brought with them many Chinese officials and soldiers. A great number of businessmen and ordinary people who were against the Chinese Communist Party also fled to the island with the KMT. This large-scale retreat brought numerous immigrants from China, resulting in a clear

---

[48] See Ng (1998) for the history of Taiwanese immigration to the U.S.

[49] In 1979, the United States broke off formal diplomatic relations with Taiwan to establish them with China. Since then, Taiwan has become an "invisible country" hidden in the shadow of China.

ethnic distinction between Mainlanders and Taiwanese on this island. Nevertheless, Chinese immigration to Taiwan had a long history beginning in the sixteenth century. Early immigrants (before 1949) were mostly from Fujian and Guangdong in contrast to the heterogeneous later immigrants who were from all parts of Mainland China. The Fujianese and the Hakka[50] composed the majority of the population on the island, and became the so-called *benshengren* or "local people."[51] Although they speak different languages (Taiwanese and Hakka), the Fujianese and Hakka have lived in Taiwan for centuries and, thus, regard themselves as "Taiwanese," an identity that distinguishes them from later Chinese immigrants. Mainlanders who moved to Taiwan after the end of World War II are called *waishengren* or "outside people," and they are mostly Mandarin speakers. By 1991, Taiwan's population was composed of 75 percent of Fujianese, eight percent of Hakka, 14 percent of Mainlanders, and two percent of aborigines (Lin and Lin 1993).

The Mainlanders who followed the KMT government to Taiwan were an advantaged ethnic group on the island. They had better access than Taiwanese to political and social resources, because most policies (such as those on language, education, and the law) established by the KMT regime were based on Mainlanders' interests. Taiwanese were considered a subordinate group, and many considered themselves oppressed under KMT rule. The ethnic differentiation between Mainlanders and Taiwanese also caused tensions and social problems. The "incident" that occurred on February 28, 1947, and is known as "2-28," was one of the most serious interethnic conflicts in Taiwan's

---

[50] The Fujianese outnumber the Hakka and are the ethnic majority in Taiwan. These two ethnic groups speak different languages, Taiwanese and Hakka, and embrace distinct ethnic identities.

[51] It has been argued in contemporary Taiwan that the aborigines, people of Austronesian origin, are the "real local people" in Taiwan because they were the original inhabitants of this island. When early Chinese immigrants (mostly Fujianese and Hakka) moved to Taiwan, the aborigines were forced to retreat to the mountain areas. They were regarded by the Taiwanese people as uncivilized and, as a subordinate group, and they had very few resources in society. Yet, since the 1980s, the government and scholars have begun to realize the importance of preserving aboriginal culture. Several aboriginal reservations have been established, and aboriginal traditions and culture are gradually gaining respect.

history. It was triggered by the arbitrary killing of a Taiwanese by the police, led to an angry mass reaction and rebellion by the Taiwanese, and was followed by government reprisals. Thousands of Taiwanese were killed, and the gulf between Taiwanese and the Mainlanders widened. The KMT's monocracy in Taiwan lasted more than fifty years, until Chen Shui-bien, the candidate of the opposition Democratic Progressive Party (DPP), won the presidency in 2000. Ethnic tensions have lessened but remain despite the end of the facto KMT rule with this election.

THE TAIWANESE EXODUS TO THE UNITED STATES

The complex historical and political background of the island became one of the most important factors that "pushed" Taiwanese to the United States. Facing political instability and uncertainty both inside (KMT's colonization and ethnic tensions between *waishengren* and *benshengren*[52]) and outside the island (the threat of China) after 1949, a great number of Taiwanese people began to consider immigration as an option (China Post 1990; Hing 1998; Ng 1998). The impetus to emigrate heightened in 1979, when the United States ended formal relations with Taiwan, terminated the Mutual Defense Act[53] between the two, and established diplomatic relations with China. This political change in U.S. policy intensified Taiwanese people's anxieties and

---

[52] The KMT government considered Taiwan as a "temporary" retreat where it prepared for regaining mainland China. Therefore, it implemented martial law and kept the island on constant alert. Patriotism and anti-communism was inculcated through media and educational systems monopolized by the KMT regime. Anti-government discourses were forbidden and suspicious dissidents were under close surveillance by plain-clothes police.

[53] Because of the Mutual Defense Treaty established in 1954, American soldiers were stationed in Taiwan to protect the island after the Korean War and during the Cold War; many of them married Taiwanese women. When these service personnel returned to the America, their Taiwanese spouses accompanied them and, consequently, composed a special group of immigrants during the 1960s and 1970s.

fears about the island's security. As a result, many chose to move to the United States. (Ng 1998: 17-18).

Before the lifting of martial law in 1987, overseas Taiwanese students were under close surveillance by the KMT government, and those who criticized the government were forbidden to return to Taiwan. As a result, many Taiwanese were actually "forced" to settle in the United States and become Americans. This group of Taiwanese Americans, most of whom tended to have a strong Taiwanese identity, later became an important social force, promoting Taiwan's independence and international status. They raise funds and campaign for American senators who recognize and advocate Taiwan's independence. They also maintain a close relationship with the DPP in Taiwan, and offer it political counsel (Shu 2001).

Several other factors also impelled the Taiwanese exodus to the United States. First, as early as the Qing dynasty (1644-1911) in China, overseas studies became a pattern of behavior among the elite. During the Japanese colonial period in Taiwan (1895-1945), a number of people went to Japan to study, although acquiring education there was a privilege for only a few who were either outstanding students or from wealthy families. Allied with the U.S. after World War II, Taiwan began to adopt the American model of education, and the United States began to replace Japan as the most favored country for studying abroad. Those who studied in the U.S. were not necessarily well off in the 1950s and 1960s. Many of them roomed together and shared the cost of food, cooking, and meals (Ng 1998: 15-16). In a study of the brain-drain flow from Taiwan to the U.S., Chang (1992) reports that during 1960-1979 only 12 percent of overseas Taiwanese students in America returned to Taiwan, and the majority of the non-returnees were graduates in the fields of engineering and science. Seeking higher education in the U.S. continues to be a predominant trend in contemporary Taiwan, and a great number of Taiwanese professionals are American trained. Upon finishing their education in the U.S., some of these students return to Taiwan while others find jobs in the U.S.

Second, it was difficult for highly educated individuals to find employment opportunities in Taiwan from the 1960s to the 1980s. Similar to many other developing countries, jobs lagged behind the growth of a professionally trained class in Taiwan. As a result, highly educated students, especially those trained in the U.S., sought employment in the United States. A flow of people, labeled the "brain drain," from Taiwan to the United States, therefore, began as early as the 1960s (Tseng 1995). Those who were less advantaged simply felt that economic conditions in the U.S. were more favorable than those in Taiwan. They came to the U.S. to work, mainly finding jobs in the service sector or in Chinese restaurants (Ng 1998).

Third, some Taiwanese emigrated because of their increasing dissatisfaction with the quality of life on the island (Lin 1990). Taiwan is a small island (approximately 245 miles in length and 90 miles in width) with a huge population (21 million). Environmental problems, such as over-exploitation of land, over-crowded residential areas, and air pollution, inevitably emerge in a region of such high density. Many people on the island, therefore, desire to migrate overseas. Countries with a spacious living environment and fresh air, such as the United States, Australia, and Canada, thus, became desirable destinations of migration (Hsiao 1991).

Fourth, the U.S. Immigration Act of 1965 ended the exclusion laws that restricted Asian immigration to the U.S. and, consequently, numbers of immigrants from various regions of Asia have increased since then (Espiritu 1997; Hing 1993, 1998; Kanjanapan 1995; Ng 1998; Ong and Liu 1994; Wong 1998). This new legislation raised the annual quota of Chinese immigrants from one hundred to twenty thousands, and the provision for family unification was not restricted by any quota. The Immigration Act also set up a system of preferences, and people who had vital and exceptional skills in preferred areas were permitted in greater number than others to migrate to the United States. A fair number from Taiwan entered the United States through these preference categories, among whom many were classified as professionals and managers (Ng 1998: 16-17). In fact, Taiwan has become one of the major countries that contribute to the "brain-drain" to the U.S. (Portes and Rumbaut 1996: 18).

Finally, Taiwanese also migrated to the U.S. for the sake of their children's education (Ng 1998: 19). The educational system in Taiwan is very competitive, and opportunities for a university education are rather limited. Students have to pass several standardized entrance exams at different levels of schooling, and this rigid screening process often becomes a nightmare for adolescents. Studying becomes the major (even the only) activity in most high schools, and passing the entrance exam turns into a measure of success for youth. In contrast, the United States has a great number of universities and colleges, and the competition for admission is not as stiff as that in Taiwan. Compared to the anxieties associated with competition in Taiwan's high schools, the relaxed learning atmosphere in the U.S. is appealing. Therefore, a fair number of parents in Taiwan migrate to the U.S. for the sake of their children's education. Some adolescents even are sent to board with relatives or at schools, and their parents travel back and forth between the U.S. and Taiwan to visit.

In sum, various combinations of "push" and "pull" factors in different historical and social contexts propelled the Taiwanese exodus to the Unites States. The reasons for Taiwanese emigration to the U.S. were complex, ranging from political to environmental and from job-related to educational. While some left Taiwan because of a lack of confidence in the government's ability to handle political instability, others were forbidden to return because of their patriotic criticism; some left the island to study, but others did so with a meticulous plan for a better educational milieu for the next generation; the U.S. Immigration Act of 1965 also opened the door for "chasers of the American dream," allowing numerous Taiwanese people to enter in pursuit of better job opportunities and life environment in this "promising land."

DEMOGRAPHY AND GEOGRAPHY OF TAIWANESE AMERICANS

According to the 1990 census data, 73,778 Taiwanese Americans lived in the U.S., including 37,051 men (50.22%) and 36,727 women (49.78%).[54] By 2000, this population had increased to 118,054.[55] These statistics, however, may underestimate this ethnic group because many people whose country of origin is listed as Taiwan identify themselves as Chinese Americans. Compared to other ethnic groups of East Asian origin, such as Chinese, Koreans, and Japanese, the Taiwanese

---

[54] Source: 1990 Census 1990 Characteristics of the Asian and Pacific Islander Population in the U.S.; Social Science & Government Data Library, University of California at Berkeley, http://sunsite.berkeley.edu/SGML/.

[55] Source: U.S. Census Bureau. Census 2000 Summary File, Table PCT5.

constitute the smallest population (see Table 5-1). Again, this number could be an underestimation since many Taiwanese are listed in the Chinese category. Further, these figures are absolute numbers of population counts that do not take into account the size of the country of origin. Taiwan is a small island, and its population is just about 1.62 percent that of China (roughly 1.3 billion). Therefore, the huge discrepancy between American populations of Chinese and Taiwanese origin (2,198,350) is actually not as enormous as it appears. In contrast, the ratio of Taiwanese Americans to Taiwanese, 0.56 percent (118,054/21 million), is actually greater than that of Chinese Americans to Chinese, 0.18 percent (2,316,404/1.3 billion). In fact, a slightly larger proportion of Taiwanese than Chinese are included in the U.S. population.

Table 5-1: Americans of East Asian Origin

Ethnicity	Population	Percent (%)
Chinese	2,316,404	53.8
Korean	1,077,116	25.0
Japanese	796,951	18.5
Taiwanese	118,054	2.7
Total	4,308,525	100

Source: U.S. Bureau of Census, Census 2000 Summary File.

An analysis of the population attributes of Taiwanese immigrants to a large extent helps us comprehend the characteristics and backgrounds of Taiwanese Americans as an ethnic group. In an analysis of the 1977's immigrant cohorts from all over the world to the United States, the U.S. Immigration and Naturalization Service (INS) reported that Taiwan had the highest percentage of migrants who had become U.S. citizens (78.1%). This percentage is much higher than the average of all other countries (45.9%) in the INS record.[56] If we look at longitudinal changes during the 1990-2000 period, we can see that the number of Taiwanese immigrants admitted over the years did not fluctuate much, compared to other groups from East Asia (see Figure 5-1).[57] Immigration trends from China and Korea varied more than related trends from Taiwan during this phase, and Japanese immigration was the lowest and least varied among these four groups (see Table 5-2). Immigration from China fluctuated significantly over this time period. This population peaked in 1993, decreased until 1995 (when immigration rose again), and then declined again before rising again in 2000.[58] After 1990, Korean immigration tended to gradually decrease, although it rose a little in 1996. Trends in the immigration rates of Taiwanese and Japanese were relatively more stable than comparable trends in the other two groups, with only some small fluctuation during this time frame. From 1992 to 2000, immigration trends from Korea, Taiwan, and Japan did not differ much (see Figure 5-1).

---

[56] This information was acquired on October 16th, 2001, from http://www.ins.usdoj.gov/graphics/aboutins/statistics/299.htm, the website of the U.S. Immigration and Naturalization Service.

[57] Here, "Taiwanese immigrants," refers to immigrants whose region and country of birth is Taiwan. This category, which excludes *waishengren* who were born in China and then retreated to Taiwan with the KMT government, underestimates the population of immigrants from Taiwan.

[58] During the mid-1980s and the early 1990s, the U.S. media linked a number of criminal and violent episodes with Chinese-American society, jeopardizing this community's public images. In 1993, the freighter *Golden Venture* with 288 illegal Chinese immigrants was grounded in New York City. This event exposed large-scale smuggling operations in the Chinese community and alarmed the public (Kitano and Daniels 1995: 38-55). These factors may contribute to more rigid regulation and surveillance by the INS of the U.S.-based Chinese community and, thus, lead to a future decline in immigrants from China.

Table 5-2: Immigration Trends from East Asia (1990-2000)

Region/ Country of Birth	Total Number of Immigrants Admitted	Range	Standard Deviation	Variance
Taiwan	121504	9630	3562.4	12690514.6
China	456388	33763	10341.9	106955680.6
Korea	203624	19461	5858.8	34325908.4
Japan	67206	6811	1850.5	3424390.1

Source: U.S. Department of Homeland Security. 2004 Yearbook of Immigration Statistics, Table 3: Immigrants Admitted by Region and Country of Birth.

Figure 5-1: Immigration Trends from East Asia (1990-2000)

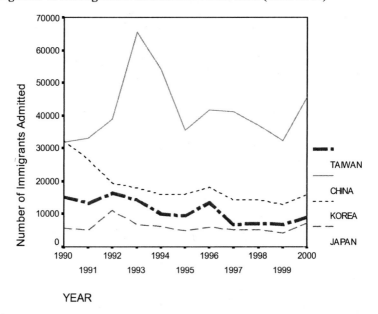

Source: U.S. Department of Homeland Security. 2004 Yearbook of Immigration Statistics, Table 3: Immigrants Admitted by Region and Country of Birth.

Who migrated to the United States from Taiwan? According to the INS data, Taiwanese women constituted a slightly greater percentage of these immigrants than did men (on average, women: men= 55.5%: 44.4% over this decade). During the 1990-2000 period, the sex ratios of admitted Taiwanese immigrants varied from 75.6 (in 2000) to 87.3 (in 1990), with an average of 80.1 (see Figure 5-2).[59] From Figure 5-2, we can also see that, over the years, the sex ratios tended to decline, except for the significant rise in 1998, suggesting a feminization trend of Taiwanese immigrants (see Figure 5-2).

Figure 5-2: Sex Ratios of Taiwanese Immigrants (1990-2000)

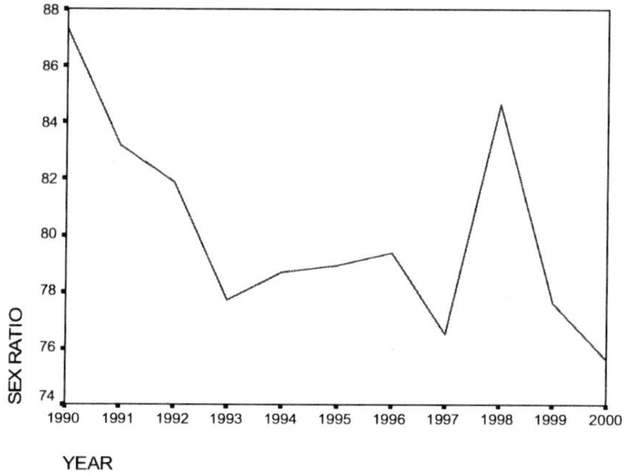

Source: U.S. Immigration and Naturalization Service. Statistical Yearbook 1990-2000.

Moreover, the occupations of 16.8 percent of Taiwanese immigrants admitted to the United States were classified as professional, specialty, and technical while 11.3 percent were executive, administrative, and managerial (see Table 5-3). In the two categories, the percentage for Taiwan was the highest among the four East Asian groups. Compared with other occupational groups, these two categories also represent those in the "brain-drain" sector because the

[59] Sex ratio=male: female /per 100.

corresponding jobs require professional and managerial skills. Therefore, Taiwanese experienced a greater "brain-drain" than Japanese, Chinese, and Koreans.

If we look at how Taiwanese immigrants were admitted to the U.S., the top three modes were through family sponsorship (40.8%), employment-based preferences (32.6%), [60] and immediate kin relationship to U.S. citizens (25.4%). These three categories made up 98.8 percent of this group and thus clearly dominated among the means used by Taiwanese to obtain immigration admission to the United States (see Table 5-4). Immigrants from other East Asian countries had somewhat different modes of entry according to the INS. A little less than half (42.7%) of the immigrants from China were placed in the employment-based preferences category, and China had the highest rate of refugees (1.9%) compared to Taiwan, Korea, and Japan. Koreans had a significant percentage (23.9%) of immigrants who were categorized as legalized population through the Immigration Reform and Control Act of 1986 (IRCA),[61] while almost half (49.5%) of the Japanese were admitted as immediate relatives of U.S. citizens. Among the four East Asian countries, Taiwan had the highest rate of family-sponsored immigrants, which may imply that Taiwanese have stronger family values and family bonds than other groups (see Table 5-4).

---

[60] Employment-based preferences comprise five categories: priority workers; professionals with advanced degrees or aliens of exceptional ability; skilled workers, professionals, needed unskilled workers, and those under the Chinese Student Protection Act; special immigrants; and those involved in employment creation (investors) (INS 1996: 15).

[61] The U.S. government passed the Immigration Reform and Control Act (IRCA) of 1986 in order to control and deter illegal immigration to the United States. Its major provisions stipulate the legalization of undocumented aliens, the legalization of certain agricultural workers, sanctions for employers who knowingly hire undocumented workers, and increased enforcement at U.S. borders (INS 1996: 19).

Table 5-3: Comparison of East Asian Immigrants by Major Occupation Group and Region/Country of Birth (1990-2000)

Region and Country of Birth	Total	Professional specialty and technical	Executive, administrative, and managerial	Sales	Administrative support	Precision production, craft, and repair	Operator, fabricator, and laborer
Taiwan	121494	20363	13773	2393	6787	519	733
		16.8%	11.3%	2.0%	5.6%	0.4%	0.6%
China	456388	58435	25093	5505	15374	5954	24009
		12.8%	5.5%	1.2%	3.4%	1.3%	5.3%
Korea	203624	14952	7708	2708	6246	2426	4470
		7.3%	3.8%	1.3%	3.1%	1.2%	2.2%
Japan	67206	5494	6859	1142	2670	507	326
		8.2%	10.2%	1.7%	4.0%	0.8%	0.5%

(continued…)

Table 5-3 (continued)

Region and Country of Birth	Farming, forestry, and fishing	Service	No occupation or not reported
Taiwan	1177	2916	72843
	1.0%	2.4%	60.0%
China	34728	20289	267001
	7.6%	4.4%	58.5%
Korea	5711	5632	153711
	2.8%	2.8%	75.5%
Japan	370	4661	45177
	0.6%	6.9%	67.2%

Source: U.S. Immigration and Naturalization Service. Statistical Yearbook 1990-2000.

Table 5-4: Comparison of East Asian Immigrants by Class of Admission and Region/Country of Last Permanent Residence (1992-2000)*

Region and country	Total	Family-sponsored preferences	Employment-based preferences	Immediate relatives of U.S. citizens	Refugee and asylee adjustments	Diversity programs	IRCA legalization	Other
Taiwan	108275	44173	35252	27457	71	77	169	1076
		40.8%	32.6%	25.4%	0.1%	0.1%	0.2%	1.0%
China	337396	85833	143967	98151	6540	128	115	2662
		25.4%	42.7%	29.1%	1.9%	0.0%	0.0%	0.8%
Korea	138736	42733	39804	54391	27	49	477	1255
		30.8%	28.7%	39.2%	0.0%	0.0%	23.9%	0.9%
Japan	62342	2255	20332	30867	113	8308	95	372
		3.6%	32.6%	49.5%	0.2%	13.3%	0.2%	0.6%

* The categorizes before and after 1992 in INS data are different, so this table does not include the information during 1990-91, a period that was comprised in Table 5-3.

Source: U.S. Immigration and Naturalization Service. Statistical Yearbook 1992-2000.

Statistics on the foreign-born population in the 1990 and 2000 census data also help depict the social characteristics of Taiwanese Americans who were first-generation immigrants. [62] Among the Taiwan-born people who had become U.S. citizens by 2000, 44.5 percent were men and 55.5 percent were women (sex ratio = 80.1). According to the 1990 census data, the sex compositions in different age groups were about equal except for the 25-44 age bracket, in which women outnumbered men by 20 percent (see Figure 5-3). After 1990, both the total numbers and the sex ratios of Taiwanese immigrants gradually decreased (see Figure 5-1 & Figure 5-2). The shortage of male Taiwan-born U.S. citizens in the 25-44 age bracket may reflect these trends because more young professional men than before returned to Taiwan after their graduate education in the United States. In contrast, their female counterparts continued to prefer emigration either for their career development or as an escape from Taiwan's patriarchal environment. Moreover, nowadays more Taiwanese women than before become U.S. citizens through interracial marriage.

Figure 5-3: Age-Sex Composition of Taiwan-born U.S. citizens

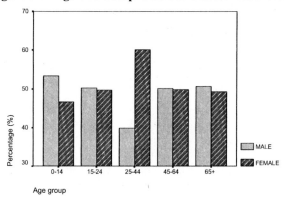

Source: U.S. Bureau of the Census. 1993.

[62] The statistics on the foreign-born population in the 1990 and the 2000 census data differ to some extent. Some detailed information, such as that in Figure 5-3 and Table 5-5, cannot be found in the 2000 data. Therefore, while using the most recent data to depict Taiwanese Americans here, I also present information from the 1990 data to supplement this description.

Women had notably higher percentages than men in the separated, widowed, and divorced populations (see Table 5-5). These huge discrepancies may suggest that, once widowed or divorced, Taiwanese American women are less likely than their male counterparts to re-marry. These discrepancies may also suggest that (1) widows are brought to the U.S. by sons who care for them upon the death of the sons' fathers; and (2) women who are separated and divorced emigrate to escape the stigma attached to these statuses in Taiwan.

Table 5-5: Sex-Marital Status of Taiwan-born U.S. Citizens

Marital Status	Total	Male		Female	
Never married	22320	11652	52.2%	10668	47.8%
Now married, except separated	63128	27046	42.8%	36082	57.2%
Separated	621	154	24.8%	467	75.2%
Widowed	1169	127	10.9%	1042	89.1%
Divorced	3592	900	25.1%	2692	74.9%
Total*	90847	39896	43.9%	50951	56.1%

* 15 years and over

Source: U.S. Bureau of the Census. 1993.

The sex ratios among the four East-Asian-born U.S. citizens were quite different. The Chinese sex ratio (the number of males per 100 females) was the highest (89.7), followed by Taiwanese (80.1), Koreans (73.4), and Japanese (56.5).[63] The significant low sex ratio of

---

[63] Historically, men had outnumbered women among Chinese immigrants (Kitano and Daniels 1995). By 1990, the Chinese sex ratio was 101.7 (U.S. Bureau of the Census 1993). The reversal of sex ratios, from 101.7 in 1990 to 89.7 in 2000, suggests a significant change in the sex compositions of the Chinese.

the Japanese is, in part, the result of women's marriage to American servicemen stationed abroad (see Table 5-6).[64]

Table 5-6: Sex Ratios of East-Asian-born U.S. Citizens

Region and Country of Birth	Taiwan	China	Korea	Japan
Total	326215	1192435	864125	347540
Male	145070	5639000	365695	125415
Female	181145	628535	498430	222125
Sex ratio	80.1	89.7	73.4	56.5

Source: U.S. Bureau of the Census. 2003. The Foreign-Born Population: 2000, Table FBP-1.

Among Asian Americans born in East Asia, the Taiwanese stand out as the largest "brain-drain" group; almost two-thirds (64.6%) of this population were employed in managerial and professional occupations (see Table 5-7). These individuals plus those who held sales and office occupations comprise more than four-fifths (86.6%) of Taiwan-born U.S. citizens, suggesting the predominantly middle-class backgrounds of first-generation Taiwanese Americans. This finding is consistent with the data on Taiwanese immigrants' occupations shown in Table 5-3. Immigrants from Taiwan are mostly members of the professional middle-class, a status that Taiwanese Americans continue to have in the United States.

---

[64] The sex ratio of Japanese has remained relatively low since 1980. According to the census data, it was only 28.5 by 1990. In addition to women's marriage to American servicemen stationed abroad, high male mortality also plays a part in this result (Barrigner et al. 1993: 97-100).

Table 5-7: Occupations of East-Asian-born U.S. citizens

Types of Occupation	Region and Country of Birth			
	Taiwan	China	Korea	Japan
Management, professional, and related occupations	123370	320365	167065	79645
	64.6%	49.3%	37.8%	50.5%
Service occupations	14670	111545	67000	24440
	7.7%	17.2%	15.1%	15.5%
Sales and office occupations	42020	116910	132875	38945
	22.0%	18.0%	30.0%	24.7%
Farming, fishing, and forestry occupations	80	660	825	400
	0.0%	0.1%	0.2%	0.3%
Construction, extraction, and maintenance occupations	2860	17195	17985	3695
	1.5%	2.6%	4.1%	2.3%
Production, transportation, and material moving occupations	8115	83130	56650	10520
	4.2%	12.8%	12.8%	6.7%
Total*	191120	649805	442405	157645

* Employed persons 16 years and over

Source: U.S. Bureau of the Census. 2003. The Foreign-Born Population: 2000, Table FBP-2.

Other East-Asian-born U.S. citizens had rather different occupational compositions than the Taiwanese. For example, the Koreans had the highest percentage (30.0%) in sales and office occupations, followed by Japanese (24.7%) (see Table 5-7). Small businesses have been the foremost characteristic of the Korean immigrant community in the U.S., so the high percentage of Koreans working in sales and the retail market is somewhat expected. The percentage of Koreans who worked in production, transportation, and material moving occupations was also the highest among the four groups (equal to that of Chinese), reflecting Koreans' need for, and attraction to, laborers from the same ethnic group in the retail market.

Chinese had the highest percentages in the two categories: service occupations and production, transportation, and material moving occupations. Historically, Chinatown has been an ethnic enclave where Chinese immigrants tend to work and dwell. It is also a community that attracts a great number of newcomers, unskilled workers, and undocumented immigrants from China. This characteristic of Chinatown also is reflected in the high percentages of Chinese who work either in service industries or as laborers, as shown in Table 5-7. In addition, one half (50.5%) of Japanese Americans held management and professional occupations, only second to the Taiwanese. This percentage plus that of sales and office occupations comprise approximately three-fourths (75.2%) of Japan-born U.S. citizens.

A comparison of the class of workers among these four groups shows that the majority were private wage and salary workers (percentages range from 74.7 to 81.9%). Similar to Chinese, Taiwanese comprise a very high percentage (81.8%) of private wage and salary workers but a low percentage of self-employed workers and of unpaid family workers (see Table 5-8). These data may reflect Taiwanese immigrants' occupational background before and after entering the U.S. As shown above, Taiwanese constitute the largest "brain-drain group" among East-Asian Americans because Taiwanese make up the highest percentage of the professional middle-class (see also Table 5-3 and Table 5-7). They tend to be white-collar workers in professional, managerial, technical, and administrative positions, rather than in self-employed business people. In contrast, Koreans constitute a significantly higher percentage of self-employed and unpaid family workers than other groups, reflecting their tendency to be self-employed entrepreneurs in the retail market.

Table 5-8: Class of Workers among East-Asian-born U.S. citizens

Class of Workers	Region and Country of Birth			
	Taiwan	China	Korea	Japan
Private wage and	156305	532210	303475	128605
salary workers	81.8%	81.9%	74.7%	81.6%
	21630	78320	39225	15950
Government workers	11.3%	12.1%	8.9%	10.1%
	11960	35740	66360	12385
Self-employed workers	6.3%	5.5%	15.0%	7.9%
	1220	3540	6340	705
Unpaid family workers	0.6%	0.5%	1.4%	0.4%
Total*	191120	649805	442405	157645

* Employed persons 16 years and over
Source: *U.S. Bureau of the Census. 2003. The Foreign-Born Population: 2000, Table FBP-2.*

The geographic distribution of Taiwanese Americans is significantly skewed. Slightly more than half of this group (52.8%) lived in California while the remainder were scattered throughout the United States, with no more than six percent residing in a single state (see Table 5-9). [65] Nevertheless, this disproportionate distribution does not differ much from that of Asian Americans. Historically, the majority of the Asian American population has been heavily concentrated on the West Coast, especially in Washington and California (Barringer, Gardner, and Levin 1993: 106-133).

California has long been a "paradise state" for Asians. First, California is separated from Asia only by the Pacific Ocean, making travel to the western state relatively inexpensive. This topographical advantage is appealing to many Taiwanese immigrants who wish to travel back and forth between the two lands. Second, the huge Asian population in this state has created an Asian-friendly environment and atmosphere. Numerous Asian

[65] These figures are based solely on the numbers for one Asian category (i.e., Taiwanese). They do not take into account the combination of one or more Asian categories and any combination (e.g., Taiwanese and Korean; Taiwanese and Chinese).

restaurants, shops, and grocery stores in this region, as well as the convenience of the exchange of information in ethnic communities, help immigrants to settle in and adapt to the host society faster and easier than would be the case in areas with small Asian populations. Third, Silicon Valley offers numerous employment opportunities for scientists and hi-tech personnel and has attracted numerous technical professionals from Asia, including Taiwan.

Table 5-9: Top Ten States in Which Taiwanese Americans Reside

Rank	State	Population	Percentage
1	California	62,317	52.8%
2	New York	7,095	6.0%
3	Texas	6,931	5.9%
4	New Jersey	5,879	5.0%
5	Washington	4,019	3.4%
6	Illinois	3,427	2.9%
7	Maryland	2,408	2.0%
8	Massachusetts	2,364	2.0%
9	Michigan	2,103	1.8%
10	Pennsylvania	1,950	1.7%
Total		118,054	100%

Source: U.S. Bureau of Census, Census 2000 Summary File.

To sum up, the population data of both the INS and the Census Bureau show that Taiwanese Americans had the following characteristics. First, Taiwan's immigration trends from 1990 to 2000 were relatively stable, compared with other East Asian groups. The numbers of Taiwanese immigrants to the United States during this period ranged from 6,714 to 16,344, with an average of 11,046 each year. In other words, immigrants from Taiwan have become a steady and important (in terms of their brain drain feature and potential contributions) flow into the U.S. Their significance and their visibility as an ethnic group in American society are therefore increasing.

Second, the majority of Taiwanese immigrants were admitted through family sponsorship (40.8%) and employment-based preferences (32.6%). They had the highest rate of family sponsorship among East Asian groups, suggesting their strong family values and ties. Family, therefore, is a core context in which one can acquire a rigorous understanding of Taiwanese Americans' migration background, cultural values, and social relations.

Third, Taiwanese Americans constituted the largest "brain-drain" group among East Asians, both before and after they became U.S. citizens; their population included the highest percentage of professional, technical, managerial, and administrative personnel. This demographic feature suggests that Taiwanese Americans are an ethnic group that is relatively homogenous compared to Chinese, Japanese, and Korean Americans. Because of their notable professional background, Taiwanese Americans also are more likely than their East Asian counterparts to reside outside ethnic enclaves and to assimilate into the mainstream.

Fourth, the sex ratio of Taiwanese Americans was 80.1, lower than that of the Chinese (89.7), but higher than those of Koreans (73.4) and Japanese (56.5). A comparison of individuals by marital status reveals that Taiwanese American women had a much higher percentage of widows (78.2% higher) and divorcees (49.8% higher) than their male counterparts. These discrepancies suggest that once divorced or widowed, Taiwanese American women are less likely than men to re-marry. This may also imply that (1) widows are brought to the U.S. by sons who care for them upon the death of the sons' fathers, and (2) women who are separated and divorced emigrate to escape the stigma attached to these statuses in Taiwan.

Fifth, more than half of Taiwanese Americans (52.8%) resided in California; the remainder were scattered throughout the United States while no more than six percent lived in a single state. California's Asian-friendly environment, hi-tech industries, and geographical distance from Taiwan (in terms of travel) all contribute to this skewed population distribution. The setting of this study, Chicago, illustrates a geography that is different from other metropolitan areas – such as San Francisco, Los Angeles, or New York City – that assemble a great number of stratified ethnic Chinese. For instance, Little Taipei in Los Angeles and Flushing in New York exemplify two large communities of Taiwanese immigrants that make room for a variety of occupations and social classes. In contrast, Taiwanese immigrants in the Chicago area are, as a group, neither sufficiently large nor sufficiently aggregated to form a visible ethnic enclave. Most of them reside in this region either to meet job demands or to be close to family members. This Taiwanese population is therefore less stratified than its counterparts in Los Angeles and New York and is more emblematic of Taiwan's brain drain. Without a surrounding ethnic enclave, Taiwanese immigrants in Chicago are forced to interact with "mainstream America" more or less in their everyday life.

SOCIO-CULTURAL ORIGINS AND CHARACTEERISTICS OF THE TAIWANESE

It is not an easy task to portray a culture, especially a society with a complex historical background like Taiwan. Although inheriting traditional Chinese culture, Taiwan's history of being colonized by the Dutch (1624-61) and Japanese (1895-1945), and massively subsidized by the U.S. during its industrialization, [66] has infused a variety of cultural elements into its tradition. As Harrell and Huang (1994) observe, Taiwan's contemporary culture reflects its interlocking context of historical, political, and economic processes. Taiwan is both traditional and progressive; a continuity of the past and a discontinuity from that legacy; unique and related to the cultures with which it interacts (Harrell and Huang, 1994). Contemporary Taiwanese culture, therefore, is built on a constant ambivalent struggle between convention and modernity, native and foreign, and local and cosmopolitan. These contradictory tendencies inevitably are reflected in social attitudes

---

[66] The KMT government adopted a policy of industrialization through export in the 1960s, with massive infusions of aid from the U.S., to transform Taiwan from a developing island to a "newly industrialized country" (N.I.C.). By 1990, Taiwan was the 13th-largest trading economy, and a producer and exporter of high-technology and consumer goods (Harrell and Huang 1994). Taiwan's economic development during the 1960s-1980s, therefore, greatly relied on the U.S. This "dependent development" of its economy also affected Taiwan's culture. Through the diffusion of mass media and direct contacts with Americans (the U.S. army was stationed in Taiwan until 1979 and many American ministries have come to Taiwan since the 1960s), Taiwanese have absorbed a certain degree of American culture. Particularly, a great number of highly-educated Taiwanese are U.S. trained. These people, who often occupy high rungs in the ladder of stratification in the society, are affected by American culture. Their values and practices may also have social influences on the island.

and cultural practices. Acknowledging the complexity and instability of Taiwanese culture, however, I believe that traditional Chinese culture that is based on Confucian teaching sustains its influence on the core values of Taiwanese people.

Because the majority of Taiwanese people migrated, although in different periods, to the island from mainland China, traditional Chinese culture has a great influence on the Taiwanese, and Confucianism continues to shape social norms in Taiwan. As Tu (1994) demonstrates in his usage of "cultural China," people who are of Chinese origin, including those of Chinese nationality (*zhong guo ren*), people in Taiwan, and overseas Chinese and Taiwanese (*hua qiao*), are all to some degree influenced by traditional Chinese culture that is based on Confucian teaching. Below I briefly illustrate some of the social values and norms that are relevant to this study (e.g., gender roles, family values, social relations, etc.) and discuss the so-called "Taiwanese or Chinese culture" thereby illustrating the socio-cultural characteristics of the Taiwanese and Taiwanese Americans.

Family Values, Gender Roles, and Inter-generational Relations

The family is the foundation of Chinese society. The importance of Confucian values, such as filial piety and veneration of age, is highlighted in Taiwanese family practices. Confucian principles of filial piety demand obedience and devotion to parents, obligating children to repay parents for caring for them and ensuring the elderly support in their later years. Three-generation cohabitation (patrilocal), thus, is highly valued because it reflects this Confucian teaching. Veneration of age demands a similar obedience. It requires children to honor the strategic knowledge and skills of their elders with deference, respect, and compliance. Extended families centered around patrilineal kinship are the primary circle of social relations, and age, sex, and generation construct authority hierarchies in them. In other words, the family is hierarchical and respects seniority. A generation should respect the generations above it. Inter-generational relations, therefore, are authoritarian.

Similar to China and other Asian societies, patrilineality is the primary organizing principle of Taiwanese life, and social institutions are mainly structured around men. According to Confucian teaching, a woman should follow *San Zhong* (three principles of obedience): obey her father when young, obey her husband when married, and obey her son after the death of her husband. Even in modern time when the influence of this traditional idea has decreased, men's status continues to be higher than that of women. A woman is expected to be a virtuous wife and good mother (*xian qi liang mu*), and to subordinate her well-being to her family's. Although women's status increases with age and the birth of sons, it remains lower than that of any man. Men are accorded a variety of privileges both legally and socially. They are more powerful in the public arena, more advantaged in the economic sphere, and more influential in the kin group and community than are women. They also have more control over the fruits of their labor and more access to important resources than do women. Despite the fact that some middle-class men have become aware of gender inequality and are willing to concede opportunities to women in the productive and reproductive spheres, society continues to grant men more respect and privilege than women. Social and economic marginality marks women's experience in Taiwan (Gu and Gallin 2004).

Value of Education

Confucian teaching prioritizes education. Taiwanese children are expected to devote themselves to study from a young age, and parents are usually involved in their children's education. Students must pass rigid entrance exams in order to attend high school, college, and graduate school, and the intense academic competition brings a great deal of pressure on the youth. Many teenagers spend most of their leisure time in private after-school programs that prepare them for exams. Parents are willing to invest financially and educationally in their children, especially boys, and consider their children's academic achievement as a parental accomplishment.

Social Relations

Guanxi, interpersonal relations, is essential in Taiwanese social life. Maintaining good interpersonal relations is beneficial in many ways, such as getting promotions, finding jobs, asking for favors, doing business, and obtaining a good reputation in the community. To establish good social relations, people must participate in social events frequently and form acquaintances with others, especially those who are in powerful positions or who are resourceful. Sending gifts, visiting on holidays, doing favors, and dining together, are all the ways used to establish *guanxi*. Associations organized on the basis of school, region, district, ethnicity, surname, or occupation, are also important in making connections.

CONCLUSION

In this chapter, I examined the historical context of Taiwanese immigration to the United States. I also analyzed demographic and geographic characteristics of Taiwanese Americans, and provided comparisons with other East Asian groups. Key social norms and values in Chinese culture were introduced in order to illustrate the socio-cultural origins and characteristics of the Taiwanese. All of this information furthers understanding of the people of this study, thereby serving as the foundation for the next chapters.

CHAPTER 6

A JOURNEY WITH WONDERING

"The decision to relocate one's self, family and community to a new setting and society is one of the most drastic social actions people may take during their lifetime, making motives for migration a worthy topic for study" (Gold 1997: 410). Why did Taiwanese people want to move to the United States? Did they have any hesitation about settling in a new country? How was the decision to migrate made in the family and who made the decision? Did the decision to migrate affect Taiwanese immigrants' psychological well-being? Why and how? These are the questions I answer in this chapter.

This chapter is composed of two major parts. In the first section, I explore the informants' motives for immigration, both for initial emigration and permanent settlement, and who made the decision to migrate for the family. Two different units of analysis are used in this section. The examination of motives is based on individuals, but the investigation of decision-making power on immigration is family-based.[67] I also analyze commonalities among and differences between informants who occupy different social locations (e.g., gender, class, ethnicity of origin, and decade of migration). The purpose of this analysis is to establish the social location within which individuals experience, interpret, and cognitively respond to

---

[67] Although every immigrant has his or her own motives for immigration, not everyone makes the decision to migrate independently. In fact, many immigrants, especially men, play the role of the primary decision-maker to relocate their families in a foreign country. Their motives are, therefore, often different from those of other family members such as their wives. Examining who in the family is the primary decision-maker helps to investigate a couple's gendered power structure, and to better understand the differences between men and women in their motives for emigration and settlement.

125

life events, thereby producing varying states of mental health. In the second section, I discuss how the decision to migrate affected informants' mental health.

THE DECISION TO MIGRATE

In Chapter Five, I synthesized various push and pull factors of Taiwanese immigration to the U.S. that have been discussed in the literature. In this section, I report a "real case," examining the informants' motives for initial emigration and permanent settlement, and exploring who in the family was the primary decision-maker to relocate to a new society.

Immigration Motives

Motives for immigration not only can be used to examine transnational practices, but they also can illustrate the meaning of immigrants' presence in the United States (Gold 1997). While the initiation of emigration does not always contribute to permanent settlement, I argue that two aspects of immigration motives, initial emigration and permanent settlement, should be examined separately in order to capture the whole picture of immigration incentives.[68]

In this section, I examine informants' major motives for initial emigration as well as those for permanent settlement.[69] In both analyses, I

---

[68] Broadly defined, international migration involves moving from one nation to another. According to this definition, students who study abroad are considered immigrants, even though not all of them intend to settle permanently in a foreign land. For those who do, their motives for settlement might be different from the ones that propelled them across national borders. Therefore, it is necessary to distinguish between incentives for emigration and settlement in order to acquire a comprehensive understanding of immigration motives.

[69] Subjects in this study included both first- and second-generation Taiwanese Americans. Since second-generation informants were not the ones who made the immigration decision, I analyze their parents' motives, based on what their children reported. Discrepancies may exist between these children's and their parents' perceptions. Moreover, all the second-generation informants reported their fathers were the primary decision-maker about immigration. This tendency may to some extent neglect their mothers' incentives and perceptions.

illustrate how subjects in different social locations (e.g., gender, class, and ethnicity) parallel or differ in their motives. In addition, as shown in Chapter Five, the push-pull factors of immigration vary in different historical contexts. I therefore investigate if informants who migrated to the U.S. in different decades (i.e., in the 60s, 70s, 80s, or 90s) had different motives for initial emigration and permanent settlement, and discuss how these differences reflect larger structural changes in Taiwan and the U.S.

Motives for Initial Emigration

The majority (35 individuals, about 65%) of the 54 informants first came to the United States to study (primarily for postgraduate education) and at the time of their move, most did not intend to stay permanently (see Table 6-1).[70] The high regard accorded to American education in Taiwan, and the fact that there are far fewer graduate schools in Taiwan than the U.S. may be the "push" and "pull" factors that led to this phenomenon.

Table 6-1: Motives for Initial Emigration

	Frequency	Percent
Study	35	65%
Family Reunion	11	20%
Work	5	9%
Children's Education	3	6%
Total	54	100%

In contrast, eleven informants (20%) came to join husbands or siblings who had migrated earlier (see Table 6-1). As noted in Chapter Five, most Taiwanese Americans were admitted to the U.S. through family sponsorship. Family reunion was informants' second top motive for initial emigration, illustrating the importance of kinship ties and family values in

---

[70] Although most informants provided only one major motive for their initial immigration, some mentioned several reasons. I asked those who provided multiple motives to name one as their primary incentive.

the Taiwanese immigrant community. Informants who chose to migrate for work in America (5 individuals, 9%) were all *benshengren*, among whom three were physicians. They migrated during the 1960s and 1970s, when the U.S. was in great need of medical professionals (the "pull" factor) and an era when the political environment on the island was unstable (the "push" factor).

Gender differences:
The information second-generation informants provided regarding their parents' motives were those of their fathers, thereby increasing the number of male subjects in this analysis (37 men and 17 women). When a comparison was made of individuals by gender, men and women differed significantly in their motives for emigration. More than two-thirds (26 individuals, about 70%) of men came to the U.S. to study, far exceeding the percentage of the women who came for the same reason (9 individuals, about 53%). Nevertheless, a majority (9 individuals, about 53%) of women moved to further their education. In other words, study was the primary motive for emigration among men, women, and the entire sample. In contrast, over one-third (6 individuals, 35%) of women came for the purpose of family reunion, while only 14 percent of men (5 individuals) moved for the same reason (see Table 6-2).

Table 6-2: Gender and Motives for Initial Emigration

	Men	Women
Study	26 (70%)	9 (53%)
Family Reunion	5 (14%)	6 (35%)
Work	4 (11%)	1 (6%)
Children's Education	2 (5%)	1 (6%)
Total (54)	37 (100%)	17 (100%)

These gender differences reflect two traditional cultural values in Taiwanese society. First, Taiwanese parents tend to invest more financially in boys than in girls because sons carry on the family's "blood" (Gu and Gallin 2004). Because sending children abroad to study is expensive, parents thus are more willing to make such an "investment" in boys rather than girls. This value may result in the trend in which many more men than women go overseas for education. Second, in Taiwan, women are expected to be virtuous wives and good mothers (*xian qi liang mu*), even if they are highly educated (Tzou 1999). They are also taught by Confucian morality to embody the strengths of "obedience, timidity, reticence, [and] adaptability" (Lang 1946: 43, quoting Confucius) and to accept an image of themselves as less important than men. Thus, once married, women are expected to follow their husbands wherever they move (*jia ji sui ji, jia gou sui gou*), and to put their well-being behind that of their husbands and children. This cultural value undoubtedly explains the finding that a higher percentage of women than men emigrated to reunite their families.

Only a few informants migrated to work and to seek a better educational environment for their children, and the differences between men and women were far less evident as those in motives for study and family reunion. As noted above, most men initially moved to study, yet surprisingly, they were as likely as women to report that they emigrated primarily in order to find better educational opportunities for their children. This similarity between men and women suggests the great regard for and important value of education among Taiwanese parents, both fathers and mothers, across social class and ethnicity.[71] Lower-class parents left their

---

[71] The two men who reported that they emigrated to seek a better educational environment for children were both *benshengren*. One of them was middle class, and the other lower class. The one woman who reported the same motive was middle-class *waishengren* who was married to a *benshengren*. The lower-class couple worked in a carry-out Chinese food store. One middle-class man, whose wife was a homemaker, was a high school teacher in Taiwan. He worked as a salesman for a health insurance company after moving to the U.S., a social status that was far less privileged than that he held in Taiwan. In the other middle-class family that emigrated for children's education, the husband quit his job as a manager in a private company in Taiwan at the age of 40, and entered the U.S. as a graduate student. He worked for a large company after getting his M.A, and had become a manager at the time I interviewed his wife. The wife worked as a secretary in a small business in Taiwan. After moving to the U.S., she became a homemaker and supervised her children's education for years until she acquired U.S. citizenship. She began to take part-time jobs after her children entered school, and finally found a

home country, enduring labor-intense work and the hardship to survive in the host society, and their middle-class counterparts quit white-collar jobs on the island, starting over in a new land in their middle age. Both were willing to subordinate their own well-being to that of their children's.

Class differences:
Despite the small number of lower-class informants in this study (6 individuals, 11%), the major motive for initial emigration of this group followed the same trend. Almost all (five out of six subjects) moved for the purpose of family reunion (see Table 6-3). The one woman who came to work as a nanny migrated because she disliked Taiwan's political environment. During my interviews, I heard a number of stories about Taiwanese who migrated to broaden their vision or to experience a different life world. In fact, many people who migrated to the U.S. through family sponsorships came just to "see the world outside Taiwan," as an informant said, and to "see if they can survive here." Sharing a mentality of "walk and see," most of these people started their immigrant life by taking temporary jobs such as waiting tables, babysitting, or data entering. In contrast, the majority of middle-class subjects (34 individuals, 71%) came to study (see Table 6-3), primarily for postgraduate education.

Table 6-3: Social Class and Motives for Initial Emigration

	Lower Class	Middle Class
Study	0 (0%)	34 (71%)
Family Reunion	5 (83%)	7 (15%)
Work	1 (17%)	4 (8%)
Children's Education	0 (0%)	3 (6%)
Total (54)	6 (100%)	48 (100%)

full-time job as an accountant for an airline company through the networks of other Chinese immigrants.

Ethnic differences:
The majority of both *benshengren* and *waishengren* informants initially came to the U.S. to study (67% and 60%, respectively), but these two groups differed significantly in their other motives for migration. More *benshengren* than *waishengren* (13% more) emigrated to seek work. In contrast, a greater percentage of *waishengren* than *benshengren* (18% more) moved to the U.S. to reunite their families (see Table 6-4). These findings suggest that because of their history of migrating from China to Taiwan, *waishengren* tended to perceive Taiwan as a temporary retreat and were, therefore, more likely than *benshengren* to move their whole family out of the island. It is also possible that *waishengren* were more likely than *benshengren* to practice "chain migration" through kinship if they had relations in the U.S. at outset. Moreover, some *waishengren* might choose to come to the U.S. rather than Taiwan after the defeat of KMT. Or, some students might be caught in the U.S. during wars.

Table 6-4: Ethnicity and Motives for Initial Emigration

	Benshengren	Waishengren
Study	26 (67%)	9 (60%)
Family Reunion	6 (15%)	5 (33%)
Work	5 (13%)	0 (0%)
Children's Education	2 (5%)	1 (7%)
Total (54)	39 (100%)	15 (100%)

Decade of Migration Differences:
Motives for emigration varied in different periods, as the social and political contexts that "pull" and "push" international migration changed over time. To examine such change, I divided the 54 families into four groups based on the decades they migrated to the U.S., and analyzed the fluctuation of their emigration motives in order to sketch a quasi-longitudinal trend. As shown in Table 6-5, study was the primary motive for emigration to the U.S. over the four decades, but its importance decreased over time (82% in the 1960s, 74% in the 70s, 56% in the 80s, and 33% in the 90s). In contrast, the percentages of those who relocated internationally for the purpose of family reunion (9% in the 1960s, 16% in the 70s, 28% in the 80s, and 33%

in the 90s) or children's education (0% in both the 1960s and 70s, 6% in the 80s, and 33% in the 90s) increased constantly. In the 1990s, studying, family reunion, and children's education became three equally significant motives for emigration (all were 33%), whereas no one emigrated to seek work (see Table 6-5).

Table 6-5: Decade of Migration and Motives for Initial Emigration

	1960s	1970s	1980s	1990s
Study	9 (82%)	14 (74%)	10 (56%)	2 (33%)
Family Reunion	1 (9%)	3 (16%)	5 (28%)	2 (33%)
Children's Education	0 (0%)	0 (0%)	1 (6%)	2 (33%)
Work	1 (9%)	2 (11%)	2 (11%)	0 (0%)
Total (54)	11 (100%)	19 (100%)	18 (100%)	6 (100%)

The trend of informants' motives for initial emigration, as shown in Figure 6-1, reflects an important change in the structural contexts that affected Taiwanese people's incentives to move out of the island. First, the number of graduate schools in Taiwan has been increasing, so studying abroad is no longer the only or major option for students who wish to pursue advanced education.[72] The return rate among Taiwanese students who studied in the U.S. also has been increasing since the 1980s (Chang 1992). Second, the gradual increase in the numbers of informants who migrated for family reunion implies that family values continue to be held in high regard in contemporary Taiwan. International migration has been a family, rather than individual, process for Taiwanese. Moreover, most Taiwanese Americans were admitted to the U.S. through family sponsorship. This trend may continue to be the primary channel for immigrants from Taiwan.

---

[72] According to the Executive Yuan, R.O.C. (1992: 73, Table 4-8), the number of graduate institutes in Taiwan has been continuously increasing since the 1960s. By 1991, 1,668 graduate schools had been established on the island, approximately 15 times more than that in 1971 (110) and 45 times more than that in 1961 (37).

Figure 6-1: Trends of Motives for Initial Emigration

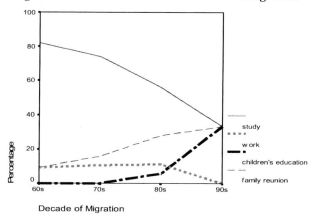

Decade of Migration

Third, the continuous rise in the number of informants who migrated for the purpose of children's education suggests that a poor educational environment in Taiwan was a push factor for Taiwanese immigration to the United States. Taiwan's educational system was totally controlled by the state until 1994, when educational movements became a well-organized social force on the island. Such authoritarianism was a defining feature of Taiwan's educational environment and it created numerous unhappy young children, the major problem educational activists wished to solve (Xue 1996). The characteristics of liberalism and flexibility, emblematic of U.S. education, mirrored the goals of educational movements in Taiwan and reflected Taiwanese parents' hope for the next generation. Sending children overseas for education, therefore, became an alternative option for many middle-class families. Fourth, the fact that fewer and fewer informants migrated to the U.S. to work reflects the economic growth of and increasing employment opportunities in Taiwan, especially after the 1980s. As Ng (1998) points out, it was difficult for highly-educated people to find employment opportunities in Taiwan from the 1960s to the 1980s, but the situation improved in the 1980s. Seeking job opportunities overseas, therefore, was no longer a major reason for Taiwanese to migrate to the U.S. The change in informants' emigration motives to seek work corresponds with such a transformation.

Motives for Permanent Settlement

In contrast to the motives for emigration for which informants could easily identify a major reason, when asked why they decided to stay in the U.S. permanently, subjects often provided multiple reasons. In addition to documenting these reasons, I asked the informants to identify one as their major motive for settlement on which my analysis in this section is based. In general, better job opportunities was the predominant determinant for informants to settle permanently in the United States; nearly three-fifths (31 individuals, about 57%) decided to stay primarily because they found good jobs here (see Table 6-6).

Table 6-6: Motives for Permanent Settlement

	Frequency	Percent
Job Opportunity	31	57%
Family Reunion	10	19%
Children's Education	7	13%
Political Factors	5	9%
Better Living Environment	1	2%
Total	54	100%

Nevertheless, those informants who settled down permanently did not intend to do so when they first emigrated (mostly to study); nor did they actually explore opportunities in both Taiwan and the U.S. in order to choose the best place. In fact, "better job opportunities" were more a presumption than an investigated fact. Since most of the subjects found jobs immediately after graduation, settling down "naturally" became the next step after starting to work. As a result, most informants did not really go through a decision-making process concerning permanent settlement. Rather, they regarded it as a "normal path" in the life course. As a 53-year-old male professor (*waishengren*), Kuo-Hwa, said, "I didn't have any specific goal at that time. I thought I'll just wait and see." Similarly, Min-Hui, a 39-year-old male engineer (*benshengren*), explained:

People don't usually decide to stay permanently at first, including us. At that time, my daughter was one and an half years old, about two. So, I thought I'd take this job first, and see how it goes.... So we didn't think too much. We were young at that time, so we thought we'd work here for a while and see how it goes. But our intention was not [to stay here forever].... We are not like Chinese students [from the PRC]. They usually want to stay here, and never go back to China. **Returning to Taiwan is always one of my options**. (emphasis added)

Three male *waishengren* mentioned the ethnic discrimination they encountered at work in Taiwan, which also propelled them to the U.S.[73] For instance, Chia-Lung, a 48-year-old man who migrated in the early 1980s and worked at a carry-out Chinese food store, told me:

Generally speaking, I came to America because my relatives were here. In addition, in Taiwan, it has something to do with ethnicity. I am *waishengren*. It was difficult for *waishengren* to find a job [in the private sector] at that time in Taiwan.... At that time, most of the job ads on the newspapers were limited to "*benshengren* only" or "Taiwanese speakers"... . All types of jobs were like this... . Under that kind of atmosphere, I thought it'd be better if we moved to America. We might have better opportunities here. That's why we moved here.... Until today, it's always a pain in my heart.... I really don't understand why speaking Taiwanese was the requirement of being hired. After moving to America, I feel I'm emancipated from that problem.

In a similar vein, Hung-Wei, a 47-year-old male computer programmer who migrated in the late 1970s, said:

I worked in the construction industry for two years after graduation. At that time, you had to speak Taiwanese if you wanted to get a job. We were required to speak Taiwanese at work. But, I am a

---

[73] The years these *waishengren* migrated, ranging from 1977 to 1981, were all very close. This was a period during which ethnic relations remained intense in Taiwan (see Chapter Five).

waishengren, and I can't speak fluent Taiwanese…. This is part of the reason, although not the major one, that I moved here. Given that kind of situation, you would think, maybe you would have better opportunities overseas than in Taiwan.

This finding is surprising. Historically, the political arena in Taiwan was monopolized by the KMT regime, and the officials, soldiers, and supporters it brought from Mainland China had been the privileged class in society. As the "ruled," *benshengren* were oppressed, and ethnic tension on the island usually was considered the result of *waishengren*'s superiority. Thus, the discrimination these informants experienced at work may reflect the larger social structure in Taiwan. As early as the Land Reform during 1951-53, the KMT government compensated *benshengren* landlords whose land was expropriated by giving them land bonds and shares in government enterprises. This encouraged many former landlords to move from the rural area to the city where they entered business. In addition, because *waishengren* monopolized the government bureaucracy and education, *benshengren* were forced to go into business and medicine as a path to prosperity.[74] These factors created an economically sectored segregation by ethnicity on the island. As the "minority" in the economic section, therefore, *waishengren* may have encountered structural constraints (such as a glass ceiling) or intentional exclusion by *benshengren*. Moreover, because most businesses in Taiwan are family owned, they tended to employ kin in high positions. It was therefore difficult for *waishengren* to move up the hierarchical ladder of job in these family-owned, and mostly *benshengren*-owned, firms (just as it was for non-kin *benshengren*).

Family reunion was the second most frequently mentioned motive for permanent settlement, indicating the important value Taiwanese immigrants place on "binding the whole family together." Almost two-fifths (10 individuals, about 19%) of the informants decided to stay in the U.S. either because their spouses had made the decision or their siblings had already migrated (See Table 6-6).

In addition, some subjects (7 individuals, about 13%) settled in the U.S. in order to give their children better educational opportunities than were

---

[74] As early as the first decade of the 1900s, during the time of Japanese occupation, becoming a physician has been a major avenue via which *benshengren* acquired high social status.

available in Taiwan, while others (5 individuals, about 9%) were not willing to return to Taiwan which was facing political uncertainty and instability under China's threat (see Table 6-6). Ethnic tension between *waishengren* and *benshengren* also led to the settlement of a few *waishengren*; the better living environment in the U.S. appealed to some, whereas others were forced to stay abroad because they were on the KMT government's "blacklist."[75]

Informants' motives for permanent settlement in this study were fairly consistent with the push-pull factors of Taiwanese immigration to the U.S. discussed in Chapter Five. Interlocking political (e.g., the unstable political situation facing Taiwan, martial law and oppression, ethnic conflicts), economic (e.g., limited job opportunities), and social factors (e.g., children's education, quality of living environment) all contributed to the Taiwanese exodus and settlement abroad. While the U.S. Immigration Act of 1965 was crucial in increasing the number of immigrants from Asia, none of the subjects in this study regarded this pull factor as one of the major reasons for emigration or settlement. In contrast, family reunion, a social factor that often has been overlooked in previous studies of Taiwanese immigration, was an important factor leading to informants' decision to settle in a foreign land. This finding suggests the importance of family values in the Taiwanese immigrant community.

Similar to their incentives for initial emigration, informants' motives for permanent settlement differed in terms of gender, class, ethnicity, and decade of emigration. Below, I describe these differences.

Gender differences:
A comparison of settlement motives by gender showed that men were significantly more concerned than women with economic prospects such as

---

[75] Taiwan began moving toward democracy after martial law was lifted in 1987. Prior to the initiation of this process, the KMT government sent many secret agents to the U.S. as "professional students." These secret agents held student visas to disguise their true identities, and registered in universities. Their major duty was to report suspicious anti-government talk and actions among overseas Taiwanese student to the government. Once reported and recorded on these secret agents' "blacklists," the students were not allowed to return to Taiwan permanently. As a result, many overseas Taiwanese who had ever criticized the KMT government were forced to stay in the United States.

job opportunities (68% and 35%, respectively), while women cared more about social   factors (e.g., 24% for family reunion, 17% for children's education, and 6% for better living environment) and political factors (18% for political instability and uncertainty in Taiwan) (see Table 6-7). As illustrated earlier in this chapter, many more men than women first came to the U.S. to study. Men, therefore, were also more likely than their female counterparts to find jobs because of their education background. Although as many as one-third of women (6 out of 17; 35%) decided to stay in the U.S. permanently because of good job opportunities, the rest primarily considered family well-being (see Table 6-7).

Table 6-7: Gender and Motives for Permanent Settlement

	Men	Women
Job Opportunity	25 (68%)	6 (35%)
Family Reunion	6 (16%)	4 (24%)
Children's Education	4 (11%)	3 (17%)
Political Factors	2 (5%)	3 (18%)
Better Living Environment	0 (0%)	1 (6%)
Total (54)	37 (100%)	17 (100%)

Several possible factors contributed to these gender differences in motives for permanent settlement. First, from a psychological view, men tended to be self-oriented, whereas women were other-oriented. Men, therefore, were more likely to put their own interests ahead of others in a major decision such as settlement, while women tended to consider other family members' well-being. Second, because in most cases men had job offers after their graduation, this "fact" reinforced and legitimated their wish to stay. It also became a convincing discussion point when they were persuading their wives to acquiesce to their wishes to settle in the U.S. Since their husbands had found jobs, married women may have thought of other "benefits" accompanying this decision and therefore reported them as motives. Third, family reunion and children's education were the secondary and third motives for settlement both among men and women, suggesting the importance of family well-being and education on the informants' deliberations about immigration. In other words, investing in one's human capital produced dividends for more than the individual. It also increased the chance that the family would prosper.

Class differences:[76]
Middle-class informants chose to settle in the U.S. permanently primarily because they acquired good job opportunities (30 individuals, about 63%). Lower-class subjects, in contrast, stayed mainly for children's education and family reunion (see Table 6-8).

Table 6-8: Social Class and Motives for Permanent Settlement

	Lower Class	Middle Class
Job Opportunity	1 (17%)	30 (63%)
Family Reunion	2 (33%)	8 (17%)
Children's Education	2 (33%)	5 (10%)
Political Factors	1 (17%)	4 (8%)
Better Living Environment	0 (0%)	1 (2%)
Total (54)	6 (100%)	48 (100%)

These class differences reflect how social location shaped individuals' decisions to settle. Middle-class informants' SES backgrounds granted them advantages in the labor market, which eventually became a major reason for their settlement. In contrast, lower-class subjects were not as advantaged. They usually had to struggle to survive, and to endure hardship to sustain family well-being. In other words, in contrast to their middle-class counterparts who just "followed the natural path of life" to settle, lower-class informants had to exert a lot of effort to "earn" the opportunity of settlement. No matter how difficult the process of adaptation was, they were

---

[76] As noted in Chapter Four and above, the comparison of social class may be problematic because of the small number of lower-class informants in this study (6 individuals, 11%). This comparison therefore is made only for reference. Sometimes when a discrepancy between two social classes is evident, such "analysis for reference" can provide useful information.

determined to stay in the U.S. For them, immigration was a "must-do," which was not necessarily so for their middle-class counterparts.

Ethnic Differences:
Benshengren were more likely than their *waishengren* counterparts (24% more) to consider job opportunity as the primary factor for settling in the U.S. (see Table 6-9). In contrast, a greater percentage of *waishengren* (30% more) than *benshengren* considered family reunion as a major reason to settle, although this incentive was as important as job opportunity in their deliberations (see Table 6-9).

Table 6-9: Ethnicity and Motives for Permanent Settlement

	Benshengren	*Waishengren*
Job Opportunity	25 (64%)	6 (40%)
Family Reunion	4 (10%)	6 (40%)
Children's Education	6 (15%)	1 (7%)
Political Factors	3 (8%)	2 (13%)
Better Living Environment	1 (3%)	0 (0%)
Total (54)	39 (100%)	15(100%)

Consistent with the findings in the analysis of motives for initial immigration, family reunion was, again, a noteworthy reason for *waishengren*'s settlement decision. Such a tendency of "chain migration" among *waishengren* may also partly result from their fear or worry concerning the political instability facing Taiwan. While the percentages of *waishengren* and *benshengren* who settled for political factors (13% and 8%, respectively) were close, the concerns of these two groups in this motive differ. *Waishengren* tended to consider Taiwan as a temporary retreat from the Mainland, and feared the Communists' threat to the island. In contrast, *benshengren* resented the oppression of the KMT regime, and considered immigration emancipatory.

Decade of Migration Differences:
Like motives for initial emigration, informants' intentions for permanent settlement may vary in different time periods due to the change in historical and social contexts. Analyzing the subjects' settlement motives based on the decades of their migration, I found such variance over time. From the 1960s to the 1990s, the percentages of informants who settled in the U.S. primarily because of job opportunities gradually declined (82% in the 1960s, 74% in the 70s, 33% in the 80s, and 33% in the 90s). The decrease is especially noticeable from the 1970s to the 1980s, with 41 percent fewer, reporting this as a reason (see Table 6-10).

Table 6-10: Decade of Migration and Motives for Permanent Settlement

	1960s	1970s	1980s	1990s
Job Opportunity	9 (82%)	14 (74%)	6 (33%)	2 (33%)
Family Reunion	0 (0%)	2 (11%)	7 (39%)	1 (17%)
Children's Education	1 (9%)	0 (0%)	3 (17%)	3 (50%)
Political Factors	1 (9%)	2 (11%)	2 (11%)	0 (0%)
Better Living Environment	0 (0%)	1 (5%)	0 (0%)	0 (0%)
Total (54)	11 (100%)	19 (100%)	18 (100%)	6 (100%)

This decrease, as described above, indicates that the rapid growth and development of industry and advanced technology in Taiwan after the 1970s created more job opportunities and a better economic environment than existed in the preceding decades. As a result, fewer people sought jobs overseas afterwards. Almost all subjects in this study who worked in the U.S. private sector reported a dramatic decrease in the number of Taiwanese co-workers in the 1990s. They mentioned that since the 1990s, students from Taiwan tended to return to the island, and thus a "cohort gap" had appeared in the Taiwanese immigrant community.

In contrast to those who settled for good job opportunities, the percentage of informants who stayed to reunite the family constantly increased from the 1960s to the 1980s (0% in the 1960s, 11% in the 70s, and 39% in the 80s), and then dropped thereafter (17% in the 1990s). In the 1980s, family reunion (39%) even transcended job opportunities (33%) as a motive for settlement, and it became the most common incentive for permanent settlement (see Table 6-10).

Figure 6-2 illustrates these changes over time. In this figure, the contrast between economic (job opportunity) and social factors (family reunion and children's education) was fairly evident during the period from the 1970s to 1980s. While the percentage of informants who settled for economic reasons dropped dramatically (from 74% to 33%), those who settled for the purposes of family reunion and the next generation's education greatly increased (from 11% to 39% and from 0% to 17%, respectively, see Figure 6-2). The rise of these two motives for settlement in the same period was also found in the subjects' incentives for initial emigration. In other words, after the 1970s, family reunion and children's education were two rising motives for both initial emigration and permanent settlement. Family reunion as the primary drive for settlement peaked in the 80s and then dropped in the 90s, but consideration of children's education continued to increase at a fast rate after the 1980s (see Figure 6-2).

Figure 6-2: Trends of Motives for Permanent Settlement

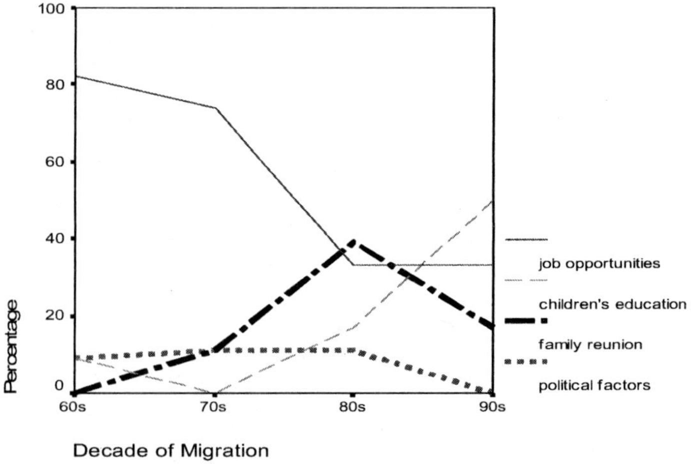

Compared to other motives, the change in political considerations over time was not as remarkable. The percentage of informants who settled in the

U.S. because of the political instability facing Taiwan remained about the same from the 1960s to 1980s (9% in the 60s, and 11% in the 70s and 80s), and then dropped thereafter (0% in the 90s). The decline in the 1990s reflects the change in Taiwan's political arena. Since the lifting of Martial Law in 1987, Taiwan has moved toward democracy, and many political regulations of the past have been rescinded and oppression declined. This transformation may contribute to the decreasing number of people who chose to settle in the U.S. for political reasons.

Patterns and Comparisons of Immigration Motives

Figure 6-3 provides a summary of the above analyses. I synthesize the informants' primary motives for emigration and settlement, as well as to compare motives among people in different social locations (see Figure 6-3).

In general, the primary motives for initial immigration and permanent settlement were study and job opportunities, respectively (see Figure 6-3, General). With the exception of the lower class, "move to study and then settled because of jobs" was the primary pattern in the sample and across subgroups.[77] This finding, however, does not support those of numerous other studies which show that women primarily migrate to join husbands and to create families (Lee 1966; Houstoun et al. 1984; Tyree and Donato 1986; Watts 1983). In general, both women's and men's motives for initial migration and permanent settlement took the "education and migration pattern (see Figure 6-3, General). Women as well as men were representative of the "brain drain" characteristic of Taiwanese immigration.

---

[77] In this study, lower-class Taiwanese immigrants both migrated and settled primarily for non-economic reasons. This tendency is fairly different from the immigrants in earlier turn-of-the-century and those from China, who mainly come to America to look for "streets that are paved with gold." Moreover, none of the lower-class informants expressed regrets that they had not been financially successful in the U.S., despite of the hardship they faced for surviving.

Figure 6-3: Synthesis and Comparison of Informants' Immigration Motives

Motives		Initial Emigration	Permanent Settlement
General		1. Study 2. Family Reunion	1. Job Opportunities 2. Family Reunion
Gender	Both	Primarily for Study	Primarily for Job Opportunities
	Men	More for Study	More for Economic Factors (job opportunities)
	Women	More for Family Reunion	More for Non-economic Factors (family reunion, children's education, political factors, and better living environment)
Class	Middle	Mostly for Study	More for Economic Factors (job opportunities)
	Lower	Mostly for Family Reunion	More for Non-economic Factors (family reunion, children's education, and political factors)
Ethnicity	Both	Primarily for Study	Primarily for Job Opportunities
	Benshengren	More for Work	More for Economic Factors (job opportunities)
	Waishengren	More for Family Reunion	More for Family Reunion

In the case of subgroups of individuals, two parallel clusters emerged from the comparisons of motives for initial emigration and permanent settlement. First, men and middle-class informants had the same pattern. Compared to their counterparts, they were more likely to first migrate to study and then to settle for job opportunities, a tendency that resembles the primary pattern of the entire sample. While *benshengren* also tended to settle for job opportunities, as did men and the middle-class, they were more likely than their *waishengren* counterparts to migrate for work. Second, compared to their male counterparts, women, lower-class, and *waishengren* informants tended first to migrate to unite their families, and then to consider non-economic factors (e.g., family reunion, children's education, political instability, better living environment) in their motives for settlement.

As shown in Figure 6-3, both commonalities and differences existed in the informants' major reasons for initial emigration and permanent settlement, suggesting the complexity of motives and of the structural effects (both push-pull factors and individuals' social locations) on people's deliberations about immigration. Nevertheless, despite the multiplicity of personal motives, the process that determines who became the primary decision-maker about immigration remains unsettled, and I turn to this issue in the next section.

Whose Decision to Settle?

Despite the variety in individuals' motives for emigration and settlement, not all informants themselves made the decision to stay in the U.S. permanently, especially those who were married.[78] While settling a family in a foreign land is a drastic social action, who makes the decision reflects the balance of power between individuals in a couple.[79] In fact, I found the major pattern of decision making about

---

[78] Not all informants were married at the time they left Taiwan, but most (51 out of 54 families) were when they were considering settling down in the U.S. (although a few got divorced afterwards). Here I analyze who in a couple controlled more power when deciding to relocate the family in a foreign land.

[79] I consider decision making about settlement as a reflection of power relations in the family, the individuals I am analyzing are partnered. The unit of analysis in this section is therefore the family (conjugal relations).

settlement among Taiwanese American couples was "men were pioneers, women followers." Moreover, most husbands (31 out of 54, about 61%) made the decision to settle their families in the U.S. permanently. While about one-third (17 couples, 33%) of the couples made this decision together, in only three (6%) families did the wife play the role of major decision-maker about settlement (see Table 6-11).[80]

Table 6-11: Decision-Makers about Settlement

	Frequency	Percent
Husband	31	61%
Wife	3	6%
Joint Decision	17	33%
Total	51*	100%

* Among the 54 informants I interviewed, two were never married and one migrated after her husband died. The analyses on decision-makers, therefore, includes only 51 cases.

Although one-third (33%) of the couples were fairly egalitarian in making decisions about settlement, the majority (31 families; 61%) were male-dominated. In most (61%) of the cases in which the husbands were the major decision-maker concerning settlement, the husbands first came to America for graduate studies, and their wives

---

[80] The three couples in which the wives were the major decision-maker about settlement were all middle-class. Two of them were married at the time they left Taiwan. One couple came to the U.S. together to study, and then settled down permanently. Another moved to the U.S. in middle age, because the wife's parents and siblings had already migrated. The third couple met each other in the U.S., after the husband ended his second marriage and the wife terminated her first. When they got married, the wife insisted that they settle in the U.S. so that they would not have to face past bad memories of her first marriage in Taiwan and relatives' gossip about her remarrying.

(sometimes with their children) eventually followed from Taiwan. These men had graduated from good universities in Taiwan, and pursued the "American dream," as did many others who were part of the flow of the "elite trend" of Taiwanese immigration. During or after their studies, those who were already married asked their wives to come, while others who were still single, returned to Taiwan, married, and brought their brides to the United States. In spite of the fact that not all of these male students had decided to become American citizens at that time, the good job opportunities they found after graduation as well as the effortless procedure of legalizing their status in the 1960s and 1970s were key factors in their decision to settle down on foreign soil.

To reunite the family, these men's wives had to quit their jobs, many of which were well paid and high status. After following their husbands to the Unites States, they became stay-at-home mothers until their children entered school. [81] Some of these women returned to school or started to work after their children entered school, but a few (mostly physicians' wives) remained homemakers for the rest of their lives. Regardless, the women did not speak English as fluently as their husbands, nor did they initially fit into the host society as well as their husbands. Even among those wives who went to the U.S. primarily for their studies, similar patterns tended to emerge. For example, 16 wives went to graduate school in the U.S., and five of these women had a Ph.D degree. [82] Nevertheless, 12 of the 16 wives (two-thirds) stayed permanently because their husbands decided to settle down in a foreign land. Because settlement was not in their original plan, most of these women worked in fields that were different from their majors in graduate school. The jobs of only four women (three Ph.D.s and one

---

[81] Wives usually did not work after their arrival for several reasons. Most of them had pre-school children at home who needed attention. Their status also usually had not yet been legalized, thereby making them ineligible for employment. In addition, because they had not been educated in the United States, many lacked fluency in English, thereby constraining their job opportunities.

[82] Among the 16 wives who were U.S. educated, 9 came to study at the time of their move. The rest migrated with their husbands, and went to graduate school after their children entered school.

MA) were related to their majors, and three of these women followed their husbands wherever the men went when searching for jobs.

Commonalities among and Differences between Informants

While male-dominance describes the general pattern in the sample about making the decision to settle, below I compare families in different social locations. These analyses demonstrate how an individual's structural position shapes power relations in marriage, and how the dynamics of this relation affect decision making in the family.

Class Differences:
When a comparison of individuals by social class was made, the data showed an interesting result. All the husbands in lower-class families made the decision to settle in the U.S., while the situation in middle-class families was more diverse.[83] Despite the fact that husbands in the majority of middle-class families (27 families, 57%) remained the major decision-maker, more than one-third of the couples (17 families, 36%) made their settlement decision together and three wives (6%) played the role of decision-maker (see Table 6-12). This difference suggests that gender relations in middle-class families are more egalitarian than those in lower-class families.

Table 6-12: Social Class and Decision-makers about Settlement

	Lower Class	Middle Class
Husband	4 (100%)	27 (57%)
Wife	0 (0%)	3 (6%)
Joint Decision	0 (0%)	17 (36%)
Total (51)	4 (100%)	47 (100%)

Major components of social class, including education, earnings, and occupational prestige, are resources individuals use to negotiate

---

[83] All the four lower-class couples were married at the time they left Taiwan.

their share of housework (Kamo 1988; Presser 1994; Ross 1987). These resources also translate into personal power in making a family decision that is favorable to oneself. This factor may explain the class difference in making the decision to settle, as noted above. In other words, middle-class women had more resources than their lower-class counterparts in negotiating with their husbands about family decisions, including the decision to settle. In addition, middle-class men may have been more likely than their lower-class counterparts to hold egalitarian attitudes because of their higher education, thereby respecting their wives' opinions more in making family decisions (Chen, Yi, and Lu 2000).

Ethnic Differences:
In a comparison of family ethnicity, the husbands in *benshengren*, *waishengren*, and interethnic families continued to be the primary decision-makers, as were those in middle- and lower-class families.[84] This consistent finding across social class and ethnicity suggests men's dominant position in deciding the family's movement patterns.[85] It also reflects the cultural value in Chinese tradition that married women should follow their husbands wherever they move. In contrast, the two couples who were in interracial marriages made their settlement decision together (see Table 6-13).[86] This finding suggests that interracial couples might have been influenced by western culture and were therefore more egalitarian than their Taiwanese counterparts. Alternatively, while "marrying out" usually means "marrying far away from home" in the Taiwanese case, women who marry someone of a different race might be more independent and assertive than those who marry within their race.

---

[84] The seven interethnic families within which the husband was the major decision-maker all included *waishengren* husbands and *benshengren* wives.

[85] Despite the fact that men maintained their dominant position across class and ethnicity, middle-class and *benshengren* couples were relatively less dominant than their counterparts.

[86] Both of these couples were families in which Taiwanese women had married American (Anglo) men.

Table 6-13: Ethnicity and Decision-makers about Settlement

	Benshengren	*Waishengren*	Interethnic	Interracial
Husband	20 (59%)	4 (80%)	7 (70%)	0 (0%)
Wife	1 (3%)	1 (20%)	1 (10%)	0 (0%)
Joint Decision	13 (38%)	0 (0%)	2 (20%)	2 (100%)
Total (51)	34 (100%)	5 (100%)	10 (100%)	2 (100%)

Decade of Migration Differences:
A comparison of different decades of immigration showed an interesting change over time. After the 1970s, more and more Taiwanese couples jointly made the decision to settle together (11% in the 1970s, 44% in the 1980s, and 75% in the 1990s), while the percentage of families within which the husband was the major decision-maker decreased remarkably (83% in the 1970s, 44% in the 1980s, and 25% in the 1990s; see Table 6-14).

Table 6-14: Decade of Migration and Decision-makers about Settlement

	1960s	1970s	1980s	1990s
Husband	7 (64%)	15 (83%)	8 (44%)	1 (25%)
Wife	0 (0%)	1 (6%)	2 (11%)	0 (0%)
Couple	4 (36%)	2 (11%)	8 (44%)	3 (75%)
Total (51)	11 (100%)	18 (100%)	18 (100%)	4 (100%)

If we assume that individuals who migrated in different decades represented different generations or age cohorts, then this trend suggests that younger Taiwanese immigrants were more egalitarian than older generations. This tendency reflects the effect of modernization or westernization on the informants' gender attitudes, as the younger cohorts seemed more liberal-minded than their older counterparts.[87] Younger cohorts also might be more open to new ideas (transmitted by modernization or American culture) than their older counterparts, thereby less insistent on traditional gender roles. In contrast, the change in the percentages of female decision-makers, was not as evident over time. Although the percentage gradually increased from the 1970 (6%) to the 1980s (11%), it dropped in the 1990s (0%). This finding suggests that even though many women participated in important decision making such as settlement, they had not yet become as dominant as men were in the family. Figure 6-4 illustrates these changes.

Figure 6-4: Trends of Decision-makers about Settlement

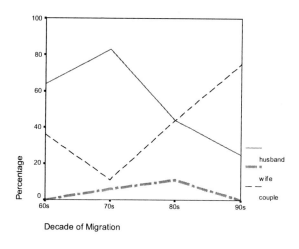

---

[87] Here I do not intend to dichotomize tradition and modernity, or oriental and western societies, nor do I consider Chinese culture as patriarchal/traditional/oriental and American cultural as egalitarian/liberal/western. In fact, these seem-to-be dichotomous characteristics can exist in the same culture. It is especially difficult to distinguish cultural boundaries and the impact of different cultures on individuals in a global era. Yet, as I demonstrated in Chapter Three, treating these two cultures as a dichotomy in discussion helps to highlight the contrasts between the two systems of cultural values and norms.

As shown in above analyses, social location shapes decision making, disadvantaging some while advantaging others. Among the variations created by different social locations (e.g., gender, ethnicity, class, decade of migration), gender stands out as the most discriminating factor. With the exceptions of interracial families and those couples who migrated in the 1990s, men across sub-groups dominated decision making about settling down in the U.S. This gendered power relation inevitably affected men's and women's emotional life in different ways after the decision was made. In the next section, therefore, I focus on gender in my discussion of mental health, pointing out instances when class and ethnicity make a difference.

WAS IT A GOOD DECISION TO MIGRATE?

Did the decision to migrate and to settle in the U.S., and the social location of the decision maker affect informants' mental health?[88] The answer is yes, but the impact appeared minimal because the informants tended to describe their distress relevant to their immigration decision as "not so distressed" and in terms such as "regrets," "wondering," "doubts," and "concerns." Below I discuss these informants' concerns and distress.

"I would've had a career in Taiwan" – Immigration as a Source of Distress for Married Middle-Class Women

Not having a career in the U.S. was a common regret among married middle-class women. In the sample, 21 wives (about 41%) quit their professional jobs, such as high school teachers, accountants, business mangers, or nurses, before migrating to the United States. In most of these cases, husbands first came to America to study, and later decided to permanently settle down in the U.S. because they found good jobs

---

[88] Although I distinguish motives for initial emigration and permanent settlement in previous section, here I examine how the informants' mental health was affected by international immigration in a general sense (since the decision to settle had been made and all the informants had become U.S. citizens).

after graduation.[89] Initially hoping that their husbands would come home after a few years of study, these married women faced an unexpected change in their life situation; they had to move halfway across the globe to unite the family.[90] Rather than a "choice to migrate" as was their husbands', such a change in their life situation was more a "choice to follow [their husbands]" to these married women because the decision was already made (by their husbands) and the job offers their husbands acquired strongly legitimized this decision. In other words, married women in this situation encountered an issue of how to manage and maintain family life, and all but one in this study decided to go along with their husbands' decision to settle in the U.S.[91]

"After getting married, you've got to follow wherever your husband goes," explained A-Mon. She earned her Bachelor's degree in a highly respected university in Japan, which only outstanding students or people from wealthy families would have been able to achieve during the 1960s in Taiwan. Her marriage was arranged and she married her husband soon thereafter. Before entering the labor force, A-Mon moved to America to join her husband who was a Ph.D. student at that time. She stayed home before her husband got his degree, and worked in a grocery store afterwards. Later, they opened a small grocery store in suburb of Chicago, but their financial situation was not good from the very beginning. Economic burdens often caused

---

[89] Three couples, both quit their jobs in Taiwan and migrated to the U.S. in order to pursue a better educational environment for their children.

[90] These couples got married at different stages of the husbands' study. Moreover, some wives initially accompanied their husbands abroad; some only came to visit for short terms, while others remained separated from their husband throughout his education abroad.

[91] Although this pattern was fairly common among married couples, an exception existed. One married woman, Li-Hung, remained separated from her husband, who studied in and migrated to the U.S., for twenty years. Li-Hung worked as an English teacher at a high school in Taiwan, a job she liked too much to give up. Her two daughters moved to the U.S. to live with their father at the ages of 14 and 16. Despite being separated, Li-Hung and her family visited each other during summer and winter vacations and maintained good relationships. Not until her husband passed away did Li-Hung move to the U.S. to live with her daughters.

arguments between the couple, but A-Mon never thought about leaving her husband or the U.S. She believed that it was her fate and duty, as a married woman, to follow her husband's footsteps and endure whatsoever difficulties the decision might entail.

Another female subject, Li-Ju, quit her job and moved to the U.S. at the age of 41 because "My only wish was that our family be together, no matter it's in Taiwan or in America."[92] Thus, to unite their families, married women quit their jobs, many of which were well-paid and high-status, and resettled in a foreign country. Compared to their male counterparts who were educated in the U.S. and were the major decision-maker of settlement, married women who followed their husbands to the new land were disadvantaged in many ways. They usually did not speak English as fluently as their husbands, and they required more time and effort to adapt to the host society. Consequently, most of them ended up taking jobs that were not well-matched with their educational backgrounds and ability. For instance, Mei-Li, a major in education, became an administrative staff member in a bank; Hsiao-Fen, a major in accounting, became a technician in a pharmacy department; and Shu-Mei, with a Master's degree in nursing, became a computer programmer. Even those women who entered graduate schools after their children grew up pursued a post-baccalaureate degree primarily to prepare them for the U.S. job market. For example, several informants studied computer science in order to find white-collar jobs. Because of immigration, these women were unable to develop careers, but rather had to accept whatever jobs were available in the new environment. As Mei-Yu said, "Here, what I do is just a job, one that brings some extra money to my family. If I didn't move here, I would've had a career in Taiwan."

Although the label "women followers" describes both middle- and lower-class married women in terms of their decision to migrate, only middle-class women regretted not having a career in the U.S. Such a

---

[92] Li-Ju worked as a nurse in her family-owned clinic in Taiwan. Because her in-laws had already moved to the U.S. in the 1970s, Li-Ju and her family migrated through family sponsorship in the early 1980s. After migration, she worked as a medical techinician intern at a Taiwanese-owned clinic in Chicago, but became a homemaker seven years later when she was diagnosed with breast cancer.

class difference can be attributed to the fact that in general, middle-class women, because of their higher social-economic status, had the ability to pursue careers, but the opportunity structure available to them in the U.S. did not allow them to fulfill their desires. Regardless of this dissimilarity, these two classes of married women shared a fatalistic attitude about their life situation resulting from international immigration because both believed it was (married) women's destiny to follow their husbands wherever they migrated. However regretful they were, these women tended to consider their move "the right thing to do" and an attribute of "appropriate womanhood." Such a fatalistic attitude reflects traditional Chinese values that, once married, women are expected to follow their husbands wherever they move (*jia ji sui ji, jia gou sui gou*), and to put their well-being behind that of their husbands and children. Moreover, *benshengren* constituted the majority (five out of six) of the "women followers" of their husbands and those who uttered regrets about not having a career, suggesting that *benshengren* women may be "more Chinese" than their *waishengren* counterparts in their gender role attitudes.[93]

Similar tendencies existed not only among the women who migrated to unite their families, but also among those who initially came for their studies. Eight of the nine female informants who first moved to the U.S. to study continued to stay primarily because their husbands wanted to settle down in this foreign land.[94] All these women looked for jobs that were close to those of their husbands, around whom their lives were centered. Three women did not finish their degrees because of the interruptions caused by either childbearing or moving (to the city where her husband worked). These situations suggest that married Taiwanese immigrant women to some extent were all "followers" of their husbands in the process of migration, either

---

[93] It is possible that because *benshengren* have larger kinship networks than *waishengren* in Taiwan, they are more likely to preserve marriage, whatever the costs (e.g., quit their jobs and become followers of their husbands), to avoid divorce and gossip of others. In other words, *benshengren* face more social pressure than their *waishengren* counterparts to follow traditional norms.

[94] One woman decided to stay because she and her husband had a mutual understanding and long discussions about the better working environment (for both of them) in the U.S. than Taiwan.

within or crossing national boarders. Many of them gave up good job opportunities, both in Taiwan and in the U.S., just to be close to (their husbands') "home," and many worked in the host society primarily to supplement family income rather than to fulfill their career ambition. As a result, married women were more likely than their male counterparts to encounter circumstances that required compromises and the sacrifice of their well-being (in terms of job opportunities and choices) in order to ensure family prosperity, leading to their greater likelihood of regrets as noted above.

Regretted or not, or however regretted, married women's perceptions of their "compromises" and "sacrifices" were fatalistic, and their responses to their "fate" were redirective. In general, women were more satisfied than their male counterparts with their work, even when the job was a "compromise" of their immigration life (see Chapter Eight). They also tended to consider the flexibility of their job conditions (when to enter and leave the labor market; working full-time or part-time, etc.) as a good way to take care of their families. Many were very active in the Taiwanese immigrant community and frequently participated in organizational activities.[95] In other words, these women redirected their regret at career interruption into devotion to other aspects of social life such as family and community. Their agency in this experience of distress was, therefore, redirective.

"I'd have more freedom if I stay here [rather than returning to Taiwan]" – Immigration as an act of "de-stress" for divorced women

In contrast to their counterparts whose careers were interrupted by immigration, the two divorced women in this study considered migrating to the U.S. an "emotional rescue" because it "blocked" potential stress generated by their relatives in Taiwan. Despite the fact that they came to unite families when their husbands decided to settle in the U.S., Min-Feng and Chia-Ling refused to go back to Taiwan when their marriages were terminated. In contrast, both of their ex-husbands returned to the island and remarried. "It would be very

---

[95] Several married women who followed their husbands to migrate served as president of social organizations in the Taiwanese immigrant community.

shameful in Taiwan if people know that I'm divorced," said Ming-Feng, a 50-year-old divorcee. After her divorce, Min-Feng had to work two jobs in order to raise two daughters, given the small amount of child support she received from her ex-husband ($100 per month). Nevertheless, she did not want to return to Taiwan because of the stigma attached to a divorced woman in Chinese culture. Similarly, another 41-year-old divorced woman, Chia-Ling, told me,

> At that time [after my marriage was over], I didn't think of going back to Taiwan. On the contrary, I wanted to stay here. Because... how to say this?... I'd have more freedom and be more likely to adjust myself well if I stay here [than return to Taiwan]. If I went back to Taiwan, the stress would be too overwhelming. My relatives would give me plenty of pressure. So, I didn't think of going back to Taiwan at all. Instead, I wanted to stay here for sure. It would be very annoying if I moved back to Taiwan, because I would need to deal with relatives' questions and gossip [about my divorce]. It's less stressful staying here.

Another informant, Jeff, was raised in a single-parent family after his father left home when he was seven. His mother, like Ming-Feng, had to take two jobs in order to survive. In addition, financial aid from grandparents (maternal) and loans from the bank helped Jeff's family in a substantial way. Despite the hardship of raising two children by herself, Jeff's mother was unwilling to return to Taiwan because of the cultural stigma attached to a divorced woman. A similar pattern was reported by Chuan-Chung, a 50-year-old chiropractic physician, who met his wife ten years ago, after she was divorced. His wife wished to stay in the U.S. in order to escape the gossip and the devaluation of a remarried woman in Chinese culture, so Chuan-Chung migrated and became a U.S. citizen.

These stories reveal another gendered prejudice in Chinese tradition. Chinese culture stigmatizes divorced women but not men. In ancient China, men (especially the rich) could legally marry several women. Men also could divorce their wives by writing a "divorce paper" without any legitimate reasons or their wives' consent. Once divorced, a woman was considered by her parents and society "abandoned" and "a family shame." While it was common for men to re-marry, divorced women were expected to stay single for the rest of their lives. Despite the fact that in modern times laws have been enacted to ensure monogamy and legal regulation of divorce, such a cultural belief continues to shape people's prejudice against divorced women. Just as the informants explicitly stated in the above stories, cultural stigma explained why they were reluctant to return to Taiwan. For divorced first-generation women across social classes, international migration became a way to escape (from cultural stigma) and heal (emotional wounds resulting from a broken marriage).[96] It "rescued" them from cultural stigma, helping to "de-tress" rather than to engender distress. Despite being followers of their husbands in the beginning of immigration, divorced women were determined to continue this journey after their husbands had left.[97]

"Why people at school make fun of me?" – Immigration as the origin of second-generation children's emotional struggles

International migration involves changes of citizenship and adaptation of a new status, sometimes giving rise to an identity crisis. My data show that different generations had dissimilar problems with identity as a result of immigration. First-generation subjects did not encounter as great or as severe an emotional struggle as their children's generation concerning self-identity -- wondering "Who am I?" One reason contributing to this difference was that first-generation informants, in contrast to second-generation subjects, tended to attach themselves more to the Taiwanese immigrant community than to U.S. society. Although most families in this study lived in areas where the majority of residents were Caucasian and worked in predominately White settings, the social circles first-generation Taiwanese participated in remained mostly Taiwanese.

---

[96] These divorced women included both middle- and lower-classes, but they were all *benshengren*. It is possible that because *waishengren* have smaller kinship networks in Taiwan, they are, therefore, less likely to face censure under such circumstances than their *benshengren* counterparts.

[97] None of the divorced women in this study ever re-married.

In addition to their involvement in various social activities within the Taiwanese community, first-generation informants tended to identify themselves as Taiwanese or Chinese, rather than as Americans.[98] Despite being American citizens, they always said "We Taiwanese" (or "We Chinese") and "They Americans" during interviews and my field observations. Sometimes when reporting experiences of racial discrimination in the workplace, subjects used terms such as "We foreigners..., they Americans..." to describe their relations with co-workers (see Chapter Eight). This distinction in informants' terms of reference, whether conscious or unconscious, suggests that first-generation informants tended to retain an "outsider mentality." In the view of many first-generation subjects, the act of immigration meant "selecting another place to live" rather than "shifting or adjusting self-identity in a new society." As a result, they seldom reported identity struggles related to their immigration decisions. Despite the fact that many parents were concerned about their children's identity struggles, they tended to consider this problem an inevitable result of immigration rather than a source of distress. Only one woman, Wan-Jen reported her emotional struggles when debating if immigration was a right decision. She said,

> I love my country, so the only question in my mind [when considering settling down in the U.S.] was that, "Do I really want to become an American? Do I really want my children to become Americans?" That's my question.

Although Wan-Jen was struggling emotionally, her husband made the decision to stay in the U.S. the moment they left Taiwan and his determination never relented. Both of them became U.S. citizens

---

[98] First-generation men, in particular, showed this tendency more evidently and consistently than their female counterparts. They tended to identify themselves as Taiwanese or Chinese both within the family and at the workplace. In contrast, while women also frequently referred to themselves as "Chinese" or "Taiwanese" in unspecified contexts, they showed a dual identity (either as Chinese/Taiwanese or/and American) in relational contexts such as in their relationships or interactions with family members and co-workers (see Chapters Seven and Eight).

several years later, but the identity question never faded from Wan-Jen's mind. After being an American for more than two decades, Wan-Jen's anxiety concerning the vanishing of her and her children's Taiwanese heritage continued to exist.

The action of "choosing another place to live" in the view of first-generation informants created a unique life situation for their children – membership in a minority group was a life situation that they would not have had to face if their parents had not migrated. In contrast to most first-generation informants who did not have to confront issues of self-identity, children of Taiwanese immigrants frequently encountered challenges in maintaining a positive self-image and a firm sense of self from the time they were young. Living in White neighborhoods, most second-generation subjects had experienced being picked on in school.[99] Because they looked different from other kids, many were called names and excluded by their peers, which sometimes diminished their self-esteem and created an identity crisis. Several informants recalled their unhappiness and denial of their Taiwanese background at elementary and high school, a result of being made fun of by other kids. Fortunately, for most, this problem just "naturally" went away after they entered college because their peers were more mature than teenagers. Many of them joined Asian American organizations and began to learn about their culture of origin. A few turned to religion (mostly Christianity) for comfort because "everyone is unique in God's eyes," as Mike said. In the view of Christians such as Mike, the struggle to accept that they were Taiwanese, and were different from other children was made easier by the belief that they were unique and treasured by God. These children therefore devoted themselves to religious activities and helped other youngsters who went through similar struggles to find peace.

Despite the fact that most second-generation informants successfully coped with their self identity, for some the discomfort of "being different" led to their denial of Taiwanese identity and a confusing self-image. For instance, Jane went through a long period of denying her Taiwanese background during her teenage and college years. In school, she hid her lunch bag to prevent classmates from

---

[99] Most of the 20 second-generation informants grew up in areas where Caucasians were the majority. Only four subjects lived in non-White areas.

seeing, in her words, her "funny lunch" (Chinese-style sandwiches). She made friends only with non-Asians, and denied her Taiwanese heritage. It was not until adulthood, with the growth of maturity, that Jane began to appreciate her cultural background. In contrast, Robert, a 19-year-old college freshman, joined a ROTC program because he wanted to show people how American he was. For him, being in the U.S. military was a symbol of "Americaness" that went beyond skin-color. When asked why he joined the navy, Robert explained,

> People assume things about you, basically, and you look different than other people. So, they always think different things. That's the thing that bothers me. I just want to be treated equal, you know.... I thought it shows people that I'm American, I guess. I thought that's the right thing to do, you know, join the navy, and show people I'm American, I fight for this country, too.

Although the decision to migrate did not generate mental distress for most first-generation informants, several subjects (mostly middle-class *benshengren*) admitted that they did not realize the profound impact of immigration until their children encountered issues with their identity, evoking some to wonder if immigration had been a good decision. [100] In dealing with their children's emotional struggles, Taiwanese parents (both fathers and mothers) adopted different strategies. Some told their teenagers to ignore other kids' stupidity and walk away, while others sent their children to summer camps established by Taiwanese American organizations (e.g., the Taiwanese

---

[100] Most parents who reported such wonderings were middle-class *benshengren*. Because *benshengren* and middle-class subjects were more likely than their *waishengren* and lower-class counterparts to take the path of "education and immigration," most of them did not take into account their children's identity issues when they decided to settle. In contrast, *waishengren* and the lower-class tended to practice "chain migration," and the decision to settle was often made before moving to the U.S. They therefore seldom wondered if it had been a right decision to settle when their children encountered identity issues because immigration had been a "must-do" for them.

American Association and Taiwanese American Foundation) to learn about Taiwanese culture and make friends with other second-generation teenagers whose parents were also from Taiwan. [101] For many second-generation Taiwanese, these camps helped relieve the distress caused by their racial and immigrant background. According to John, the experience of participating in the Taiwanese American camp filled the missing part of his heart.

> I think the event that sparked it [how I got to know myself better and began interested in learning about Taiwanese culture], that started it all, is that Taiwanese American camp I went to when I was thirteen, the summer right before high school. Simply because it [the camp] finally filled the void. Like, **there's always this missing part of my life, which was, Who am I? Am I Taiwanese? Am I Chinese? Is it ok to be like that? How come, why people at school make fun of me? So once I went there, I felt like that hole's sealed. Like, you're Taiwanese, you have a history. And look, look, other people, they are all there, there are several hundreds, and there are a lot in the Untied States. So finally I figured, wow, I'm part of the group.** And so starting from there, from being part of the group, then I wanted to know more about this group. Otherwise, I can't define it [myself and my cultural heritage]. I needed to define it, I needed to say what it is like, how did it get here.... I saw all my friends, they were in the same boat. They didn't know where they came from, and so to see them going through the same struggle I was going through before, gives me the motivation to try to share what I've learned with them, too. That helps them a lot, too.
>
>   (emphasis added)

---

[101] These camps and organizations are primarily funded by first-generation Taiwanese. As parents, they devoted their time and money to help the next generation deal with questions of identity and learn about Taiwanese culture. Participants in these summer camps and organizations were mostly from middle-class families because of the large registration fees (usually several hundred dollars per activity).

Realizing that they were not actually "that different" by knowing other teenagers of similar background, these children of Taiwanese immigrants began to free themselves from the emotional struggles concerning their identity. Many of them became good friends or married after these camp activities, and some began to develop a strong sense of Taiwanese pride. In other words, second-generation informants adopted an extensive range of strategies, utilizing various resources available to them when dealing with the distress resulting from issues associated with self-identity. Both boys and girls exhibited such a "strategic" style of exerting agency, but middle-class parents tended to provide their children more assistance than did their lower-class counterparts.[102]

SUMMARY AND CONCLUSION: A JOURNEY WITH WONDERING

In this chapter, I described the informants' motives for both initial emigration and permanent settlement, and discussed the gendered power structure of decision making in the family relevant to the decision of migration. Contrasts among informants of various social locations were provided in my analyses. I also showed if and how the decision to migrate as well as who was the decision-maker affected the subjects' mental health. In sum, Taiwanese Americans' immigration motives generally supported what Chang (1992) calls a pattern of "education and migration." Individuals of various social locations, however, migrated and settled for varied reasons that were affected by social factors (e.g., position in structural hierarchies, push-pull factors) or/and cultural (e.g., Chinese values of family and appropriate womanhood, American ways of education) factors. In other words, the structures that led to Taiwanese Americans' immigration and settlement were socially and culturally transnational.

The decision to migrate impacted, although not drastically, the informants' psychological well-being in different ways. Immigration created a minority status for second-generation children who struggled with their self identity; it also engendered regrets among married

---

[102] Because all second-generation informants in this study were middle-class *benshengren*, I was unable to examine differences across social locations.

women (across ethnicity, but mostly middle-class) about not having a career in the host society. The former situation caused some parents (mostly middle-class *benshengren*) to wonder if their immigration had been a good decision for the next generation; in the case of the latter, middle-class women (across ethnicity) wondered about their unachievable ambitions. International migration, therefore, became a journey of wondering for these Taiwanese Americans. In contrast, the action of immigration served as a means of "de-stress" for divorced *benshengren* women across social class because it prevented them from being stigmatized by Chinese culture.

Among the issues of distress revealed in this chapter, middle-class married women's regrets were directly related to the power imbalance between the partners in a couple in making the decision to migrate. As I have pointed out, husbands were the primary decision-maker in the family across various social locations. This tendency led to a gendered context within which married individuals made the immigration decision; men chose to move while (married) women chose to follow. Moreover, within this context, gendered distress (women's mental health was impacted more than their male counterparts) was created. Chinese cultural norms of appropriate womanhood, however, legitimated the gendering of migration choices. The differences between men's and women's motives for emigration and settlement also provided a supplementary illustration of such a context. Power also contributed to second-generation children's emotional struggles of self-identity. Their distress was produced by their position in the racial hierarchy of the host society, a power relation marked by the dominance of the White population and the subordination of the "other."

Individual agencies were exhibited in diverse ways within different contexts in reacting to the distress engendered by power relations. Married women followers re-directed their career ambitions to social activities in their ethnic community. Both parents and children adopted a range of strategies, either actively or passively, to ease inner struggles resulting from contradictory self-identities.

Emotional transnationalism to some extent was a part of second-generation children's struggles. While some were embarrassed by their Chineseness (e.g., hiding their Chinese-styled sandwiches), others were eager to demonstrate their Americaness (e.g., joining the ROTC), and still others contested their dual characteristics throughout their lives. In contrast, women followers did not experience such emotional transnationalism because only Chinese culture was involved in their power relations with their husbands in making the decision to migrate. Lacking conflicting standards from American culture, these women's experiences of distress did not result from emotional transnationalism that involves ambivalence when attempting to accommodate two conflicting value systems.

CHAPTER 7

AMBIVALENT CULTURAL TUG

The immigrant family is a place where there is a dynamic interplay between structure, culture, and agency. (Foner 1997: 961)

As demonstrated in Chapter Two, sociologists in the areas of mental health research and immigration studies all emphasize the importance of family structure and context for examining individuals' psychological well-being. Situated in a transnational context, the practices of Taiwanese American families are affected by both the sending and receiving societies. As Foner (1997) correctly points out, immigrant family patterns are shaped not only by the social practices and cultural meanings immigrants bring with them from their home countries, but also by social, economic, and cultural forces in the receiving society. It is therefore important to investigate Taiwanese Americans' family dynamics and their impact on mental health in a transnational milieu.

In this chapter, I discuss my analysis in two major parts: (1) the gendered power structure of Taiwanese American families, and (2) how familial relations conjoined with emotional transnationalism generate mental distress. First, I explore how Taiwanese American couples made important decisions about family finances and children's education, and how they divided domestic labor. I focus on spousal relations in this analysis, examining power relations between husbands and wives. I also compare similarities among and differences between various sub-groups. Second, I explore the mental distress Taiwanese Americans experienced in the family, and provide illustrations of the dynamics within which such psychological suffering occurred. This investigation extends to familial relationships other than conjugal (e.g., in-law and generational relationships). I discuss how power in these familial

167

relationships, in some contexts interwoven with emotional transnationalism that is a result of clashing values of cultural identifications, produces mental distress.[103]

GENDERED POWER STRUCTURE IN THE FAMILY

The household division of labor and decision-making are two of the most important elements of marital arrangements that affect individuals' well-being (Van Willigen and Drentea 2001). Both aspects of family life are an outcome of the gendered power structure of conjugal relationships. In Chapter Six, I discussed how the decision to migrate was made in the Taiwanese immigrant family and its implications for mental health. Below I examine how domestic labor was divided among Taiwanese American couples, and who made important decisions about finances and children's education. I also compare groups occupying different social locations to explore variations in the way this division and decision making were done.[104]

Gender Division of Domestic Labor

The gender division of domestic labor is a complex issue, involving different factors and tasks. A great number of scholars have contributed to the exploration of this subject, although how housework is conceptualized and measured varies from study to study (Shelton and John 1996). While acknowledging its complexity, I investigate and

---

[103] Following Brubaker and Cooper (2000), I use the term "identification," instead of "identity," to emphasize the fluid and changeable nature of identity.

[104] I did not have sufficient data to analyze second-generation informants' spousal relationships because only one woman was married (to another second-generation Taiwanese American) in the sample, and another was cohabiting with a Caucasian. Both of them were childless. The interracial couple shared domestic labor, but surprisingly, the second-generation woman who married another second-generation Taiwanese did all housework. She considered this unequal division a practice of Chinese cultural norm. As she said when explaining why she did all housework at home, "... gender roles, I'm definitely more Taiwanese[Chinese], definitely."

discuss the gender division of domestic labor in a rather limited sense for the purpose of this study. I adopted a "proportional measure," as Shelton and John (1996) describe, to examine how housework was divided between the couple, asking informants to indicate whether the wife did all, wife did most, both wife and husband shared, husband did most, or husband did all household task.[105] My analysis is, therefore, based on these self-report data and does not describe the nuances of housework such as detailed divisions of household tasks, rationales for such divisions, associated gender ideologies, and perceptions of fairness.

In almost one half of the households (47%), domestic labor was divided between the couple. One-third of the wives (34%) did all the housework, and another one-fifth (19%) were responsible for most of it (see Table 7-1). The two categories, wives did all and most housework, made up slightly more than one half of the families (53%) within which the wife was primarily responsible for housework. This general pattern in the entire sample suggests that the division of domestic labor in a Taiwanese American family is not uniform across couples.

As many studies have repeatedly pointed out, whether employed or not, women continue to do the majority of housework (Brines 1993; Marini and Shelton 1993; Shelton and John 1996; Robinson 1988). This study once again supports this observation, as more than a half of the women were responsible for most domestic labor at home.[106] This tendency to some extent forecasts the consequent vulnerability of women's mental health (see next section).

---

[105] I used a proportional measure primarily for two reasons. First, the purpose of this study was to obtain a general idea about the gender division of household labor in the family, rather than to investigate detailed task distributions between the couple. Second, because this theme was only a small section of my interview schedule, using a proportional measure that did not induce long answers helped to control the length of interviews.

[106] I used a proportional measurement in this study, thereby leaving detailed task division of domestic labor between the couple un-examined. I anticipate that the portion of "shared" category would decrease if exact tasks men and women did and the time they spent per day on housework were taken into account, because the meaning of "shared" may vary from one couple to another and differ for men and women.

Table 7-1: Gender Division of Domestic Labor

	Frequency	Percent
Wife does it all	16	34%
Wife does most of it	9	19%
Shared/Divided	22	47%
Total	47*	100%

* Among the 54 families, two women were widowed, two were divorced single parents, and two were never married. In addition, one family hired a housekeeper to take care of domestic labor. For the purpose of examining power dynamics among the couples, I excluded the above cases and the total number in this analysis therefore became 47.

Class Differences:

To explore why couples might adopt different patterns, I compared various social characteristics of families. The data in Table 7-2 show that wives in lower-class families were solely responsible for housework (100%). The tendency in middle-class families was fairly similar to that in the general pattern as shown in Table 7-1; about one half of the couples (51%) shared domestic labor equally, while in the other half (49%) the wives did all or most of the housework (see Table 7-2).

Table 7-2: Social Class and Gender Division of Domestic Labor

	Middle Class	Lower Class
Wife does it all	12 (28%)	4 (100%)
Wife does most of it	9 (21%)	0 (0%)
Shared/Divided	22 (51%)	0 (0%)
Total	47 (100%)	4 (100%)

Three factors possibly contribute to this difference between the two classes. First, because of their higher education, middle-class men's perceptions of gender roles might be more egalitarian than their lower-class counterparts and thus they are more willing to "help" with housework (also see Chen 1992). Second, compared to their lower-class counterparts, middle-class women might bring greater resources, such as money and education, to the marriage, thereby buttressing their power in the family. As scholars who adopt the relative resources explanation argue, income, education, and occupational prestige reflect resources men and women bring to relationships, affecting how a couple divides housework (see Blair and Lichter 1991; Kamo 1988; Presser 1994). Third, according to Chen (1992), husbands in middle-class families usually have more time than their blue-collar counterparts, who work long-hours, to do housework at home.

The issue of power is evidently involved in the above explanations. On the one hand, middle-class women's high social-economic status enhances their power in negotiating a more equal distribution of domestic labor. On the other, lower-class men tend to select a traditional value to adhere to in the private (family) arena in which they can exert power as a way of compensating for their powerlessness in the workplace (i.e., lack of autonomy and control of their labor) and in the larger society.

Ethnic Differences:
Ethnicity engendered more variations among couples than social class. Among the 54 families, only *benshengren* couples resembled the trend found in the entire sample and middle-class families; 15 of the couples (50%) shared housework, and among the other 15 couples, the wives were primarily responsible for domestic labor (see Table 7-3). In contrast, the two interracial couples (Taiwanese wives and Caucasian husbands) equally shared their housework. In comparison, *waishengren* families were less "egalitarian" than interracial couples, but more "egalitarian" than *benshengren* couples and interethnic couples. In fact, interethnic families showed the strongest patriarchal tendency. Eight of the ten wives did all or most of the housework while only two couples

(in which all included *waishengren* husbands married to *benshengren* wives) shared the task (see Table 7-3).[107]

Table 7-3: Ethnicity and Gender Division of Domestic Labor

	Benshengren	*Waishengren*	Interethnic	Interracial
Wife does it all	10 (33%)	1 (20%)	5 (50%)	0 (0%)
Wife does most of it	5 (17%)	1 (20%)	3 (30%)	0 (0%)
Shared/Divided	15 (50%)	3 (60%)	2 (20%)	2 (100%)
Total (47)	30 (100%)	5 (100%)	10 (100%)	2 (100%)

Some scholars in Taiwan (e.g., Lin and Lee 1999; Lin 1998; Huang 2000) point out that *waishengren* husbands are more likely than their *benshengren* counterparts to share domestic labor with their wives, although others find no differences (e.g., Lee, Yang, and Yi 2000). In this study, while a slightly greater percent of *waishengren* than *benshengren* couples (10% more, see Table 7-3) shared housework, having a *waishengren* husband did not "guarantee" equity in the gender division of household labor. Among the eight interethnic families within which the wives did all or most housework, five included *waishengren* husbands with *benshengren* wives (about 63%). Despite the fact that some couples (e.g., middle-class, *waishengren*, interracial) divided domestic labor more equally than others (e.g., lower-class, *benshengren*, interethnic), women continued to do more housework than men in most families, producing a negative effect on women's mental health. Overload of housework, therefore, became a predictable source of distress among married women (see below).

Sociological studies in Taiwan have repeatedly shown that despite improvements in women's social status, education, and the increasing rate of women's participation in the labor market, the gender division of domestic labor in the family remains grounded in traditional cultural

---

[107] Among the 10 interethnic couples, seven were *waishengren* husbands with *benshengren* wives, and three were *benshengren* husbands with *waishengren* wives.

norms, and women continue to do more housework than men (Huang 2000; Lee, Yang, and Yi 2000; Lu and Yi 1996). The mixed pattern of household labor among the informants, however, suggests that Taiwanese Americans might be slightly more egalitarian than Taiwanese people on the island. Taiwanese scholars Lai and Huang (1996) and Lee (1993) argue that husbands tend to do little housework in three-generation-cohabitation families because the older generation tends to impose traditional gender roles on the couple. The absence of parents in the U.S. context may play a role in the informants' division of household labor. Because most parents of first-generation Taiwanese Americans did not migrate with their children, conjugal families predominated in the sample.[108] In the absence of the traditionalism of the older generation and in the presence of the egalitarianism of American culture, Taiwanese American men were more likely than their Taiwanese counterparts to do housework. Although this explanation needs further study to determine its validity, social practices in the immigrant family are eventually products of transnational cultural norms.

Decision-making Power

Decision making can be a mechanism of control and, as such, reflects power relations within a family (Allen et al. 2001; Bloom, Wypij, and Gupta 2001; Van Willigen and Drentea 2001). According to Chen, Yi, and Lu (2000), Taiwanese couples consider children's education and family finances as the two most important decisions in the family. I therefore examine Taiwanese American couples' gendered power structure by analyzing who in the family controls more or less decision-making power on these two issues.

Financial Decisions

Financial decision-making is a complicated issue, involving both management and control, and a wide range of nuances in its forms and

---

[108] Among the 54 families, four were living with the men's mothers and another two had ever lived with them.

practices are prevalent in the family.[109] Acknowledging its complexity, I examine financial decision-making at a rather surface level for the purpose of this study. Similar to the proportional measurement I used for understanding informants' division of domestic labor, I asked subjects to report if their major financial decisions were primarily made by the husband, wife, or jointly. In other words, I again used a proportional measurement to identify the general power relations between a couple concerning their financial decision-making, investigating *who controlled money* in the family.

Overall, a slightly higher percentage of husbands than wives took charge of financial decisions alone (46% and 40%, respectively), although some couples (14%) jointly managed family finances (see Table 7-4). This result suggests that financial decisions in most Taiwanese American families were the responsibility of either a husband or a wife.

---

[109] A couple may adopt one or more than one system of financial management. For example, some couples practice a system of "household allowances" in which the husband gives his wife a portion of his income to take care of the house but retains money to which she has no access. While the wife may skim some money out of this household allowance, thereby saving money for her own use, the husband still controls major financial decisions. Some couples contribute all or part of their incomes to a common pool (pooled income) to which they both have access. Still among other couples, each partner keeps her or his own wages and the costs of various household expenses are divided (separate budgets), with one partner paying some and the other one paying others. In addition, financial decisions take various forms that may differ substantially, thereby impacting family life differently. For instance, deciding what to buy for dinner is a different decision than buying a car or taking a vacation.

Table 7-4: Decision-makers of Finances

	Frequency	Percent
Husband	24	46%
Wife	21	41%
Couple Together	7	14%
Total	52*	100%

* Two informants were single, so the total number of cases in this analysis became 52.

Interestingly, such a pattern is a reverse of the finding of Chen and her colleagues (2000) about how Taiwanese couples make financial decisions. Analyzing a national-scale survey conducted in Taiwan, Chen, Yi, and Lu (2000) report that joint decision-making was the major pattern Taiwanese couples adopted to manage family finances (about one half of the sample), followed by the form in which the wife made sole decisions (slightly less than one-third). Only 16 percent of the husbands were the primary decision-maker of finances (Chen, Yi, and Lu 2000). In addition to these general tendencies, Chen and her colleagues found different patterns in urban areas, where sole responsibilities (either the wife or the husband took charge of family finances) prevailed in most cases (ibid.). While Chicago is also a metropolitan region, its urban settings are different from those of Taiwan. Therefore, although Taiwan's urban case resembles the findings of this study, the factors that contribute to their similarities are rather difficult to conclude.[110]

---

[110] A great number of the major cultural characteristics that distinguish urban from rural societies, such as individualism, liberalism, and modernism, to some extent also permeate the differences between U.S. and Taiwanese societies. The question, if it is the urban or American environment that affects how Taiwanese immigrant couples arrange financial decisions, therefore, requires further investigation.

Class Differences:

The overall pattern in the whole sample changed when social class and ethnicity were considered. As shown in Table 7-5, decisions about finances in the five lower-class families were all under the control of husbands, suggesting that patriarchal relations prevailed within the couples. This finding, the absolute dominance of lower-class husbands in financial decision-making, is consistent with that of migration decision-making shown in Chapter Six. In contrast, women in middle-class families appeared much more powerful than their lower-class counterparts; almost one half (21 individuals, about 45%) were the financial decision-maker. I believe that middle-class women's higher educational background and economic status, compared to that of lower-class women, gave them more power in negotiating their role in family financial decisions. Middle-class men's egalitarian ideology, due to their higher education than the lower-class, might also contribute to this class difference. Middle-class families, however, were not as egalitarian as I expected because only 15% (7 families) of the couples jointly made financial decisions. Almost as many (40%) middle-class men solely took charge of finances as women (45%, see Table 7-5).[111]

Table 7-5: Social Class and Financial Decision-makers

	Lower Class	Middle Class
Husband	5 (100%)	19 (40%)
Wife	0 (0%)	21 (45%)
Couple Together	0 (0%)	7 (15%)
Total (52)	5 (100%)	47 (100%)

---

[111] Four wives were homemakers in this study, among whom two were lower-class and two middle-class. Both the two lower-class *benshengren* homemakers subordinated major financial decisions to their husbands (one was *benshengren*, the other *waishengren*). One of the middle-class *benshengren* homemakers, who was married to a *benshengren* physician, took charge of finances at home, while the other (*benshengren*, married to a *benshengren* businessman) abided by Chinese tradition (according to her interpretation of this arrangement) and submitted to her husband's decisions in major aspects of family life. In other words, a patriarchal tendency was more consistent in lower-class than middle-class families.

Ethnic Differences:
When a comparison was made by family ethnicity, a range of differences emerged. First, husbands in *benshengren* and *waishengren* families (53% and 50%, respectively) were more likely than those in the other two types of couples (30% in interethnic and 0% in interracial families) to play the role of major financial decision-makers (see Table 7-6). Second, wives in interracial marriages (Taiwanese women married to Caucasian men) dominated financial decisions. Third, *waishengren* and interethnic couples were more egalitarian than the other two types of families; more of them (33% and 30%, respectively) made financial decisions jointly than did *benshengren* and interracial couples (6% and 0%, respectively; see Table 7-6).

Table 7-6: Ethnicity and Financial Decision-makers

	Benshengren	*Waishengren*	Interethnic	Interracial
Husband	18 (53%)	3 (50%)	3 (30%)	0 (0%)
Wife	14 (41%)	1 (17%)	4 (40%)	2 (100%)
Couple	2 (6%)	2 (33%)	3 (30%)	0 (0%)
Total (52)	34 (100%)	6 (100%)	10 (100%)	2 (100%)

Compared to immigration decisions in which only six percent of the wives made the decision alone, Taiwanese American women appeared to have more control over finances than did men; two-fifths (41%) of the wives were independently in charge of financial decisions for their families. My data suggest that perhaps because money is a sensitive subject, most first-generation informants were somewhat reserved when talking about this issue. Whenever asked why a certain person took care of the money issues, first-generation informants were fairly vague. Often, they would say, "She just likes to manage it.", "It's just the way it is.", or "I don't know." Most of them also said they were satisfied with their way of managing finances. Nevertheless, quite a few second-generation informants mentioned that their parents frequently fought about money, suggesting that the issue of financial control might be more complex than what my informants revealed to me in this study.

Despite the fact that almost half of the wives were the primary financial decision-makers, the idea of women controlling money appeared "unconventional" to many informants, especially the second generation.[112] When they were asked why their wives took charge of finances, first-generation men tended to speak hesitantly and reservedly. [113] Second-generation informants were rather direct, and some showed surprise and puzzlement when their mothers took charge of finances. For instance, a 21-year-old second-generation *benshengren,* Joseph, said,

> I think, In Taiwanese family, the women always seem to be the strength, or a main person in the family structure.... For me, it seems always like, my Taiwanese friends, they're always like, "Who is more powerful? Your mom or your dad?" It's always the mom.... I think in Taiwanese families, it's more like this than everything else. Like, for example, Korean, I think the man is more dominant, but Taiwanese, no, the woman is more dominant, you know, in my little conversations, you know, seems that, even the mother doesn't do the work bringing in the money, she always manages the money, you know, it's kind of [she is the one] who tells everyone what to do.

Katherine, a 30-year-old second-generation *benshengren,* also described an everyday life situation in her family.

> I don't know why [my mother is in charge of finances] (smile). I think it's really funny (smile). Yes, my father is the one who

---

[112] Informants tended to consider men controlling money a "norm." When a wife dominated financial decisions in the family, men and second-generation children tended to show surprise, puzzlement, or embarrassment about such an arrangement.

[113] During interviews, I sensed that male informants tended to consider wives taking charge of finances a case of "losing face," so they felt embarrassed and hesitant to explain further about their family's arrangement.

brings, you know, most of the income home. But he will give the check to my mother, and he gets [an] allowance from my mother, and so.... so, maybe.... just recently when I was home, my father said he needed more money, and then my mother would say, "Well, I just gave you twenty dollars!" And then he had to itemize, where he spent his money. So, he had to go to the gas station and I [the speaker] didn't have any money for lunch, so he gave me some money. So he had to explain, where every dollar goes. So, that's the arrangement.

Both Joseph and Katherine were from middle-class, professional, dual-income *benshengren* families. Although their fathers were the primary breadwinners, their mothers controlled family finances. This pattern was especially common in physicians' families. Even though most physicians' wives did not work, they were the ones who took care of finances. Did Taiwanese immigrant women have a tendency or interest to look after money? Did they control money because it was a "compensation" for their "loss" or "sacrifices" resulting from following their husbands to migrate? Might any cultural reasons be at play in this tendency? [114] Most children of immigrants did not know why their mothers controlled family money, nor did I find evident explanations in my interview data.

As shown in Chapter Six, interracial couples were the most egalitarian in making migration decisions. In the case of finances, however, Taiwanese wives were the primary decision makers, to some extent reflecting their ability to hold sway in decisions that had a potential impact on the security of the family. For instance, Ya-Chi, a 39-year-old professional *waishengren* woman who married a Caucasian, told me,

---

[114] In Chinese culture, paying for friends at a restaurant (sometimes at other places or occasions) is one of the common ways men adopt to show their generosity and "face." Being stingy (*hsiao chi*) is often considered a "violation" of manhood. To reduce the chance that their husbands might spend too much "unnecessarily" (in women's eyes) money in such culture, many wives control family finances in order to ensure the security of the family. Men might be concerned about the security of the family as well, thereby ceding authority to their wives.

Oh, it's me who is in charge of finances, yeah. We didn't
really "discuss" who ought be the one that manages money,
because there's nothing to be discussed about. He doesn't
know how to handle money, so of course it should be me who
takes charge (smile)...... As I know, many Taiwanese wives
who married Caucasians are all like this (smile). First of all,
they [Caucasians] are not good at math (laugh).... Yes, it's all
like this.... I have been managing his money since long time
ago.

To Ya-Chi, her role as financial manager seemed to be "natural"
and "normal," an arrangement that did not need to be discussed or
decided. Although compared to her Caucasian husband, Ya-Chi was
disadvantaged in terms of her race and gender, her power in controlling
family money suggests that she was not a subordinate in the conjugal
dyad. Another middle-class professional *benshengren* woman who
married a Caucasian was in a similar situation. She controlled the
family's money and arranged the couple's social activities, while her
husband cooked and cleaned the house. These two cases contradicted
the stereotypes of the "obedient Asian woman" and "oriental bride,"
suggesting that social class and nation of origin might be two factors
that affect power relations in interracial marriage. While the number of
interracial couples in this study was too small to generalize any
findings, the conjugal relationships of Taiwanese immigrant women
with their Caucasian husbands would be an interesting subject for
further investigation.

In sum, managing family finances among Taiwanese Americans
showed the influences of both power and transnational contexts. While
power balances marked the differences between social classes,
transnational contexts played a role in families of different ethnicities.
While some couples revealed a continuity of Chinese tradition in
arranging family finances, others represented a discontinuity from "the
tradition."

Decisions about Children's Education

As I explained in Chapter Five, Chinese culture places a high value on
seniority, thereby engendering authoritarian parenthood and

hierarchical relations within the family. In addition, Confucian teaching prioritizes education, thereby making children's educational attainment a major concern and responsibility of Taiwanese parents. Fully aware of the importance of education and having grown up in an educationally competitive society, Taiwanese parents tend to emphasize educational achievements above everything else in their practices of parenting. As Chen and her colleagues (2000) point out, according to the findings of their Taiwan survey, children's education is the most important family decision in Taiwanese couples' views (Chen et al. 2000). Moreover, Taiwanese parenting styles, shaped by traditional Chinese culture, also tend to take the form of authoritarianism, thereby putting enormous pressure on the next generation.

This tendency of authoritarian parenthood that emphasizes education appears to be sustained in overseas Taiwanese communities. As Ng (1998: 42) humorously describes, "studying, studying, and studying," are the three "hobbies" Taiwanese immigrant parents typically expect their children to adopt; one of the hopes second-generation children have is that their parents do not "ask where the other point goes when they come home with a 99 course grade on the report card." Undoubtedly, children's education is the primary concern of Taiwanese immigrant parents, a concern that prioritizes academic achievement. Decisions about this matter, as well as who has the power to make decisions, therefore, deliver important messages about parenting styles, power relations between the couple, and the gender division of housework in the family.[115]

To understand Taiwanese immigrants' parenting styles, I used a proportional measurement, analyzing if the husband, the wife, or the couple jointly played the role of primary decision-maker about

---

[115] I do not take decision-making power about children's education as a direct representation of gendered power relations. Based on my observations and interview data, in many families, women were allocated the "power" to govern children's education because it was considered "a women's task" rather than "an important family decision." Such a tendency was particularly evident in lower-class families within which gender relations were patriarchal.

children's education.[116] In the sample, joint decision-making was the major pattern (18 families, about 46%), followed by the mother alone (14 families, about 36%). Only seven husbands (about 18%) played the leading role in this matter (see Table 7-7).

Table 7-7: Decision-makers of Children's Education

	Frequency	Percent
Husband	7	18%
Wife	14	36%
Couple Together	18	46%
Total	39*	100%

* Because three informants were single and another three had no children, only 48 cases are valid in this analysis. Nevertheless, nine of the 48 informants reported that their children made their own decisions about education (see below). Because the focus of analysis is to examine the gendered power structure that shapes decision making, I exclude these nine cases and the total number is therefore 39.

Moreover, among the nine cases in which parents did not intervene in children's education decisions, six were middle-class *benshengren* families, one was middle-class interethnic, one was lower-class interethnic, and one was a lower-class *benshengren* family. Factors attributed to the differences among ethnicity were not evident, but   middle- and lower-class parents did not intervene for different reasons. While middle-class parents intended to show their liberal attitudes, their lower-class counterparts admitted that they lacked the ability (e.g., fluency in English, comprehension of the U.S. educational system, good educational background) to make decisions about their children's education.

---

[116] I asked informants to report who was the primary decision-maker regarding major issues of their children's education, such as to which school should children go; what major should they choose; what courses should they take; what extracurricular activities should they attend; and who in the family was responsible for "supervising" their children's academic progress.

This pattern shows that Taiwanese American couples were fairly egalitarian, as joint decision-making was the primary trend. Nevertheless, the number of mothers (14, about 36%) who were in charge of children's education was double that of fathers (7, about 18%), suggesting authoritarian motherhood prevailed in more than one-third of the informants' families. It would be rash, however, to conclude from this gender difference that women were more powerful than their male counterparts. While playing the role of the decision-maker for the family to some extent indicates a certain degree of power, the context in which it is situated also needs to be examined in order to further understand the meaning and latent implications of such power. For instance, in contrast to other decisions such as finances and immigration, children's education is a matter that is usually regarded as "the mother's job" in the Taiwanese family. When more wives than husbands play the role of decision-makers, it may not indicate women's power but, rather, their powerlessness in negotiating with their husbands to share the responsibility of child-raising. In other words, women's decision-making "power" in children's education in some cases can be a result of a gendered division of household labor.

Moreover, Chinese values and culture may contribute to fathers' high involvement or equal involvement with mothers in decisions about children's education. As a result, joint decision-making as the major pattern may reflect the importance of education in the view of Taiwanese parents (both fathers and mothers) in addition to the gendered power relations of a couple. It also may reflect the high regard for academic achievements that have prevailed in the surrounding culture. As Chen, Yi, and Lu (2000) state, Taiwanese people consider children's education the most important family concern, and joint involvement dominates their decision-making form about this issue.[117] Joint involvement as the major decision-making pattern is even more obvious in this Taiwan study, as two-thirds of the couples are equally involved (ibid.). Situated in a society that is more

---

[117] In this national survey in Taiwan, joint decision was the major tendency, as two-thirds of the couples were equally involved in decisions about children's education. Seventeen percent of the wives played the role of primary decision-makers, and only 10 percent of the husbands were solely responsible in this matter (Chen, Yi, and Lu 2000).

educationally competitive than the U.S., Taiwanese fathers appear to engage in more joint decisions about their children's education than do their counterparts in American society. This tendency suggests that decision making about children's education reflects not only power relations but also cultural values and educational environment. No single factor can be used to conclude the nature of conjugal relations, nor does power exist outside of (social and cultural) contexts.

Class Differences:
Middle-class families showed a very similar pattern to that of the whole sample (see Table 7-8). One half of the couples (18 families, 49%) jointly made decisions concerning their children's education, suggesting their egalitarian character in this arena. About one-third of the wives (13 individuals, about 35%) made these decisions alone, and 16 percent of husbands were decision makers. In contrast, both wives in the lower-class families played the role of primary decision-maker (see Table 7-8). Comparing these two social classes, more lower-class women than their middle-class counterparts were in charge of children's education decisions. Again, this finding may not suggest the power of lower-class women. Rather, as mentioned above, the responsibility for childcare is conventionally assumed to be a woman's. Thus, issues related to children, including their education, tend to be perceived as a mother's "natural duty."

Table 7-8: Social Class and Decision-makers of Children's Education

	Lower Class	Middle Class
Husband	0 (0%)	6 (16%)
Wife	2 (100%)	13 (35%)
Couple Together	0 (0%)	18 (49%)
Total (39)	2 (100%)	37 (100%)

Moreover, unlike their middle-class counterparts, most of whom were educated in the U.S., lower-class parents lacked adequate education and language skills to provide their children with substantial help in guiding their education. Such a situation, what Portes and Rumbaut call "generational dissonance" (Portes and Rumbaut 1996: 241), may result in lower-class parents' little involvement in their children's education. Lower-class fathers in particular, who were disadvantaged in the U.S. labor market and powerless in society, may opt for traditional values in the family, an arena where they were allowed to exert power. In other words, rather than showing their incompetence, they may cede decision-making power about children's education to their wives in order to "save face," thereby ensuring their presumed power and image of dominance in the family. Put another way, making decisions about children's education does not necessarily imply holding a powerful position in the family. It might simply reflect the traditional gender division of labor in which women are primarily responsible for taking care of matters associated with children, or a father's "strategy" to sustain his position of power in the family.

The importance of situating decision-making power in context can be illustrated by comparing decision-making styles on different issues among lower-class families. As discussed in Chapter Six and earlier in this chapter, lower-class husbands had absolute power in making both immigration and financial decisions. Yet, the situation was totally reversed when it came to children's education issues; the power of decision making shifted to the wives. In explaining such a power shift, I argue that we must situate the matter of children's education within the context of the gender division of labor in the family. As noted above, domestic labor in lower-class families was completely relegated to wives. It is therefore possible that a husband's low involvement in children's education represents a patriarchal arrangement, rather than an example of authoritarian motherhood. In other words, we need to take into consideration how men and women divide housework at home and the ideology that underpins their arrangement, in order to re-examine the power structures reflected in the decision-making styles of children's education. For instance, if the wives of lower class were "assigned" to the child-related arena, then the authoritarian motherhood shown in this matter could be a false representation. In addition, the issue of men's "face," inherited from Chinese culture, may lead to their transfer of decision-making power to their wives in order to conceal their incompetence and powerlessness in the host society. In other words, when taking social and cultural contexts into account, the patriarchal power structure of lower-class families may not actually be shaken, but once again confirmed.

It has been widely documented that, despite the fact that lower-class Asian immigrant women's economic contributions to the family are equal to and sometime are greater than their husbands, they tend to maintain patriarchal traditions at home because the traditional family system provides them with male economic protection, and important sources of support and authority (as mothers) over the younger generation (Donnelly 1994; Glenn 1983; Kibria 1990, 1993; Loo and Ong 1982; Morokvasic 1984). In other words, by accepting the traditional male-dominant system, lower-class immigrant women are able to preserve a strong and intact family that serves as an important source of support to sustain them in the work world (Morokvasic 1984). I believe this is also true in the case of lower-class Taiwanese immigrants. In particular, the traditional ideologies of gender roles in Chinese culture legitimate the "norm" of the patriarchal system of the family, thereby leaving unequal gender relations unchallenged.[118]

Ethnic Differences:
A comparison of decision making by family ethnicity showed that most *benshengren* and *waishengren* couples tended to jointly make the decision about their children's education (52% and 66%, respectively), suggesting their egalitarian characteristic and high regard for education. This tendency was consistent with those in the whole sample and middle-class families. The two interracial families in this study were childless, so they could not provide a comparison with other families. Among interethnic families, wives constituted the majority (5 out of 8 families) of decision-makers. Two of the eight husbands played the leading role in this matter, while only one couple jointly made the decision (see Table 7-9).

---

[118] In this study, two lower-class families encountered financial difficulties at times, and both wives' parents provided substantial financial aid to the couples. Despite their economic contributions, these two wives accepted their subordinate status in the family and regarded their husbands as the heads of household.

Table 7-9: Ethnicity and Decision-makers of Children's Education

	Benshengren	Waishengren	Interethnic
Husband	4 (16%)	1 (17%)	2 (25%)
Wife	8 (32%)	1 (17%)	5 (63%)
Couple	13 (52%)	4 (66%)	1 (12%)
Total (39*)	25 (100%)	6 (100%)	8 (100%)

* For the purpose of examining the gendered power structure among couples, this table excludes cases in which children made their own decisions.

Only in interethnic families did the wife play the role of primary decision-maker about children's education (5 out of 8 couples). This finding was consistent with that of Chen, Yi, and Lu's Taiwan study (2000). Among the five interethnic couples within which the wives were the primary decision-makers, three of the husbands were *waishengren* and the other two were *benshengren*. The influence of having a *waishengren* or *benshengren* husband on the form of decision making, therefore, was not evident.

Patri-Egalitarian Orientation in the Taiwanese American Family

Decision making can be a mechanism of control and, as such, reflects power relations within a family (Allen at el. 2001; Bloom, Wypij, and Gupta 2001; Van Willigen and Drentea 2001). Similarly, how a couple divides domestic labor can reflect power (im)balances in role-negotiation (Emerson 1962; Kamo 1988; Stafford, Backman, and Dibona 1977). In previous chapters and here, I have analyzed these two forms of power. Here I synthesize these analyses to provide an overview of the gendered power structure in Taiwanese American families.

Figure 7-1 summarizes the findings of this study concerning how Taiwanese American couples made major family decisions and managed domestic labor. In sum, husbands were more powerful than their wives in the decision to migrate (see Chapter Six) and making financial decisions. Joint involvement was the primary form decisions took about children's education. Most wives were in charge of housework but, as demonstrated above, this tendency suggests a patriarchal arrangement because women are traditionally "assigned" this task.

I use the term, patri-egalitarian orientation, to describe the overall gendered power structure in Taiwanese American families. As shown in Figure 7-1, gender relations between Taiwanese Americans couples in the entire sample were either male-dominated (immigration, finances, and domestic labor) or egalitarian (decisions about children's education). Moreover, joint involvement was the secondary form decision-making took in immigration and domestic labor, and quite a number of wives controlled finances and decisions about children. These findings suggest that the power structure within Taiwanese American families was both patriarchal and egalitarian. Regardless of this general tendency, families in varied social locations showed differences in power relations (see Figure 7-1).

Figure 7-1: Gendered Power Structure in Taiwanese American Families

Issues	International Migration	Family Finances	Children's Education	Division of Housework
Entire Sample	1. Husband *2. Joint	1. Husband 2. Wife	1. Joint 2. Wife	1. Wife 2. Shared
Class				
Middle	1. Husband 2. Joint	1. Wife 2. Husband	1. Joint 2. Wife	Shared
Lower	Husband	Husband	Wife	Wife
Ethnicity				
Benshengren	Husband	1.Husband 2.Wife	1. Joint 2. Wife	1. Shared 2. Wife
Waishengren	Husband	1. Husband 2. Joint	Joint	1. Shared 2. Wife
Interethnic	Husband	Wife	Wife	Wife
Interracial	Joint	Wife	N/A	Shared

* A secondary pattern is listed when the percentage of the form is larger than or equal to one-third of the sum.

Power relations in marriage do not emerge in a contextual vacuum. While structural positions (e.g., gender, class, race, and ethnicity) affect how men and women negotiate power in the family, cultural values about gender roles and parenthood also exert pressures on men's and women's social practices. As Strober and Chan (1998) argue, egalitarian ideology in the greater society is an important factor that affects the extent to which men participate in domestic labor. Its influence transcends that of educational level (Strober and Chan 1998). More specifically, the life world of immigrants crosses two countries. Cultural systems in both the sending and receiving societies affect a couple's power relations in different aspects of family practices. In other words, patriarchy in Taiwan and egalitarianism in the U.S. both exert influences on Taiwanese immigrants, but the impacts of transnationalism vary in different families, differ in the case of different issues, and change by context.

For instance, as I have demonstrated earlier in this chapter, the relations of Taiwanese immigrant couples were more patriarchal in the presence of a husband's mother, but more egalitarian in the older woman's absence; interracial couples were the most egalitarian because, within them, Taiwanese wives did not have to conform to the gender roles prescribed by Chinese culture; lower-class families were the most patriarchal because husbands opted for traditional values in the family, where they could exert power, thereby compensating for their disadvantage in the greater society; and Taiwanese parents' joint involvement in children's education was sustained both in Taiwan and the U.S., suggesting their constant concern about and continued emphasis on educational achievement. Transnational context, therefore, shapes power relations in the Taiwanese American family, and spousal relations are a product of transnationalism as well as power.

DYNAMICS OF FAMILY LIFE AND MENTAL HEALTH

As noted above, in general, Taiwanese American couples' gender relations were patri-egalitarian, although variations existed among sub-groups. This characteristic affected how men and women experienced their family lives and distress. Below I first examine how informants' psychological well-being was impacted by the gendered power structure analyzed above, i.e., the division of domestic labor and decision-making power. Next, I explore other aspects of distress that were associated with the dynamics of family life and familial relations other than spousal (such as in-law and generational relationships). In both sections I examine if and how informants' social locations affected their distress experiences, how power and transnationalism intersected in shaping these experiences, and how individual agencies were asserted in reacting to distress.

Spousal Relations and Distress

The unequal division of domestic labor and the practice of authoritarian motherhood in the education of children were two factors that caused tension in the informants' spousal relations, thereby engendering distress. Below I describe the dynamic contexts of these two issues.

"He would never help" – Overwhelming Double-shifts of Married Women

The negative effects of housework on women's psychological well-being have been widely documented (see Glass and Fujimoto 1994; Golding 1990; Lennon and Rosenfield 1992; Kandel, Davies, and Raveis 1985; Ross, Mirowski, and Huber 1983). Similarly, the overload of housework remained a common complaint among married women, especially those of the lower class. For example, Yi-Hua and her husband both worked in a carry-out Chinese food store.[119] At the store, they both cooked, cleaned, and did dishes. But after work, her husband never "helped" with housework. Despite the fact that what this couple did at work was similar to the content of their domestic labor, the husband maintained the role of patriarch and "the face of a man" at home. When Yi-Hua complained about this to me, she said,

> After coming home, he just sits there and does nothing. Even when I ask for help, he would not even bother to move a little bit. I'm so tired…. We both do a lot at the store and both are tired every day. But after coming home, it's always me who has to do the housework. He would never help. I'm so exhausted….

Hsiao-Fen, a 56-year-old lower-class working mother in a *benshengren* family, also complained that her husband went out to play sports every night, so she had to stay home, taking care of housework and their children. She complained that she sacrificed a lot for her family, that she had never gone to a movie, nor had she ever spent a day doing things just for herself. During our interview, Hsiao-Fen repeatedly expressed regrets that all the beautiful dreams she had when young seemed so far away. In spite of such deep regrets, she believed that subordinating her well-being to the family's was her destiny and responsibility as a married woman. She told me over and over that "Once a woman gets married, all she can think of is her family, not herself." This worldview again illustrates Taiwanese American

---

[119] This was a lower-class interethnic couple. The husband was a *waishengren*, and the wife was a *benshengren*.

women's fatalism as shown in their immigration motives (see Chapter Six). Once married, women tend to accept the cultural ideology of Chinese tradition. They frequently have to compromise their own wellbeing in the interest of family stability and continuity.

The above cases echo what I discussed earlier about the gender division of domestic labor in lower-class families. Because of their powerlessness and disadvantage in society, lower-class men tended to opt for traditional values in the family within which they were able to maintain a dominant status. By so doing they were able to save face, thereby epitomizing masculinity as normatively defined in Chinese culture. Without their husbands' "help," however, lower-class women endured an overwhelming double-shift that engendered both physical and psychological hardship. Regardless of this hardship, they tended to sustain the traditional mode of family and accepted their subordinate status within it in exchange for economic protection, social support, and mothering authority. Their adoption of Chinese views of appropriate womanhood not only supported the norm of patriarchy, but also shaped the way they exerted agency in reacting to distress resulting from their subordination in the family. Despite complaining about the heavy burden of domestic labor, lower-class women did not or failed to "make a patriarchal bargain," using Kandiyoti's (1988) term, of their workload with their husbands.[120] Rather, they tended to accept their "fate" and tolerate the hardship and distress, thereby exhibiting an acquiescent form of agency.

Many middle-class professional women also faced the distress of overwhelming double-shifts, but they usually had more capital and resources than their lower-class counterparts; they thus were able to negotiate more "help" from their husbands or they hired housekeepers to relieve their workload around the house.[121] Wan-Jen, a manager in a real estate company, was a busy working mother who was also very active in the Taiwanese community.[122] Her husband was very

[120] Despite the fact that none successfully negotiated with their husbands to assume their fair share, these women's complaints, in front of their husbands or not, can be seen as a discursive form of agency.

[121] As I analyzed in the previous section, domestic labor in middle-class families was relatively equally divided by couples.

[122] Wan-Jen was *waishengren*, and her husband was *benshengren*.

supportive and encouraged her participation in social activities. She thus spent a considerable amount of time after work in organizational activities. Nevertheless, she still had to do all the housework because, according to Wan-Jen, her husband "would never help, even it was him who encouraged me to participate in those activities." She complained that her husband's support always stopped at "the verbal level," and that he never took "real action," such as sharing housework. This story represents the patri-egalitarian characteristic of Taiwanese American families. Although the husband showed an egalitarian attitude by not drawing on patriarchal norms of womanhood to constrain his wife's activities outside the home, he did not share the housework to actually practice egalitarianism. This gap between culture and conduct consequently entrapped his wife in a difficult situation as she tried to manage her everyday life. Unable to negotiate with her husband and feeling overwhelmed by the multiple burdens of work, family, and community activities, Wan-Jen hired housekeepers to clean the house and do the yard work. Nevertheless, other women who could not afford housekeepers burned the proverbial candle at both ends, and their mental health was more seriously impaired than that of their wealthier counterparts.

Apparently, the overload of domestic work was a common source of distress among women across social class and ethnicity. While lower-class wives accepted their subordination, their middle-class counterparts were able to demand more "help" from their husbands or to "contract out" their housework by hiring housekeepers. In contrast to the acquiescence of the former, middle-class women were active and strategic in exerting their agencies when distressed by the burden of domestic labor. Their social location and the relative privilege it accorded them allowed them to negotiate a more favorable outcome. Differences among women of various ethnic groups, in contrast, were not evident.

"Can they [the children] take a day off, please?" – Husbands' Feeling of Powerlessness

Many male informants who had school-age children reported that they frequently argued with their wives about their children's education. In most of these cases, the wives were predominantly in charge of supervising children's education, including schoolwork, math exercises, Chinese writing, and instrument practice. These mothers were very rigid about the setting of their children's daily schedules, making sure that their schedules and rules were followed. Yet, in reality, not every child could or was willing to do as much work on a daily basis as her or his mother demanded. Frequently, they were tired after playing sports, or just felt lazy and wanted to skip a piano practice or the like. Because their mothers were too strict, making it impossible to negotiate with them, they usually turned to their fathers for help. Out of sympathy, these fathers would try, although most of them failed, to persuade their wives that "It should be fine for the kids to take a day off." Chun-Hung, a father of two in a middle-class *benshengren* family, talked about this problem, as the following excerpt from our interview shows.

> *CH:* We have different views on teaching kids. I'm more open, but my wife is more strict. Both of our kids have been learning violin since they were five. As you know, it requires a lot of practice to play the violin well. I can't do that [watching them practice everyday], so my wife has to keep an eye on them. She is very rigid, and asks them to practice every day. But I'm more concerned about their schoolwork. I think they should do their homework first, then other stuff if they have time and energy. But my wife always insists that they should practice the violin first, then do other things.
> *GU:* How do you handle it when you have such different views?
> *CH:* I'll have to listen to her, most of the times…. (smile). It's ok. Of course, we fight about it, because sometimes, my son feels that his mother is too strict. She always asks him to do this and that, and then he would feel overwhelmed and have some emotional reaction. Then, we would have some arguments or fights about such things in our family….I don't know, I think I have a very different view from my wife's over this issue [how to educate children].

Another father, Kuo-Hua, in a middle-class interethnic family (his wife was a *benshengren*), expressed similar frustration and powerlessness when negotiating with his wife about their children's education. Although Kuo-Hua disagreed with his wife's way of training the children, there seemed little he could do to change the situation. As he said,

> *KH:* We [my wife and I] are very different. She is much more pushy than me. She demands a lot of our daughter, and wants her to become a doctor. I'm more easy-going, because I know children don't like to be pushed too much. You cannot teach your children in the Taiwanese way [i.e., demand academic achievement].
> *GU:* Do you and your wife fight about this?
> *KH:* Oh, of course, but.... this world is ruled by power. I'm the one who's powerless at home, so I have to listen to her (smile).

Like Kuo-Hua, most husbands who have disagreements with their wives about their children's education did not aggressively pursue change. Instead, they tended to accept their wives' "power" and "authority." During our interviews, they talked about how "powerful" their wives were at home, so that they could do nothing but be obedient and silent. Some husbands admitted that since their wives were the ones who actually spent time with children, they should have absolute power in deciding what was good for the children. For example, Da-Lin was a 42-year-old *waishengren* manager who migrated to the U.S. in 1982. He did not like his wife's way of training their children, which he considered "too Chinese." Learning at work the disadvantages of holding Chinese worldviews, Da-Lin realized the importance of American values for successful adaptation into mainstream U.S. society and culture. Therefore, he always wanted his children to develop American attributes. As he said,

> I don't like [the] Chinese way of education. I hope my kids will have more leadership, but leadership is learned from everyday life, so you need to constantly give them some guidance in daily life. Like myself, I think I have some inherent [Chinese] characteristics, because I was educated in a Chinese way. I don't want my kids to be that Chinese, but my

wife doesn't care about this at all. I'm worried. But, she is the
one who is with our kids everyday, so she can do her own way.
I don't think I should intervene.

Although worrying that his wife's teaching of Chinese values
would lead to his children's disadvantage in American society, Da-Lin
did not intervene. Even sometimes, when his mother (who lived with
them) complained about the way his wife taught his children, Da-Lin
would advise his mother to keep quiet and let his wife make decisions
for their children. He believed that his wife (*benshengren*), who had
studied and worked in the U.S., was "relatively more American" than
his mother, who had lived in Taiwan for more than sixty years. Unable
to spend time with children because of his busy work life, Da-Lin
completely entrusted his children's education to his wife.

Despite the fact that they sometimes disagreed with how their
wives educated children, first-generation men tended to remain silent.
In other words, they exhibited an acquiescent form of agency given
their powerlessness to prevail in this situation. Their silence and feeling
of powerless to some extent reflected their tendency to perceive
educating children as "a woman's job." It was also possible that after
weighing the negative outcome of the tension between them and their
wives against the costs of acquiescence, they decided to comply with
their wives in the face of the wrath their resistance might invoke. As
this tendency among men existed across ethnicity and social class, most
Taiwanese immigrant women therefore maintained their authoritarian
style of mothering in the family.[123] As I showed earlier in this chapter,
however, joint involvement was the major pattern of Taiwanese
American couples' decision making about their children's education,

---

[123] A second-generation woman, Andrea, talked about her mother's extreme
authority and rigidity in terms of her education. Before college, Andrea was
always asked to study and was not allowed to go out. Whenever she rebelled in
reaction to this demand, her mother would physically abuse her, which became
a psychological trauma in Andrea's life. Quite a few other second-generation
informants also complained about their mothers' strictness, but they did not
report subsequent distress as did Andrea.

followed by mothers as decision-makers. Men's feeling of "powerlessness" (especially middle-class men) in arguments with their wives, therefore, suggests that the informants' joint involvement may not actually reflect egalitarianism in practice. While inheriting Chinese values of education, (middle-class) men's participation in decisions about their children's education may be limited to their concerns rather than substantial supervision. Such a gap between men's practice and ideology also existed in their small share of domestic labor they assumed, as I have pointed out earlier in this chapter.

In the same way, women's practice of authoritarian motherhood in teaching children may not completely refer to their powerful status in the family; rather, they might simply consider child-raising (including education) a primary responsibility of womanhood as demanded by traditional Confucian teaching. The cultural norms immigrants carry from their sending society, therefore, to some extent shape their perceptions and social practices. Immigrants' transnational background needs to be taken into account when interpreting their behavior and experience of distress.

Other Familial Relations and Distress

In addition to tension over domestic labor and children's education, conflicts between parents (mostly mothers) and children as well as tensions resulting from in-law relationships were two major sources of distress in Taiwanese American families. Family conflicts have been identified by many sociologists (Portes and Rumbaut 2001; Rumbaut 1996; Wolf 1997) as a major factor that impairs the mental health of both generations, but *why* and *how* these conflicts engender distress remain under-explored. Here I present my interview data to contexualize Taiwanese Americans' family conflicts and dynamics -- between two generations and among in-laws -- that are associated with psychological well-being.

Parent-Child Conflict

"They are too Americanized!": Mothers' Disappointment
In some families, parents' "Taiwaneseness"/"Chineseness" and children's "Americaness" frequently resulted in a clash of values that

caused ruptures in relations between the two generations. [124] For example, growing up in the U.S., second-generation children valued their privacy and hoped their parents would respect it, an idea that is emphasized in "the American" value system. Yet, the authoritarian style of Taiwanese parenthood considered intruding into children's privacy (e.g., opening their letters, searching their rooms) as an expression of protection and concern. In the view of children, then, parents were supposed to learn to adjust their behavior in order to meet their children's need and request for privacy. Yet, some parents (mostly mothers) struggled with the necessity to make such an adjustment, complaining that their children were too Americanized. [125] Accordingly, they reported distress, as the following excerpt from my interview with a mother (middle-class *benshengren*) shows.

> It's very difficult to educate the children who grow up in America. What they learn in school is that parents should respect their privacy. For example, you cannot enter their rooms without knocking. We don't have such a thing in Taiwan, right? And, you cannot open their letters. So, you'd

---

[124] Although second-generation informants reported generational conflicts between them and both of their parents, most referred to the conflict between them and their mothers. Because mothers were the ones who actually "supervised" children, they were more likely than their husbands to be considered by children "the opponents" or "source of distress." In addition, among first-generation informants, although both fathers and mothers complained that their children were too Americanized, only mothers expressed their disappointment about children's Americaness. Fathers tended to adopt a rather acquiescent attitude, saying, "What can I do with it?"

[125] From my observations and interviews, many Taiwanese immigrant fathers also disliked some "Americanized behaviors" of their children. Despite the fact that a few fathers at times had serious arguments with their children because of their contradictory values (e.g., the importance of academic achievements, what major to choose, etc.), they tended to entrust to their wives the responsibility of educating children and did not necessarily confront their children in person. As a result, most generational conflicts were those between mothers and children (both boys and girls), although fathers might hold the same values or take the same stances as mothers in demanding obedience from the next generation.

think, what's up? I am your mother! Why can't I read your letters? I just want to know what kind of friends you make. I am concerned about you. But what they learn in school is different. Their teachers told them that they should have their own autonomy, and they should make their own decisions. So, we can't really change their perceptions. Whenever we try to persuade them with a different perspective, they feel resentful, and say we don't respect them.

Attempts to protect their privacy of not only teenaged but also adult children, sometimes led to considerable tension between the two generations. Tom, a 21-year-old second-generation Taiwanese American, told me that, whenever his parents wanted to visit his elder brother who lived alone in downtown Chicago, they had to make an appointment about two weeks before their expected visit. This "business-like" and "American-like" behavior made his parents very unhappy, and they could not understand at all why parents had to make an appointment to see their son. Consequently, the parents and son had been estranged for years, and the parents constantly complained that their elder son had "become American."

In spite of the disappointment their westernized children engendered, Taiwanese parents tended to accept the fact that, ultimately, "their children are American," so there is actually little they can do to "Taiwanize" the next generation. As Wen-Ting, a lower-class *benshengren* mother of three said,

At first, we fought a lot, because I couldn't stand their [my children's] behavior and attitudes [too Americanized]. For example, the way they spend money, the kind of friends they make, and the way they speak to us [lack of respect to parents] are all not what I expected. But later, I realized that it's impossible to make them like us [Taiwanese], so I told myself, maybe I should just accept it. There's really nothing I can do....

Confronting cultural differences is emblematic of a transnational context, two generations of Taiwanese Americans engaged in an endless process of negotiation in which norms, boundaries, and meanings were created, recreated, defined, and redefined in the family. Similar to the Filipino youth in Wolf's study (1997), second-generation Taiwanese often struggled to free themselves from Chinese cultural norms that they considered synonymous with their parents' control. Their parents, in contrast, suffered mental distress because they were educated in the "Taiwanese way" but confronted challenges and transformations in the way they educated the next generation. In particular, mothers tended to consider children their prime responsibility and thus were more prone to suffer than were fathers.

Among the informants who reported parent-child conflicts, no particular differences were found among those in different social locations, suggesting that common cultural conflicts between generations occur across class and ethnicity. In reacting to the distress engendered by generational conflicts, however, first-generation men and women showed distinct attitudes. Two extreme reactions occurred among men: while a few fought (verbally) with children frequently, most remained silent and entrusted this problem to their wives. In contrast, women attempted to communicate more with children, exchange strategies with other parents (mostly other mothers), and learn from books and professionals.[126] While fathers usually took a stance that was either confrontational or avoiding, mothers were rather active, engaging, and strategic. Moreover, second-generation children (both boys and girls) tended to seek comfort from other children who had similar experiences and shared understandings.[127]

"Am I not American enough?": Mothers' Anxiety
While Taiwanese immigrants complained that their children were too Americanized, second-generation children also criticized their parents, especially their mothers, for "not being American enough." Five mothers, all middle-class (both *benshengren* and *waishengren*), expressed anxiety because their children accused them of not

---

[126] A few middle-class mothers consulted with counselors in their companies (part of the benefits of their jobs) about how to deal with generational conflicts.
[127] Not only other Taiwanese American children but also other second-generation Asians, mostly Koreans, who had similar immigration background became an important source of comfort for second-generation children to talk about their confrontations with parents.

understanding American culture. All of these mothers had been working in Anglo-owned private companies for a decade or two, and were confident that they had acculturated into and adapted to American society. Yet, their children's charge of "under-Americanization" shook these mothers' self-assurance and engendered their mental distress. As Wen-Ting, a professional working mother in a *benshengren* family, told me,

> Of course, overall, we [first-generation immigrants] cannot speak English as well as Americans, nor can we compete with the next generation. So, I've seen a lot of children look down on their mothers who do not work and cannot speak fluent English. I've been working in an American company for more than ten years, and am quite content with my social skills with Americans. Yet, my daughter often criticizes that I don't understand American culture. So, I can imagine that those stay-home moms would face a more difficult and embarrassing situation when their children feel ashamed of them. I really sympathize with these homemakers.

Immigrant families that reflect dissonant acculturation have been found to show high levels of depressive symptoms (Portes and Rumbaut 2001: 192-232). In this study, despite the fact that middle-class parents were highly acculturated white-collar professionals (e.g., U.S. trained, fluent in English, and assimilated to the middle-upper class of American society), quarrels over the degree of their acculturation (e.g, being American enough or not) and consequent distress occurred more often than they did in lower-class families. I believe that in addition to degree of acculturation and contradictories of two cultural systems, the power relations between two generations played an important role in producing parent-child conflict and distress. The authoritative style of parenting in Chinese culture demands children's obedience. Surrounded by American society within which individualism and independence were highly valued, such a (Chinese) power relation engendered children's distress, provoked them to confront and challenge their (Chinese and powerful) parents, and therefore caused their parents distress.

As stated earlier, the immigrant family is a place where a dynamic interplay of structure, culture, and agency take place. It is also a location where behavioral norms, boundaries, meanings are continuously produced, reproduced, defined, and redefined within a transnational context. Taiwanese American parents and children, while representing two opposite poles of cultures, engage in an endless process of negotiating a midpoint where they can bridge the gaps that divides them.

"My parents love uncle Chen's son more!": Confusing Messages of Love and Expectation

In contrast to the abundant vocabularies and body language about emotion in western culture, the expression of love in Asian societies, including Taiwan, is rather reserved and indirect. Moreover, Taiwanese people's high regard of education places the task of imbuing this value on parents who undertake it by focusing on their children's achievement. The major way Taiwanese parents express their love to children, therefore, is to provide the best education and material life they can, and they consider children's accomplishments to be the reward of parenthood. Many parents, especially those who are lower class, are willing to sacrifice themselves by doing intensive labor and minimizing their own luxury in order to give their children the best of everything. These socio-cultural characteristics also are maintained in the Taiwanese immigrant community.

Growing up in America and acculturated by western culture, however, second-generation youth did not necessarily appreciate their parents' way of expressing love. Some even considered their mothers' intense demands for educational achievement, and their lack of verbal encouragement and recognition, as a sign of indifference and distance. Joseph, a 21-year-old second-generation *benshengren*, put it the following way during our interview.

GU: How important is family to you?
JO: Hmm…I think family is important, but I don't think, I'm relying on family, you know. I would sacrifice for the family, but I don't think I'm very, as close as could be to a family as other people are, you know, so, it's really difficult.
GU: Why?

JO: I think that's how they weren't very loving to me, you know. They didn't show very...loving support. They didn't show loving support at all. Like, everything I did was either not good enough, or so what.... I've never felt that, they were happy with my accomplishments. It's only recently that my father explained that, that was their way of, kind of, motivating me to do better, because you'd never be satisfied with your accomplishments. You'd always be great, we always want the best in you, drive me to do better. But then, they kind of realized that you know, maybe... as a kid, I was very angry. Everything I did wasn't good enough, and you know, I studied so hard, and still they think it's not good enough.

A mother of three (lower-class *benshengren*) also told me how she came to realize her children did not understand the way Taiwanese express love. She said,

They [my children] felt that, their parents always said love them, but they just couldn't feel it. They told me, "You [the speaker] always said that you love us, so you buy me the best material goods, send us to the best school, and give us all the best. But so what? My [American] friends' parents always hug and kiss them, but you've never done that. How can you say you love us?" I suddenly realized that my children wanted something on the outside, like Americans. But, we don't really know how to do that. We are so sincere... we parents just work very hard, and try to save as much money as we can in order to give them the best education. Yet, they don't seem to appreciate what we have done for them. Just because we don't hug and kiss them, they'd think we don't love them. (Sigh).... So, we had to tell them that, we come from a different culture. In Taiwan, our parents are very authoritarian and distant. We have to obey everything they say, and cannot act like their friends like American kids do to their parents. We tried to let them understand that our cultural backgrounds are different.

Cultural differences of expressing love and expectations made the feeling of closeness difficult in some families. These differences also, sometimes, became the major obstacle to mutual understanding between two generations. Tom, a 21-year-old second-generation *benshengren*, cleverly pointed out the key cause of such a communication problem in Taiwanese American families.

We Taiwanese Americans are different [from Caucasians who are very direct in communication]. If I say to my parents, "I want to study music," that's what I say. But what my parents hear is, "I want to be a poor man." Ok. See, what I say and what they hear are two totally different things. When they tell me, "You see, Uncle Chen's son won so many competitions. He is smart. You should learn from him," what I hear is, "I don't love you. I love Uncle Chen's son more. I hope to exchange you with Uncle Chen's son. You are useless." That's what I hear.

These differences of expressing affection, as noted above, caused distress to both generations. Middle-class *benshengren* (both first and second generation), in particular, reported such distress more frequently than their lower-class and *waishengren* counterparts.[128] While children did not feel loved, parents did not feel appreciated. Many informants trod a long path to finally understand such cultural differences between generations. Some tried to accept this fact and adjusted their attitudes and expectations accordingly, yet others remained distant and unconcerned.[129]Familial relationships continued to be a tough road to home and a major source of distress for both generations.

---

[128] This difference, however, may be produced by the population characteristics of the sample because all second-generation informants were middle-class *benshengren*.

[129] Informants who reported such distress adopted a wide range of strategies in reaction. No significant differences in their ways of exerting agencies were found among social classes and ethnic groups

"It took six years for them to acknowledge his existence!": Battles over Interracial/ethnic Marriage and Courtship

A common and serious battle between Taiwanese immigrants and their children arose from their different values concerning interracial and interethnic marriage. Such a battle began as early as the teenage years when young people started dating, and could last as long as years after children married. Since Taiwanese Americans were a small population compared with other Asian sub-groups in Chicago, it was relatively difficult to maintain endogamous marriage, especially for the second generation. Moreover, Taiwanese Americans in Chicago tended to reside in suburban areas that were mostly White communities, thereby reducing the opportunities to know other ethnic Chinese. Because Taiwanese American children did not face language barriers as did their parents, they also were able to expand their social circles to include member of other racial and ethnic groups. Courting someone who was not ethnic Chinese often gave rise to serious tension between the two generations in Taiwanese American families.

Judy, a 33-year-old second-generation Taiwanese from a middle-class *benshengren* family, was going to marry a Caucasian, Matt, at the time of our interview. With a "Can-you-believe-it?" tone, Judy told me the extremely long and difficult battle she had with her parents over her relationship. According to Judy, her dating a Caucasian was unpleasant for her parents from the beginning, and living with her boyfriend without her parents' consent made it more unacceptable. For six years, her parents were in denial of Matt's existence. Matt was a total stranger in the eyes of Judy's parents, even when standing in front of them. As a result, Judy was constantly fighting with her parents and avoided going home. She told me, "For many years, I was very hurt, and I was always fighting to get them to acknowledge him."

This battle and the hurt engendered by the tension between two generations continued for six years. Then finally, Judy's parents began to invite Matt over for dinner and to get to know him. They thought, a relationship of six years probably was indicative of a strong commitment on the part of Judy and Matt, and Matt might not be just a "play boy." Yet, they continued to harbor reservations about Matt, because he did not yet have a stable job; they doubted whether he would have a bright career and be able to support Judy financially. After six years together, Matt got a decent job, and Judy's parents also knew him better and finally recognized him. When Judy described the moment her parents accepted her relationship with Matt, her voice sounded so emotional that it seemed she could not believe this day had finally come. As she said,

> You know, this is nine years now. We've been together nine years. My father FINALLY said, "You know, he is a good guy." (laugh) And then, I got their approval. And he finally... a few weeks later, my mom and I were talking, [she said] "If you are ready to get married, we'd approve." So, nine years, NINE YEARS (laugh) of the approval process. It was very difficult. It's like, insane! Yeah, nine years, for them to actually have a conversation with him. Like, after the interrogation, you know, six years of interrogation, and then, you know, after that, they could at least said, "Oh, Matt, how are you?" on the phone, you know.

Although she fought for nine years to maintain her relationship with Matt and eventually received approval to marry him, Judy did not plan to get married. Her parents, however, considered cohabitation a shame and pressured her to get married. Judy admitted that she was getting married for her parents' sake because she was tired of fighting any longer. Yet, she had been arguing with her mother about what dress she should wear on the big day and other wedding details. The inter-generational battle never ended in her family.

Similar conflicts also occurred in other families within which a daughter dated or married a Caucasian, although the scale of the battle was not as great as in the case of Judy. Most parents did not really oppose interracial marriage (although they were not happy about it either), but they needed some time and adjustment to accept the reality. Yet, this problem seemed to occur only when Taiwanese daughters dated Caucasian men. As several male second-generation informants told me, when they were dating Caucasian girls, their parents seemed quite happy about it. Historically, Asian American men have been excluded from the White-based American notion of masculinity. They are depicted not only as asexual but also as threats to white women (Espiritu 1997: 90-93). Taiwanese men dating Caucasian women to a certain extent reversed such a power hierarchy of gender and race, and thus the relationship was regarded as a "symbolic triumph."

When asked about their perception of children's interracial or interethnic marriage, most first-generation respondents reacted in a cautious and indirect way. They usually said, it was not that they were "against" it but that they had some "ranks of preferences" concerning whom their children married. Acknowledging the fact that it was not easy for their children to marry Taiwanese Americans, these parents set up a schema of preference that was based on both race and ethnicity. On this hierarchy, of course, Taiwanese Americans were the number one choice. If children could not find suitable Taiwanese American partners, then Chinese Americans would be fine. But, if they could not find either Taiwanese or Chinese, Japanese Americans would become the next choice, then Korean Americans, and then Caucasians. Blacks ranked the lowest in this preference hierarchy, and none of the respondents ever mentioned Southeast Asians or Hispanics as possible mates for their children.

Among the informants, Caucasian, Taiwanese Americans, and Korean Americans most commonly were the ethnic and racial groups from which children of Taiwanese immigrants chose individuals to date or marry.[130] The gender ratio of Taiwanese American children who married Taiwanese was quite equal, but it was not the case for cross-ethnic marriages. Female second-generation Taiwanese Americans tended to marry Caucasians whereas their male counterparts were inclined to marry Korean Americans. This phenomenon apparently reflected the differential positions of Taiwanese American men and women in the marriage market based on the intersection of gender and race/ethnicity.[131] Taiwanese American men tended to "marry down,"

---

[130] Although Japanese Americans were more favorable than Korean, the number of second-generation Taiwanese Americans who were married to Korean Americans was larger than that who were married to Japanese Americans. I believe that it is caused by the fact that many more Korean than Japanese Americans are in the U.S. (see Chapter Five), making their higher "availability" than the latter in the marriage market.

[131] I acknowledge the importance of class, along with gender and ethnicity/race, in constructing what Collins (1990) calls, the "matrix of domination." I did not emphasize class in the discussion of interracial/ethnic marriage because the informants did not list it as one of their concerns, nor did respondents of various class backgrounds have different reactions regarding this issue.

whereas their female counterparts "married up" the racial or ethnic hierarchy. This tendency of *"men dang hu duei"* (to match gates) in seeking a daughter-in-law is typical in Chinese culture. As Gu and Gallin (2004) illustrate, in Taiwan, marriages traditionally are arrangements between families rather than individuals. They are usually from the same class and ethnic group in order to "match gates" of two families. While occasionally, women would marry into higher-status families, brides marrying downwards are less likely because a bride from high-status family is unlikely to adapt to humble surroundings (Gu and Gallin 2004). Apparently this cultural tradition was sustained within the Taiwanese immigrant community in the U.S.

Interethnic marriage, between Taiwanese or other Asians, was less likely than interracial marriage, primarily between Taiwanese Americans and Caucasians, to engender cultural conflicts and communication barriers within families because of shared Asian backgrounds. However, sometimes interethnic marriage also generated serious conflicts when hierarchical ethnic ideologies among sub-Asian-groups came into play. For instance, a second-generation professional Taiwanese, John Lee, told me a heartbreaking story about his family caused by interethnic marriage. The Lee family (middle-class *benshengren*) used to be a close unit centered around the youngest son, Eric, a sweet and smart young man who was a successful physician. Yet, ever since Eric's wedding day two years ago, this family had fallen apart and gone through severe psychological suffering. The tragedy began when Eric's mom asked the bride, Angela, to wear a traditional Chinese gown, Chi-Pao, on her wedding day. Angela, a one-point-five-generation Korean American, regarded this demand as an insult to her Korean heritage perpetrated by people who believed in Chinese superiority. She, thus, hated her mother-in-law. Although she did wear a Chi-Pao as requested, Angela had refused to talk with and see her parents-in-law ever since the wedding.

Angela's anger and hatred brought striking changes to the Lee family. Eric, the child who used to be the center of the family, was influenced by his wife and stopped talking to and visiting his parents.

Nevertheless, I believe that class plays an implicit role, because Taiwanese American parents in many cases also care about the financial situation and social status of their in-laws. Yet, race/ethnicity remains the key factor.

Consequently, his mother had been suffering from depression because of this traumatic change in her relationship with Eric, and the Lee family had been living in the shadow of unhappiness for two years. Even though Eric's siblings had made efforts to help by acting as mediators between the couple and the parents, the stalemate continued.

While race is a marker of difference and inequality between White and non-White populations, a similar system of stratification exists among Asian sub-groups. Such systems are produced by both the skin-color of individuals and the economic power of their countries of origin in Asia. Historically, East Asians have a lighter skin color than South and Southeast Asians, and are wealthier. As a result, people's perceptions of these countries and their emigrants are affected. For instance, Japan is the most economically powerful country in Asia, and its people have the lightest skin-color. Therefore, Japanese usually regard themselves, and are perceived by other Asians, as "the White" in Asia, a superior nationality in the region. In contrast, South and Southeast Asians' dark skin and their under-developed economies situate both the countries and their people in relatively disadvantaged positions. A "mini world system," made up of core, semi-periphery, and periphery, exists in Asia. Such a system also contributes to the construction of a perceptional schema of ethnic hierarchies among Asian Americans.

Another middle-class *benshengren* family was trapped by similar inter-generational tension because the son was dating a Vietnamese American. Even though the son was still too young (a freshman in college) to consider marriage, the courtship had precipitated numerous fights and arguments between the parents and their son. Considering Vietnamese an inferior ethnicity compared to Taiwanese, the parents were extremely upset by their son's relationship, which had engendered overwhelming distress within the family.

From the cases above, we can see two distinct world views among Taiwanese Americans concerning children's interracial or interethnic courtship or marriage. First, when children dated or married Caucasians, the parents tended to worry about the differences between two cultures, value systems, and ways of communication. Yet, when their children's partners were other Asians, Taiwanese parents showed a concern that was rooted in a hierarchy of ethnicity and economic power. Such tendencies were particularly evident in middle-class *benshengren* families, and the resulting conflicts of these tendencies occurred mostly between mothers and children.[132]

Moreover, Taiwanese immigrants' reluctance about their children dating Blacks shows what Ong (1996) calls "whitening" ideologies and attitudes.[133] In spite of the fact that both Taiwanese and Blacks are non-White, the Taiwanese perceive themselves as "relatively Whiter" than Blacks. Their racial superiority and stereotypes about Blacks have resulted in segregation, sometimes even hostility, between these two groups. In fact, a second-generation woman described her mother's reactions when she invited a male Black friend to stay with her family. She recalled how upset and nervous her mother was that night, getting up and walking around the house constantly. I believe that such feelings of insecurity and fear come from negative images about African Americans portrayed in the media both in Taiwan and the U.S. Based on my interviews, it seems that Taiwanese immigrants rarely interact with African Americans in their everyday life and do not have Black friends. As I (2000) have pointed out elsewhere, although aware of their minority status, Taiwanese immigrants construct difference based on race and ethnicity, particularly in the case of Blacks. Their resistance to the idea of their children dating or marrying African Americans, therefore, is not at all surprising.

---

[132] All the informants who reported generational conflicts over interracial or interethnic marriage came from middle-class *benshengren* families. Several middle-class *waishengren* showed racial stereotypes in their perceptions about children's courtship, but they did not actually encounter situations that engendered conflicts between two generations. Moreover, because mothers were primarily responsible for child raising in the family, they were more likely than the fathers to encounter generational conflicts over varied issues, including interracial or interethnic marriage.

[133] According to Ong (1996), racial othering is a dynamic that emerges through a variety of mechanisms that subject nonwhite immigrants to whitening or blackening processes that indicate the degree of their closeness or distance from ideal white standards.

Other Family Conflicts

"He is always right in her eyes": Distress Engendered by Mothers-in-law

Six families in this study were living or had lived in three-generation households. In most of these cases, three-generation cohabitation was initiated when a husband's father passed away; his widowed mother then moved to the U.S. to live with her son's family.[134] The time that three generations lived under the same roof generally was about ten years, although it was even longer in some families. During this period, the mother-in-law usually helped with housework and, thus, reduced her daughter-in-law's workload to a certain extent. Nevertheless, the tension between a daughter-in-law and her mother-in-law caused serious and common psychological distress in a family.

Every female informant who had ever lived with their mother-in-law told me the same story; whenever a couple had a disagreement, the mother-in-law would take her son's side and blame his wife. Consequently, the argument between a couple always turned into a fight (mostly a "cold war") between the mother-in-law and daughter-in-law. This was especially the case when a wife asked her husband to help with housework. Because traditional Chinese culture stigmatizes men who "do women's work" around the house, invariably, her mother-in-law would be angry and defend the woman's husband. As Hsio-Fen told me,

> Sometimes when I asked my husband to help me with some housework, my mother-in-law would be very angry. So, every time when I was arguing with my husband, it would turn into a situation that I began to argue with her [my mother-in-law]. It was actually a fight between my husband and me, but my mother-in-law would always intervene. She seemed unhappy that I initiated a fight with my husband, and that I asked him to do housework.

---

[134] As I described in Chapter Five, Taiwan is a patrilineal society. Married couples are traditionally expected to live with the husbands' parents as a representation of filial piety. It is, however, usually the wives who are required to take care of their husbands' parents.

Mei-Li, another female informant who had lived with her mother-in-law for more than ten years, also recalled that her

> mother-in-law was a very old-fashioned woman. In her eyes, her son was always right. For example, every time when we brought her to a friend's place for dinner, she would want to come home right after we finished the meal. But my husband liked to talk and hang out with friends longer, and didn't want to leave that early. Then, my mother-in-law would blame me, asking why I didn't want to go home. I tried to make my husband leave, but he liked to talk so much that we had to stay with him. After we came home, my mother-in-law would blame me, saying that "Women are always too talkative." In fact, it's her son who's talkative but not me. But she always thought it must be my fault. Also, every time when I had an argument with my husband, she would take his side and accuse me of causing problems in our family.

Regardless of the tension with their mothers-in-law, Hsiao-Fen and Mei-Li tried to remain obedient to them. "She was old, so I thought I didn't have to dispute her and make her angry," Hsiao-Fen said. Therefore, although having much to complain about their mothers-in-law, Hsiao-Fen and Mei-Li still followed traditional Confucian teaching and deferred to the older woman as much as they could. Even when their mothers-in-law were suffering from Alzheimer's disease and lost their ability to be independent adults, they did not hire helpers or send them to a nursing home. Instead, they took care of washing, changing, and feeding their mothers-in-law, regarding this care as their obligation as daughters-in-law. Traditional Chinese culture and the value of filial piety were sustained in these families at the expense of a daughter-in-law's mental health. Such an experience of distress prevailed among married first-generation women across social class and ethnicity. Nevertheless, accepting the demands of Chinese norms on a daughter-in-law, these women tolerated such an unfair treatment at home as well as its consequent distress. As Gallin (1995) and Yu (2001) point out, in modern time, Taiwanese women continue to follow traditional norms regarding gender roles. This tendency can also be observed in this study of immigrants.

"They are too un-Americanized!" – Distress from Relatives

Middle-class Taiwanese Americans in this study were fairly wealthy. Most of them owned large houses in the suburbs and sent their children to expensive private schools.[135] Therefore, when their relatives came to visit from Taiwan, these wealthy families usually hosted them at home. Moreover, when relatives first migrated to the U.S., they also expected that they would obtain help from kin who were already well established in the receiving society. Tensions erupted, however, when these visits occurred too frequently or lasted too long. Wan-Jen, a middle-aged professional woman (*waishengren,* married to a *benshengren)*, told me how distressed she was during the stay of her brother-in-law's family.

> My stress is that… my stress comes from relatives. You know, because the stress from Chinese relatives is more… they don't care about privacy, which is very stressful for me, like….Last year, my husband's brother and his family migrated to the U.S. We were very supportive, and welcomed them to live with us when finding a place to settle. Yet, they stayed here for six months! It's terribly too long! You know, that really ruined my entire life, you know, my family life. You know, How should I say this? Really, really significantly damaged our marriage life…. At that time, I'd already sought help from a marriage counselor, and I didn't really want to continue my marriage. Of course, it's because my husband didn't handle it correctly, but things like this…things like this… are very difficult. Now I can take a step back and see it more clearly. If it had happened today, I would have found an apartment for them in the first place, rather than inviting them to stay with us.

---

[135] Many middle-class Taiwanese immigrants resided in Jewish communities in which family values and educational achievements are highly regarded. Because their children went to the same schools with their Jewish neighbors, these Taiwanese became acquainted with some Jewish families, who also became the major source of what they learned about American culture. Many informants told me that they shared similar values of family and education with Jews, and thought that Americans were not really that different from the Taiwanese.

How can you live with a family for six months? I feel that they are too un-American!

While her relatives' stay had caused Wan-Jen serious psychological distress, she felt that she could not ask them to leave directly because of her in-law status. So she asked her husband to talk to them, but he refused. He even asked Wan-Jen not to mention this matter to them, because it would be "inappropriate." Typical Chinese culture and attitudes are evident in this situation. First, a husband's ability to do such a favor (hosting relatives in his home) not only shows his generosity but also gives him "face," a greatly valued attribute in Taiwanese society. Second, rejecting people directly is not culturally appropriate in Taiwan, because it would cause embarrassment to others. Third, a married woman is expected to be subordinate to her husband and in-laws according to traditional Chinese social norms. She is not supposed to engage in decision-making of any kind that involves her in-laws.

Wan-Jen had been living in the U.S. for almost twenty years and regarded herself as "Americanized." She was also a modern woman who knew what she wanted for herself and family, and how to get what she wanted. Nevertheless, Wan-Jen was unable to overcome the constraints Chinese social norms and cultural appropriateness imposed on her in dealing with her relatives' stay. Even though she was obviously going through psychological suffering and a marriage crisis and knew her relatives must leave to solve the problems, Wan-Jen

felt I was going crazy.... You know, when there are some guests in your home, you would not be able to sleep well, right? You would think, what they would like to eat and things like that. You would have to take care of extra things. But in my own home, I just want to relax. I want just to be free, not responsible, ok? So, that tension continued for about six months. I couldn't even sleep at night. I was so mad.... I was breaking down and couldn't relax. Later, my daughter tried to communicate with them, but she told me, "Mom, they really don't know you need privacy, I can tell. I had a discussion with them, but they didn't understand." My goodness! How can they not know I need privacy? We have a huge house, but it doesn't mean that we have the obligation to host them, you know. Later, I realized that **they thought it was my husband who made decisions for this family, so my feelings and opinions were not considered.** You know, you've got to respect me, because I contribute more than a half for this family. I mean, at least as equally as he does. You must know that. You cannot say his decision can override mine.

(emphasis added)

The above narrative reflects Wan-Jen's strong sense of individual rights and privacy in the family. Yet, facing an issue that was embedded in Chinese cultural norms, Wan-Jen felt overwhelmingly unable to speak up and confront her in-laws. She went to a marriage counselor (Caucasian) but did not find it helpful because "He (the counselor) did not understand our culture," according to Wan-Jen. Finally, she asked a friend to talk to her brother-in-law, suggesting that they should move out. Her "nightmare" eventually ended, but after this disaster her relationship with her husband was no longer the same. Unfortunately, from time to time, her brother-in-law still invited other siblings and relatives to visit and stay with Wan-Jen's family without consulting her first. Without breaking Chinese social norms and cultural standards, Wan-Jen's nightmare continued to be a ticking bomb in her life.

SUMMARY AND DISCUSSION

In this chapter, I have examined the gendered power structure of Taiwanese American families, and compared different patterns among sub-groups. Using three indicators, decision-making about finances and children's education, and the gender division of domestic labor, I analyzed how Taiwanese American men and women allocated responsibilities within their families. In general, Taiwanese Americans showed a patri-egalitarian orientation in their spousal relations. Both patriarchy and egalitarianism existed in varied aspects of spousal relations, among sub-groups and in different contexts.

In this chapter I also explored how familial relations influence Taiwanese Americans' mental health, and provided illustrations of the psychological distress women, men, and children experienced in the family. In general, first-generation women were distressed most by various aspects of family life. They had to endure distress caused by mothers-in-law, relatives (in-laws), and overwhelming double-shifts; they also were anxious about their children's Americanization and criticism. First-generation women's psychological suffering, however, did not necessarily reflect their powerlessness in the family. Rather, they were assigned authority for the supervision of children's education, and their exercise of the power inherent in this position was one of the sources of their spouses' distress. Although they usually were not the major breadwinner in the family, many women controlled finances.

To generalize an overall pattern from these findings, I argue that although disadvantages in the gendered power structure lead to certain psychological problems for men, women, and children in different aspects of family life, a lack of power alone does not necessarily contribute to mental distress. The insufficiency of power in explaining distress also can be illustrated by the inconsistencies between the informants' social and emotional lives. The gendered power structure that organizes the lives of a husband and a wife does not necessarily impair individuals' psychological well-being. Rather, many experiences of distress emerge from power relations other than spousal (e.g., generational and in-laws), and from individual struggles over contradictory cultural norms. Moreover, those who were "powerless" in conjugal relations, as analyzed in my comparisons of various sub-groups, did not necessarily experience more forms of distress or experience distress more frequently than their "powerful" counterparts. In fact, some experiences of distress were fairly prevalent (issues such as women's burden of housework, parents' ways of expressing love, women's role as daughters-in-law) across social class and ethnicity, while others occurred more often among certain groups (issues such as middle-class women's relationships with in-laws, middle-class *benshengren's* perceptions about interracial marriage). In these varied experiences of distress, cultural factors (values and norms) appeared to be an important factor that triggered emotional struggles.

In other words, in addition to power relations, I see ambivalent struggles between two cultures and value systems, inherent in the transnational structure within which Taiwanese Americans experience their family lives, as factors that provoke distress. When individuals are situated in a power relation (e.g., husband vs. wife, mother vs. child, mother-in-law vs. daughter-in-law), they tend to seek behavioral guidance, meanings, and values from their "cultural toolkit." Nevertheless, because immigrants' cultural world spans two societies, such a toolkit is inevitably transnational by nature, containing cultural elements of two societies that are not always compatible. Mental distress is produced when individuals fail to process incompatible cultural norms and values in their interpersonal interactions in which power relations are embedded. That is to say, the mental distress of immigrants and their children is a form of "transnational struggle," or what Wolf (1997) calls "emotional transnationalism," resulting from a cultural tug of "Americanese" and "Chineseness" in their interactions and relationships with family members. These familial relations also involve power.

Such a cultural tug and its consequent distress occurred particularly often and was most evident among first-generation women when they were dealing with different familial relations and their multiple roles in the family. Because most "tasks" in the family (including housework, child raising, and taking care of in-laws) were considered "a woman's job," married women encountered many more forms of relational tensions and distress than their male counterparts. In these relational tensions, on one hand, first-generation women wanted to show their children and in-laws that they were "very American." On the other hand, they also presented traditional Chinese features in their roles of daughter-in-law and sister-in-law. The processes of their cultural identifications, however, were not always smooth. These women were frequently trapped in ambivalent, troubled, and contradictory emotions. Regardless of the belief that they were Americanized and should adopt American ways, they often conformed to Chinese norms (e.g., in their submissive relations with in-laws) or practiced Chinese norms unconsciously (e.g., in their authoritarian relations with children). In both situations distress was produced, and power played a critical role in these situations (e.g., the powerlessness of a daughter-in-law and the power of a mother to demand that her children submit to her will). In other words, the situations -- what I call "contexts" – that produce mental distress involve two significant mechanisms, power relations and cultural identification.

Although frequently distressed in the family, women exhibited active and strategic styles of individual agencies. For example, they tended to directly confront their children, indirectly sought help from friends or counselors, or read self-help books. Nevertheless, their active and strategic agency styles did not always effectively relieve distress. Sometimes they were able to reduce distress and change the power relations or contradictory cultural identifications that bothered them; yet other times they reproduced power relations, went back and forth in their ambivalent cultural identifications between Chineseness and Americaness, and were trapped in continuous emotional transnationalism. In contrast, first-generation men experienced far less distress (mostly about children's education and a few about parent-child conflict) than their female counterparts. When distressed, they frequently reacted acquiescently, either ceding their authority to their wives to solve "the problem" or just "letting it be." In the family, therefore, transnational struggles and agencies are gendered.

CONCLUSION: AMBIVALENT CULTURAL TUG

Not all families share equal opportunities or equal living conditions. Rather, like individuals, families occupy particular social locations by virtue of their class, race/ethnicity, gender, age, sexuality, stage in the life cycle, and/or national origin (Baca Zinn and Eitzen 1999). Therefore, the structure of daily family life, the meanings attached to familial relationships, and the effects of social and economic changes in society all vary by a family's social location (Garey and Hansen 1998). By the same token, individuals' social locations (e.g., gender, age, race, ethnicity, class), determine their statuses within the family, shaping how they experience family life and the meaning attached to these experiences.

Taiwanese American families, within which individuals also differ in their standpoints, occupy a special social location and represent a unique ethnic culture in U.S. society. The term "creolization" has been used to describe the unique social system that blends cultures of both sending and receiving countries (Foner 1997; Mintz and Price 1992; Smith 1967). In Jamaica and other West Indian societies, a new system of social relations and cultural forms has developed. Neither African nor English, the locally produced system is completely new, created in the context of specific West Indian economic, social, and political circumstances (Mintz and Price 1992; Smith 1988). In her study of

Japanese-American kinship, Yanagisako (1985) observes that Japanese Americans construct their family lives by adopting models of both Japanese and American kinship, and create a "Japanese American synthesis." Thomas and Znaniecki (1984) also point out that Polish peasants in the U.S. create a Polish-American society, within which social structures and individual attitudes are neither Polish nor American. Rather, Polish-American culture is a completely new product "whose raw materials have been partly drawn from Polish traditions, partly from the new conditions in which the immigrants live, and partly from American social values as the immigrant sees and interprets them" (Thomas and Znaiecki 1984: 108).

Accordingly, Taiwanese American society is also a product that blends both American and Chinese cultures, a new creation within which social structures and individual attributes are neither American nor Chinese/Taiwanese. As a one-point-five-generation Taiwanese American said, "I am Taiwanese, and I am American. It's not an either-or, and it's not a fifty-fifty. I'm more like an eighty-five, seventy-five. It's more than fifty of each." The social practices and personal attributes of Taiwanese Americans, therefore, are transnational. They are not solely Taiwanese or American, nor are they simply Taiwanese "plus" or "minus" American. Rather, they are a mixed new creation, a transnational creation. It is under such a transnational structure and context that different codes, cultures, ideologies, and goals circulate in the lives of Taiwanese Americans. The power structures, roles, and kin relationships in Taiwanese American families, as a result, represent this group's transnational characteristics.

To sum up, I argue that transnational experiences, particularly the ambivalent cultural identifications resulting from these transnational experiences, intersect with power structures and relations in shaping Taiwanese Americans' emotional life within the family. Situated in a transnational structure and context, Taiwanese American fathers, mothers, in-laws, and children inevitably confront challenges of two competing systems of cultural meanings that serve as guides for carrying out social practice in the family. As Morris (1990: 2) puts it, families are "a theatre" of multiple relationships between genders and generations. Families are the major institution that provides immigrants with intimacy and protection (Parrillo 1991). Yet, while families create the ties that bind, they also are sites of intense conflict and contradictions, especially among immigrants (Rumbaut 1997). It is in the "theatre" of the immigrant family that transnational contexts, power structures, dual-cultures, and individual agency, interact in a multiple and complex dynamic to establish familial relationship among kin. The structure of family life, and the meanings attached to familial relationships and roles, are, therefore, defined, re-defined, negotiated, and re-negotiated. It is also through this multifaceted interplay of transnational power/culture/agency, as well as the ongoing process of meaning building and negotiation that mental distress is engendered.

CHAPTER 8

UNBEARABLE RACIAL OTHERING

My focus in this chapter is Taiwanese Americans' working experiences as racialized and gendered actors, and how these experiences affect their mental health. I present and discuss my findings in two sections. First, I investigate Taiwanese Americans' reported experiences of racial discrimination and sexist treatment in the workplace. Differences in gender, generation, and ethnicity are analyzed for each issue of focus. Despite the fact that social class is one of the major factors that shape variance in individual working experiences, the analysis in this chapter is primarily based on my interviews with salaried professionals because of limitations in sampling. After excluding those informants who were self-employed, home-makers, and college students, only three informants of the lower class were eligible for inclusion, and they all worked in small ethnic businesses that hired only Taiwanese or Chinese. I therefore do not present results by class due to the small number and homogeneity of lower-class subjects.

Second, I examine *if* and *how* Taiwanese Americans' racialized and gendered experiences at work provoked psychological distress. Major distress at work confronting men and women is discussed. In both sections, explanations for the findings are explored.

TAIWANESE AMERICANS' WORKING EXPERIENCES

According to the informants' descriptions, "few promotions" was the primary indicator they (both men and women) used to infer racial discrimination and sexist treatment in the workplace. Only three male professionals, all first-generation, pointed out other situations that they considered examples of racial discrimination, such as opinions discounted, low wages, and long working hours. In these men's view, such inequities were not only different forms of discrimination and unfairness, but also something inherent in the social structure about which they could do nothing. In particular, during the period when these immigrants were applying for permanent residency or citizenship through their employers' sponsorship, they felt they were forced to tolerate many kinds of unfair treatment in the workplace, such as low wages, few benefits, and long working hours.[136]

The salary gap between Asians and Caucasians is one of the major outcomes of racial oppression in the labor force. According to Ong and Hee (1994), Asian American men receive lower economic returns than White men, despite their superior levels of education. In 1990, highly educated Asian American men earned about ten percent less than their White counterparts, even though they were much more likely to have a graduate degree. Moreover, both Asian and Caucasian women face the wage gap, earning only about 70 percent of the salaries of White men with similar backgrounds, but Asian American women fared worse than their White counterparts (Ong and Hee 1994). In other words, not only race/ethnicity but also gender affects the distribution of economic rewards in the U.S. labor market. In this study, however, only men recognized this inequity. None of the female informants mentioned earning discrepancies between different races/ethnicities or genders.

Racial Discrimination: Commonly Reported Experience

More than a half (58%) of the informants reported that they experienced unfair treatment in the workplace because of their race, and another 33 percent acknowledged the existence of racial

---

[136] Feelings of deprivation and disadvantage are relative. Among middle-class professionals, for example, some informants identified their disadvantaged work situation (e.g., lower wages and longer working hours than their Caucasian colleagues) during the period when they were applying for citizenship as racial discrimination, but not as much as a problem after they became U.S. citizens, although a racial glass ceiling may continue to exist. Others thought their disadvantages remained a problem in the workplace.

discrimination, although they had not actually encountered any (see Table 8-1). These two categories made up 91 percent of the informants who reported that racism buttressed a glass ceiling in the workplace.

Table 8-1: Reported Racial Discrimination in the Workplace

	Frequency	Percent
Yes, experienced	23	58 %
Yes, but not experienced	13	33 %
No	4	9 %
Total	40*	100%

*Among the 54 informants, six were college students who had not yet had working experiences at the time of interviews, five were self-employed and three were home-makers. Thus, the total number of cases became 40 in this analysis.

Gender Differences:

When a comparison was made by gender, many more men (20% more) than women reported experiencing racial discrimination in the workplace. As shown in Table 8-2, a little more than two thirds of men (68%) said they were discriminated against while slightly less than a half of their female counterparts (48%) reported such a phenomenon.

Table 8-2: Gender and Reported Racial Discrimination

	Men	Women
Yes, experienced	13 (68%)	10 (48%)
Yes, but not experienced	5 (26%)	8 (38%)
No	1 (5%)	3 (14%)
Total (40)	19 (100%)	21 (100%)

Why were Taiwanese American men more likely than their female counterparts to report racial discrimination in the workplace? In part, the difference may be a product of the interactive effect of gender and race/ethnicity. According to McIntosh (2003), male privilege is unearned and unacknowledged. Thus, in seeking to explain inequity in the workplace, Taiwanese men may ignore their gender and attribute unfair treatment to their race or ethnicity. In contrast, Taiwanese American women are disadvantaged by both their non-male and non-White status. Race therefore may not be the only hierarchy to which they attribute the experience of discrimination. In fact, when asked about their experience of racial discrimination, many female informants neutralized this problem by using the term "unfair treatment" or by providing explanations in addition to race, such as gender, working experience, actual achievements or efficiency at work, or their employers' budget plans. In other words, women tended to attribute their unfair treatment to multiple factors, while men tended to relate problems to race.

Moreover, gender differences in the perception of racial discrimination in the workplace may also be due to the differing expectations of Taiwanese American men and women caused by their transnational experiences, especially among first-generation immigrants. Coming from a society within which almost all people are of the same race (*Han*), men in Taiwan, especially middle- and upper-class men, are the most privileged and advantaged. They expect to achieve economic success and acquire high social status without barriers; race would be the last factor that interfered with their path to success. In the United States, however, where race is a major social marker of difference, Taiwanese men encounter a predicament over which they have little control. Although considered successful by mass standards, many professional Taiwanese Americans lamented that they could have achieved more if they were Caucasian. Such regret may contribute to men's vulnerability to feelings of mistreatment in American society.

Despite the fact that women were less likely than their male counterparts to report being discriminated against, racial discrimination was a common experience among women; almost one half (10 individuals, about 48%) reported this experience. These women's reasoning of racial discrimination resembled men's, but their feelings of distress and reactions to unfair treatment differed from theirs. In the second section, I discuss these gender differences.

Generational Differences:

Reports of racial discrimination were significantly skewed in terms of generation. Almost three fourths (73%) of first-generation informants thought they had been treated unfairly, and another 12 percent acknowledged the fact of racial discrimination in the workplace, although they had not experienced it. In contrast, among second-generation adults, only 29 percent reported encountering unfair treatment at work, although all acknowledged the fact of racial discrimination against Asians (see Table 8-3).

Table 8-3: Generation and Reported Racial Discrimination

	First	Second
Yes, experienced	19 (73%)	4 (29%)
Yes, but not experienced	3 (12%)	10 (71%)
No	4 (15%)	0 (0%)
Total (40)	26 (100%)	14 (100%)

There are two possible explanations for these generational differences. First, moving from Taiwan where race is not a major hierarchical marker in society, first-generation immigrants may be more likely to feel frustrated by racism than are their children who grew up in the U.S. and have faced problems associated with race since they were young. Second, first-generation immigrants are generally less acculturated than their native-born children, leading to a more difficult process of adapting to the majority culture. Such differences, in turn, may make them more vulnerable to feelings of racial discrimination. In short, migration history and transnational background may affect individuals' perceptions of racial discrimination. First-generation immigrants whose life experiences extend across two societies are more likely than their native-born children, whose experience of transnational culture emanates primarily from their parents, to report experiencing racial discrimination in the workplace.

Ethnic Differences:
When a comparison was made by ethnicity, my data showed that more *waishengren* than *benshengren* (78% and 50%, respectively, 28% more) reported being discriminated against in the workplace because of their race (see Table 8-4).

Table 8-4: Ethnicity and Reported Racial Discrimination

	Benshengren	*Waishengren*
Yes, experienced	15 (50%)	7 (78%)
Yes, but not experienced	12 (40%)	1 (11%)
No	3 (10%)	1 (11%)
Total (40)	30 (100%)	9 (100%)

This finding may be explained in a way similar to that offered for gender differences in the perception of discrimination. An advantaged group in the sending society, Taiwan, *waishengren* tend to perceive more discrimination in the host country than do their disadvantaged counterparts. As demonstrated in Chapter Five, *waishengren* were more privileged than *benshengren* in Taiwan's history. They were, however, more likely than their *benshengren* counterparts to report being discriminated against in the U.S. Again, the "relative feeling of deprivation" resulting from migration history and transnational background shaped the informants' perceptions of their experiences in the receiving society.

In addition to this dissimilarity in reporting their experience of racial discrimination, *benshengren* and *waishengren* differed from each other in their feelings of and reactions to distress in the face of racial discrimination. Later in this chapter, I examine and discuss these ethnic differences in mental health.

Explaining Perceived Racial Discrimination

Not only did the informants report experiences of racial discrimination in the workplace, they (particularly the first-generation) also provided a great number of explanations about the reasons for it. Synthesizing their descriptions, three major explanations emerged. The first two, language barriers and life styles, reflect the cultural differences between Taiwanese and Americans, differences that are primarily representative of first-generation immigrants. The third explanation, social stereotypes, illustrates how Asian Americans, including Taiwanese, are generally perceived by American society and, accordingly, treated.

Language barriers and cultural values of self-expression:
Although they had lived in the U.S. for several decades, many first-generation informants admitted that they still could not communicate as well as native speakers.[137] This language barrier became the major obstacle to self-expression and mutual understanding in the workplace and, in turn, they argued, constrained their achievements. These informants (especially men) complained that in spite of their outstanding professional performance, they did not acquire credibility among their colleagues and the promotions they deserved because they were unable to express themselves well enough in English. "America is a society that views highly on self-expression. If you cannot present yourself well, nobody would know how good your ideas are, or how much you've done for this company," said Ren-Jer, a 42-year-old male manager in a chemical company. Another 47-year-old engineer similarly maintained,

> In American culture, if you don't speak up, nobody would help you. We Chinese are more conservative. We don't usually say more than what we can prove. So, I think, we usually don't advertise ourselves. But advertising yourself is encouraged in American society. Therefore, this cultural difference makes us disadvantaged when it comes to promotion.

---

[137] Seventeen of the 26 first-generation informants reported this language barrier, including many more men (14 individuals) than women.

In the view of Taiwanese immigrants, therefore, their inability to express themselves is due not only to the fact that English is their second language, it also is a reflection of the different values Confucian culture taught them about self-presentation.

Different life styles and social skills:
Informants in this study also considered differences in life styles and social skills important factors that contributed to racial discrimination at work. "We don't play golf, that's why," said Li-Ming, when talking about why Taiwanese, including himself, did not get promoted often. Ren-Jer further explained why playing golf had anything to do with promotion at work. According to him,

> Work performance involves interpersonal skills and many other aspects, such as family relations [socializing with co-workers' families] and personal relationships. For example, I don't play, and am not interested in playing, golf with Caucasian co-workers. So, it's very difficult for me to establish personal connections with others, including my boss. Our cultures are essentially different. Like, I'm not interested in watching football games, either, so it's difficult for me to fit into their group [Caucasian co-workers]. So, being a middle-level manager, like myself, probably would be the best we [Chinese/Taiwanese] can do here. It's impossible to get a higher position than that [because our life style and social skills are different from those of Americans].

Chinese perceptions of the self and the social are relational (Hsu 1985; Tseng 1973). In Taiwan, the human resource department in government bureaucracies and companies is called *Ren-Shih Bu* (people-job department). Interpersonal relationships are essential for securing jobs and getting promotions, because "people-job, people-job, you'd need to win people in order to earn your job," says a folk proverb. Therefore, establishing good relationships with co-workers, bosses, the chair of the *Ren-Shih Bu*, and even with some powerful local politicians is important. Sending gifts, doing favors, forming acquaintances with bosses' families, singing karaoke together, and hosting dinners are all very common among co-workers. Nevertheless, these Taiwanese ways of building interpersonal relationships seem not to work in American corporate culture. Americans establish relationships mainly through watching sports, playing golf, and commenting on politics, which are not familiar arenas for the Taiwanese. Life-style differences prevent Taiwanese Americans from "melting into" the majority culture, not to mention into close relationships with co-workers. As an engineer, Wei-Kun (54 years old, male), said,

> I think, for first-generation immigrants, the limitation [caused by race] is greater [than the second genetation]. It's because we don't understand each other. Americans don't understand us [Taiwanese/Chinese], nor do we understand them. Besides working together, you have to socialize with them [Caucasians] in order to understand their culture, so that you can become one of them. Speaking their language doesn't mean that you can certainly fit into their society. It's not enough if you don't understand their culture. You would not be able to become part of this society, and people would not consider you as one of them. Under this circumstance, they would not invite you to social occasions. I think this is the actual difficulty for the first generation. It's not that we can't compete with them in terms of professional ability. No, it's the cultural differences that separate us from them.

Cultural differences in lifestyles and social skills construct an "invisible wall" that separates Taiwanese Americans from those in the majority culture. No matter how hard they strive to maintain rapport in the workplace, obstacles hinder their efforts to establish informal connections with co-workers. They thus attribute their lack of promotion to their enculturated way of forging workplace relationships.

Social Stereotypes about Asian Americans:
Although only a few (4 out of 14, including three men and one woman) second-generation informants reported being racially discriminated against, all of them acknowledged race problems and the disadvantage of being an Asian in the workplace. In contrast to their parents, who tended to recognize the problem of "how different we

[Taiwanese/Chinese] are from them [Americans/Caucasians]," children of Taiwanese immigrants considered their racialized experiences a result of others' stereotypes about Asians in general, an issue of "how we [Asians] are perceived by others [non-Asians]." Chris, a 30-year-old finance analyst insisted that his co-workers made assumptions about him based on their stereotypes of Asian.

> In many ways, just because people have… maybe a… maybe stereotype, or pre-assumption of what Asian is, and what Asian does, like hard working, quiet, and… not really, a leader-type, or…. They don't want to be in charge of everything, so I think in a way it does affect, you know, promotions or job performance… especially in business…. There're so very few Asians in very high positions, unless it's an Asian company…. They've already had the preconception that, you know, you're quiet, submissive, and… so I think, Asians that, come out as being more successful are extremely aggressive, extremely outgoing, just very… very American…. Yeah, cause I think that, that Americans, they would think that, you know, they have the view of communication, or how you should… in a way, you know, is very aggressive, very loud, almost very… pushy, in such a corporate world. And, they can't accept that… someone who's maybe quieter or more gentle, or nicer, and… even though he, that person still gets the job done, just because his… style of communication doesn't fit with theirs, then, they don't see that person as… being able to succeed. Especially men…. maybe they expect, males to be… even more dominating, and… if a male isn't dominating, then he's weaker (laugh), incapable (laugh)….

As Tuan (1998: 154) argues, Asian Americans' class status does little to validate their authenticity as long-time Americans in the eyes of the public. Thomas (1995) also reports that a great number of Asian American professionals experience discrimination and blocked opportunities in the labor market because White employers tend to perceive them as passive and self-effacing, lacking managerial skills, and unable to communicate, command, and provide leadership. In Chris's case, the status of a native-born middle-class American man does not prevent him from being racialized. Social stereotypes of Asians (e.g., hard-working, passive, quiet, submissive, not leadership material), as well as those of men (e.g., dominating, aggressive, tough, pushy) interweave in the construction of his co-workers' presumptions and judgments. These presumptions have an effect on performance evaluations, interpersonal relationships, and communications.

As Tuan (1998: 154) states, Asian Americans are marked off and made "other." Such "otherness," however, comes not only from stereotyping, but also from cultural differences between Asians and Americans. As Sherry, a 29-year-old elementary school teacher, said,

> I don't think they tried to be unfair, but I always found it hard to communicate well, with certain kind of co-workers or managers. Because the fact that, the communication is always an issue, I think. It's always hard, because Asians are taught to be very...very... non-direct. But Americans are taught to be very direct. And that, conflicts me that you're direct the way you talk, but with Asian people, you know, how to make every people feel comfortable, or something. So it's very different. Like, communication barriers have been always a big thing.... I don't think they purposely try to be that way.... I'm the one that doesn't communicate like them, and they're usually like, ones that are managers, ones that are in authority. So, I'm the one that has to learn how to do it their way.

Similarly, Lowe (1996: 5-6) notes that native-born Asians are always seen as immigrants, as "foreign-within." Wong (1982: 79) also observes that no matter how Americanized they are, Asian Americans still are made conscious of their racial and ethnic heritage by the larger society. Socialized in Asian traditions, children of immigrants develop racial or ethnic characteristics that differentiate them from the majority White culture. This distinction both marks race and ethnicity and discourages inter-group relationships. In the above case, for instance, Sherry's "Asian style" of communication that categorizes her with other Asians, has become an obstacle in her interaction with Caucasian co-workers. In her colleagues' eyes, Sherry's "difference" may fit, or even reinforce, social stereotypes of Asians, even when the presumption is not intentionally applied.

Sexist Treatment:
Acknowledged but Not Necessarily Encountered Fact

Similar to their descriptions about racism, the informants regarded "few promotions" as the primary indicator of sexist treatment at workplace, followed by "gender stereotypes." In contrast to racial discrimination that was more broadly experienced, sexist treatment in the workplace was an "acknowledged but rarely encountered fact" for the informants. Only one second-generation man reported being treated unfairly because he was judged by social stereotypes about Asian men. The majority (85%) of the informants recognized gender inequalities in the workplace, but reported that they did not encounter any sexist treatment themselves (see Table 8-5).

Table 8-5: Reported Sexist Treatment in the Workplace

	Frequency	Percent
Yes, experienced	1	3 %
Yes, but not experienced	34	85 %
No	5	12 %
Total	40	100%

Chris, the only informant who reported being unfairly treated because of his gender, was a second-generation man. He complained that being male, he was often expected to be aggressive and domineering. Whenever Chris failed to display these masculine characteristics, he was considered weak, sissy, and, in his words, "not a leadership material." According to Espiritu (1997: 90-93), American mass culture emasculates Asian American men as asexual, passive, and malleable, and these stereotypes engender social and economic discrimination against Asian men. Even if this emasculation is not manifest, when Asian American men do not conform to White-based notions of masculinity, they are still likely to be stereotyped. This stereotyping – what Espiritu (2001) calls the "femininization of Asian men," -- can constrain their social and economic achievements.

As shown in Table 8-5, most informants (85%) in this study acknowledged gender inequalities at the workplace. This pattern is sustained in the comparison of informants by social location (see Table 8-6).

Table 8-6: Social Characteristics and Reported Sexist Treatment

	Yes	Yes, but not experienced	No	Total (40)
Gender				
Men	1	16	2	19
	5%	84%	11%	100%
Women	0	18	3	21
	0%	86%	14%	100%
Generation				
First	0	24	2	26
	0%	92%	8%	100%
Second	1	10	3	14
	7%	72%	21%	100%
Ethnicity				
Benshengren	1	25	4	30
	3%	83%	13%	100%
Waishengren	0	8	1	9
	0%	89%	11%	100%

Explaining Perceived Sexist Treatment

Despite both men's and women's recognition of the "fact" of sexism in the workplace, only male informants discussed its causes. For instance, three male subjects gave examples of women's associations in their companies to infer the existence of gender inequality. "Oh, they would not need such a group [if there is no sexist treatment at workplace]," said Wu-Hsiung, "There must be something they [members of those women's associations] want to fight for." Another five men pointed out that gender inequality was the result of the "biological/natural difference" between men and women, rather than sexist treatment. For example, according to Li-Ming, "Women have more limitations than men, in terms of childcare and family responsibilities." He continued, "Biologically, when they have kids, they inevitably would have to spend some time for the kids and family. This is a **natural** difference between men and women, so I don't consider it special at all" (emphasis added).

It was also a commonly shared belief that women face more barriers than men in achieving their career goals because "they are unable to spend as much time and energy on work once they have children and family," Min-Hui said. While this statement might reflect reality, it also suggests a traditional view of gender roles among male informants. Family matters were generally considered women's primary duty and the "inevitable" obstacle blocking their achievement. As noted in Chapter Seven, the burden of a double shift was one of the major sources of distress for Taiwanese American women. Despite the fact that their husbands understood the overload of housework and child-raising, and even in some cases encouraged their wives to participate in social activities, men did not necessarily help their wives with "women's work." The culture and conduct of men were not in sync. Moreover, not only women but also men are gendered actors, but first-generation men in this study were not aware of their gender privilege (compared with women) or disadvantages (caused by White-notions of masculinity) in the workplace.

None of the female informants in this study reported being treated unfairly because of their gender. Although widely acknowledging gender inequalities, women rarely talked about associated issues, nor did they mention the obstacles of being women in the workplace.[138]

WORKING EXPERIENCES AND MENTAL DISTRESS

Although they were both racialized and gendered actors, Taiwanese Americans' experiences of racial discrimination engendered psychological distress more significantly than did sexual

---

[138] Female informants tended to consider race the primary factor that caused unfair treatment in the workplace. Although they did not recognize gender as a "problem," women tended to attribute their experience of mistreatment to both gender and race.

discrimination. While gender inequality was broadly recognized, only one second-generation man expressed distress over sexist stereotyping.

More than half (22 out of the 40 subjects, approximately 55%) of the informants reported distress emanating from race-related problems at their work settings. Among these individuals, more men (12 out of 19, about 63%) than women (10 out of 21, about 48%) spoke about distress.[139] In contrast, while gender inequality was broadly recognized, only one second-generation man expressed distress over sexist stereotyping, although many women also attributed gender to their experience of racial discrimination. While race-related problems in the workplace were the main and prevalent source of distress for the informants, men and women differed notably in their feelings of distress and styles of exerting agencies. Below I demonstrate these gendered distress and agencies, and examine how they were affected by individuals' social locations other than gender.

"It is [racial] discrimination!"

As shown in previous analyses, racial discrimination was a common experience in the workplace. It was also a major source of distress for both men and women.[140] Similar to their reasoning of perceived racial discrimination, the informants' (especially men's) experience of distress emanated mainly from their cultural differences in the workplace.

---

[139] In addition, many more first-generation (19 out of 26, about 73%) than second-generation (3 out of 14, about 21%), as well as more *benshengren* (23 out of 30, about 78%) than *waishengren* (4 out of 9, about 47%) reported psychological distress as a result of racism in the workplace.

[140] Although also identifying race as the primary cause of their perceived racial discrimination, women tended to attribute their unfair treatment in the workplace to multiple factors (e.g., gender, working experience, and ability). Similarly, when speaking about distress, women tended to recognize racism as the primary cause, but frequently mixed race with gender and culture in their explanations.

For example, according to Confucian teaching, "Silence is golden," and "A full bottle of water does not make sound." [141] Traditional Chinese culture encourages hardwork, humbleness, and modesty. Even when you have done something incredible, you are not supposed to tell others about it. Rather, you should wait for others to "find out" and recognize your achievement. This value predisposes Taiwanese immigrants to be quiet and reserved in the workplace. They work hard but seldom ask for what they deserve; they do not aggressively propose suggestions but wait until others solicit their opinions. They hold on to the old belief that as long as you work hard and do well, others will surely recognize and praise your accomplishment. In many cases, unfortunately, "They [Americans] never found out my worth," a 47-year-old engineer said to me in a tone full of deep frustration. He continued, "I was supposed to take charge of that project because I was the most qualified, experienced, and senior in our company. But they chose an American [Caucasian]. I was very unhappy about that."

Not only men but also women experienced distress because of obstacles to promotion, misunderstanding, and unfair treatment resulting from their cultural differences. For instance, Wan-Jen, a 52-year-old female manager in a real estate company, spoke about such distress.

> Our background.... our education did not teach us how to deal with confrontation and negotiation. So, it took me a long time observing, learning, thinking, and practicing these skills.... We Chinese do not dare to ask for what we want, but you've got to. You have to tell others loudly about what you want.... **We tend to assume they should know [what we want] and don't ask for it. That's our problem.** Actually, nobody

---

[141] "A full bottle of water" is a metaphor for a person who is knowledgeable and talented. "A full bottle of water does not make sound" means that when someone is really outstanding, s/he would not boast about her/his ability or achievement. On the contrary, only those who are "half bottles" (people who know just a little bit) would make sounds loudly (i. e., brag about their knowledge). The purpose of this old saying is to encourage humbleness and modesty.

would know what you want, and nobody would promote you if you don't ask. But we don't have that kind of training [in negotiation and communication], so we don't really know how to do it. (emphasis added)

In addition to this broadly acknowledged cultural difference of self-expression and work attitudes, eight men (out of 26), all professionals, perceived language barriers as both a constraint to their promotion and a justification that Americans used to disguise racial discrimination. [142] Min-Hui, a 39-year-old researcher in a large pharmaceutical company, described his experience.

I had some experiences… like, one time, I knew a colleague was wrong, so I pointed it out at a meeting. But he pretended he didn't understand what I was talking about. Sometimes, Americans do understand you, but they would pretend not, to get you in trouble. So, sometimes, Americans ignore or dispute your opinions by telling you that they don't understand you because of your accent or language ability. Some of them are very nasty. There are some people like this, especially, in a corporation, people compete with each other. They play politics. So, we foreigners do have some disadvantages.

A male 47-year-old male programmer in a technology company also said,

If you look at your work evaluation, you'd know what problems they see in you. They often said my English was not good enough. This is discrimination! They just want to pick something to discriminate against you, that's all. Language is the most difficult thing you can improve, no matter how good your professional performance is. Biologically, our [Chinese]

---

[142] Both men and women identified language barriers and Chinese values of self-expression as a major cause of racial discrimination and distress. Nevertheless, perhaps because women in general are more skilled than men in mastering language, men appeared more distressed than their female counterparts by this communication problem.

tongues are shorter than theirs [Americans'], so it's not that
easy for us to pronounce certain English words. This is my
shortcoming, I know. I know that I have accent and can't
speak like a native. But the truth is that it's just an excuse they
use to discriminate against you. Your achievement is totally
put aside because of this language problem.

Regardless of whether language is considered an obstacle to
communication or used as a justification for racial discrimination, such
a barrier is doubtless a problem commonly facing and frustrating first-
generation Taiwanese Americans. As Cavosora (2000) reports,
discrimination based on language and accent differences is a major
issue confronting Asian Americans in the workplace. They are
increasingly frustrated by employers who arbitrarily discriminate on the
subjective basis of English fluency rather than on the quality of work.
Similarly, in this study, even when informants had high education and
professional skills, failing to speak and express themselves like a native
created a "glass ceiling" that jeopardized not only their achievement
but also their psychological well-being.

Communication obstacles distressed not only first-generation but
also second-generation informants who were native speakers, although
very few of the latter reported this distress.[143] For example, 24-year-old
business consultant Kent was distressed that he always had problems
communicating with co-workers and establishing good relationships;
John, a 31-year-old assistant professor, complained that some students
dropped out of his class because of his "thick Chinese accent," even
though he was a U.S.-born native-speaker. Because of this
communication obstacle, as well as different life styles and social
skills, as noted earlier in this chapter, Taiwanese Americans felt
discriminated against, mistreated, excluded, and alienated in their work
settings. In their view, race constrained not only their opportunities of
getting promotion, but also their likelihood of joining core social circles
in the workplace. These perceived constraints therefore led to
agonizing frustrations and enormous feeling of unfairness.

---

[143] Only three second-generation informants (two men and one woman)
reported distress resulting from their experience of racism in the workplace.

Regardless of this prevailing feeling of frustrations, nuances existed among subgroups. As noted above, first-generation and men were more likely to report distress as a result of racism than their second-generation and female counterparts. Moreover, more *benshengren* than *waishengren* (13 and 9 individuals, respectively) reported such distress. This ethnic difference, however, is inconsistent with my previous finding that *benshengren* were less likely than *waishengren* to report the experience of racial discrimination. Why did *waishengren* report more racism but less consequent distress than their *benshsengren* counterparts? I believe that *waishengren*'s transnational experience greatly contributes to this contradiction.

Recall that *waishengren* in this study migrated to the U.S. in part because they encountered ethnic conflict and oppression in Taiwan. "Uprooting" themselves from China to move to Taiwan and then to America, *waishengren* seemed to have a "diaspora mentality." Their nostalgia for their homeland continuously sensitized them to feelings of ethnic or racial distinctions and oppression, but produced contradictory reactions in different lands. In Taiwan, *waishengren* associated themselves with the ruling KMT government, so they tended to harbor feelings of superiority over the *benshengren* and perceive themselves as "the orthodox Chinese." Any ethnic exclusion from or oppression by *benshengren,* thus, became unbearable. In the U.S., however, *waishengren* were apt to normalize racial discrimination as part of the "reality." They were still disturbed by their minority status, but they considered it an "acceptable fact" in the new homeland.[144] In contrast, *benshengren* informants who were ethnically disadvantaged in Taiwan's history, expected more equal opportunities in the U.S. than on the island. They therefore were less tolerant and less accepting of racial discrimination in American society than their *waishengren* counterparts.

In reacting to their distress experiences of tremendous frustration, unhappiness, alienation, isolation, and being worn-down by their economic-social constraints at work, men and women took distinct

---

[144] Both *waishengren* men and women tended to articulate this belief. In sum, six out of the seven *waishengren* who reported being discriminated against regarded their oppressed situation as "normal." The one who did not normalize this unfair treatment put his hopes in the second generation.

actions. Men (particularly first-generation and *waishengren*) tended to consider their disadvantageous status and unfair treatment part of "the reality," something that was built into American society. By normalizing these problems encountered at work, these men obtained a feeling of comfort, thereby mitigating their distress. For instance, in reacting to their experience of racial discrimination, these informants frequently responded, "It is normal to be discriminated [against]."; "We are foreigners anyway."; "It's understandable because we are not one of them."; "It's acceptable because it's just the way it is"; or "I would have a louder voice if I were American." These responses showed that first-generation men had a tendency to normalize racial problems, thereby rationalizing the structural constraints that they thought limited their economic and social achievements. By rationalizing racial discrimination, they were able to relieve their frustration and their feeling that life was unfair, thereby justifying their acceptance of and acquiescence to unfair treatment. As Li-Ming, a 49-year-old researcher at a large pharmacy company, said,

> It's very natural that Caucasians don't promote Asians. If we [Taiwanese] were the boss, we would promote Asians first, too. **It's human nature.** It's very easy to feel frustrated under such a social structure. Your ambition would be worn out easily…. **If I were Caucasian, I would have a louder voice at work.**   (emphasis added)

Moreover, first-generation men alleviated their frustrations by putting their hopes on the next generation. "I just hope that our children won't face the same difficulties as we do," said Wei-Kun, a 54-year-old engineer. A 49-year-old scientist, Li-Ming, responded in a similar way, saying,

> You must learn how to tolerate all of these [unfair treatment and frustrations at the workplace]. Like many other first-generation immigrants, my hope is in the next generation. I hope they'll have better opportunities than I do.

It is common to read from the literature of immigration studies that millions of undocumented immigrants and boatpeople endure labor-intensive, low-paid jobs, and oppressive working conditions in the hope that their children will have better opportunities to pursue the American dream. It is also common to read that highly educated men and women from the third world work as nannies, waiters or waitress, or laborers in the United States for the same purpose (e.g., Chen 1992; Parrillo 1991; Portes and Rumbaut 1996; Wong 1982). Yet, this mentality is apparently not only seen among lower-class immigrants. Middle-class Taiwanese men of high social-economic status still find sustenance and comfort in their dreams for the next generation. This similarity across social class also signifies the shared constraints of social achievement among first-generation immigrants.

Dissimilar to their male counterparts who took these frustrations as a "fate," women tended to explore the nature of the problems that caused their distress, seek possible solutions, and take concrete actions to resolve these problems. They identified not only "the problem" but also the solution to this problem; "you've got to stand up for yourself [when being mistreated]!" many female informants said. This tendency, while commonly seen among female informants, was fairly rare among men. As a result, despite the fact that both were distressed by racial problems, men continued to be bothered, while women became content and confident once "the problem" was solved.

Compared with their male counterparts, therefore, women complained less and reported fewer feelings of distress about racial discrimination in the workplace. They also expressed a higher degree of satisfaction from work, and were more likely to defend themselves when confronting unfair treatment than were men. Unlike men who chose to normalize and accept racial problems, female informants tended to take a confrontational style of resistance against power. They often were assertive and strived for promotion, benefits, fair treatment, and a better working environment. Race was an "issue" rather than an "obstacle" for them in most cases.

Because of this gender difference, only female subjects told me about instances in which they fought for rights and fairness when handling race-related problems. Mei-Li (*benshengren*), who worked for an importing company as a data entry clerk, confronted her boss directly and explained her stance when being mistreated; Chia-Yin (a *waishengren* director in a welfare institute) and Pei-Yi (a *benshengren* manager in a pharmaceutical company) asserted their authority as managers when challenged by Caucasian colleagues; Ming-Feng, who was a *benshengren* bank teller, spoke up when her salary was unreasonably reduced due to a duty transfer; Wan-Jen, a *waishengren* manager in a real estate firm, asked for the promotion she deserved; and Ming-Feng, a *benshengren* technician in the pharmacy department in a teaching hospital, sought assistance from the Union to solve problems of unfair treatment and racial conflicts at the workplace. Although disadvantaged by both their minority status and gender, women across social class and ethnicity appeared to be more confrontational than their male counterparts in responding to mistreatment.[145]

"It's difficult for them [Caucasians] to hear Asian women say 'No'," said Wan-Jen, a 52-year-old female manager in a real estate company. Pei-Yi, another younger female manager in a large pharmaceutical firm also said, "Oh, I'm really tough at work, even though I'm Asian and a woman." Popular images of Asian women, such as passive, subservient, quiet, and docile, seem to be subverted in the case of these Taiwanese women. As a female professor, Ya-Chi, described, "They expect Asian women to be obedient and passive, but I'm not." But this "anomalous" behavior was described not only by middle-class informants. Even those who worked at the lower end of the production relationship (e.g., pharmacy technicians, bank tellers, factory laborers, and data-entry workers) also tended to show toughness when confronting racial issues in the workplace, thereby contradicting stereotypes of Asian women.

Previous studies that compare the working situations of Asian men and women argue that Asian women are more subjugated than Asian men because of their double disadvantage as non-male and non-White (Espiritu 1997; Man 2004; Ong and Hee 1994; Shin and Chang 1988). Such a double disadvantage leads to Asian women's marginalized status in the labor force, entrapping them in vulnerable positions. Not only patriarchal but also racist ideologies consign Asian women to a secondary and inferior position in the capitalist wage-labor market. As

---

[145] Only one second-generation woman reported race-related distress in the workplace. She considered this distress a result of her "Chinese style" of communication. By talking to other Asian friends who understood such a cultural difference, she was able to reduce her feeling of distress.

a result, they experience the work world as both gendered and racialized individuals, and obtain less economic resources than their male counterparts across social class (Chai 1987; Espiritu 1997: 61-85; Hossfeld 1994; Mazumdar 1989; Ong and Hee 1994; Raijman and Semyonov 1997; Shin and Chang 1988; Villones 1989; Williams 1989; Yamanaka and McClelland 1994). Nevertheless, the findings of this study illustrate that Taiwanese American women's double disadvantage in the labor force does not result in more reports of racial problems than their male counterparts. On the contrary, women (including working-class women) tended to feel more content with their working environment, were more likely to develop friendships with co-workers, and were less likely to form a social circle within the workplace composed of Asians only than were their male counterparts.

"It's impossible to fit into their [Caucasians'] social circle!"

As noted above, because of cultural differences in social skills, Taiwanese Americans (both men and women) felt not only discriminated against, but also excluded and estranged by the majority culture. Lacking "appropriate" social skills (e.g., playing golf, watching football, etc.) to mingle, Taiwanese Americans' working relations were racially or/and ethnically segregated. They (consciously or unconsciously) tended to socialize only with Asian co-workers, thereby reinforcing the racial and ethnic segregation that, in their view, was caused by the majority culture. This tendency was particularly evident among men, first-generation, and *waishengren*. [146] These three sub-groups were also less likely than their counterparts to develop friendships with co-workers. The following description provided by Wen-Ling, a female accountant in a private company, illustrates such racially or ethnically segregated social circles commonly seen at a work setting.

> We Taiwanese still get together with Taiwanese, mostly, but others are all the same…. Chinese with Chinese, Korean with

---

[146] More men than women (40%: 29%), more first than second generation (48%: 7%), and more *waishengren* than *benshengren* (50%: 30%) informants socialized only with Asians in the workplace.

Korean, White with White, and Black with Black.... Each ethnic group has its own circle. It's very common.

A few informants considered this phenomenon a "natural" result of cultural diversity. For instance, according to Chun-Hung, "You can communicate much more easily and deeply when talking to Taiwanese or Chinese. With Americans, I often don't know what to say. It's difficult to express yourself to them." A female teller in a Caucasian-owned bank, Ming-Feng, also explained:

They [Taiwanese and Chinese co-workers] understand you better because you share the same culture. For example, one time I brought some marinated chicken feet to our company. My Caucasian co-workers were scared to death when they saw that.... Ha ha.. They thought I was weird (smile)..... But my Chinese colleagues were very happy to share those chicken claws with me, and they really enjoyed it. You know how good they [chicken feet] taste, right?

In other words, the boundary between "we" (Taiwanese, Chinese, or other Asians) and "they" (Caucasians, Blacks, or Hispanics) in the workplace was fairly evident. As Min-Hui said,

At work, you have some social occasions. Like, your manager... you can feel your manager has his own people. Like, **only one or two of your co-workers are close to your boss. And, it'd never be us [Taiwanese]**.... Eventually, we have different backgrounds. **It's impossible for us [Taiwanese] to fit into their circle** very well.... But...**the good thing is that... in our company, we Chinese have our own circle of friends**.... We are closer to each other at work, compared with all co-workers in our company. Although the manager would not behave very obviously that he is closer to Americans [Caucasian] than Chinese, but you'd acknowledge this situation exists. So, **you wouldn't feel too bad if someone [Caucasian] gets promoted but you don't.** You'd feel ok, because **you're a foreigner anyway**.

(emphasis added)

Despite their differences in reasoning, many informants (especially first-generation men) felt distressed. [147] In their view, racially segregated social relations in the workplace were a result of racial discrimination and exclusion. Nevertheless, by keeping other racial or ethnic groups out of their own social circle, Taiwanese Americans obtained a feeling of solidarity and comfort. [148] This intentional or unintentional distancing from the majority culture not only eased their distress, but also served as a form of agency, resisting the power structures created mainly by race/ethnicity and culture in the workplace.

"Things could've been easier if I had a [female Asian] role model!"

Regardless of the assertiveness of female subjects at their work settings, as noted earlier in this chapter, women's lack of role models was a common pity. Several professional women (both *waishengren* and *benshengren*) stated that having a female role model would have eased frustrations and shortened their journeys to attain success. As Wan-Jen, a female manager in a real estate firm, said with a sigh,

> We're pretty much on our own, you know, there's no other Asian women in our company who I can model myself on. So, you've got to learn from your own experiences and observations. **It took me a long time and plenty of energy to achieve what I've had today. Things could've been easier if I had a [female Asian] role model**.   (emphasis added)

Chia-Ling, a female scientist in a large pharmaceutical company maintained,

> There are very few [female Asian] role models who you can follow. I would like to have a role model that I can identify with, or a path I can follow at work. It'd help me to foresee the

---

[147] Among the 14 informants who socialized only with Asians in the workplace, nine reported consequent distress. These nine informants were all first generation, including eight men and one woman, and five *benshengren* and four *waishengren*.

[148] This tendency was sustained across gender, ethnicity, and generation.

future of mine. Yet, there are very few role models for women, very few, and it's a huge limitation.

Due to the lack of role models, these professional women had to learn on their own the path to success. This disappointment, however, did not seem to obstruct them. By observing others, trying and making mistakes, and practicing what they learned in the process, these women accumulated experiences and wisdom, striving to succeed and overcome their limitations and disadvantages inherent in the social structure. Women's assertive form of agency was once again exerted in these cases.

CONCLUSION: UNBEARABLE RACIAL OTHERING

The labor market is not only gendered but also racialized (Brah 1994; Lutz 1994; Phizacklea 1994). It is also an arena to which ethnic groups bring their cultural and social orientations (Brah 1994). The workplace is therefore an institution where race/ethnicity, gender, and culture intersect to shape individuals' working experiences. As Hune (2000: 413) correctly points out, "race and gender are sites of power relations." Individuals' experiences as racialized and gendered actors in the workplace reflect their relations with co-workers, and these relations are marked by power. In this study, the informants' work experiences demonstrate that, in addition to race and gender, culture can also be an element of these power structures and relations. Chinese culture, represented through the informants' social skills and ways of self expression, become a mark of difference, disadvantage and, sometimes, inequality in co-worker relations.

International migration brought Taiwanese immigrants into a living milieu that links two socio-cultural worlds. In this transnational experience, however, men and women perceived and reacted to racial and gender discrimination differently. Although both recognized their cultural distinctiveness and that they were different from those who were in the majority culture, men tended to persist in their old "habitus" while women were apt to adjust themselves to new customs in order to fit in. For men, clearly identifying their Chineseness as the obstacle to economic achievement and joining mainstream social relations did not prevent them from emotional transnationalism. Knowing that they "should" act like Americans but "unable to do so" or "rather chose to maintain their Chinese style," men experienced ambivalent emotions that resulted from difficulties or unwillingness to cross the border of two cultural worlds. Their acceptance and acquiescence of the (racial and cultural) distinction between them and the majority culture, while in a way serving as a form of self-comfort, reproduced existing power relations at the workplace. In contrast, women tended to take a confrontational style of agency against power, thereby transforming imbalanced relations.

The informants' work experiences and consequent distress demonstrate the interplay among structure, culture, and agency. Within the racialized, gendered, and cultural structure of the workplace, Taiwanese Americans confront an on-going process of "two-way othering." On one hand, they are "othered" by co-workers' stereotypes and assumptions about Asians that sometimes lead to misjudgment or mistreatment. Taiwanese Americans are forced to deal with an "imposed racialized ethnic identity," as Tuan (1998: 157) terms it, and this is true even for some second-generation children who have lost ties to traditional cultural patterns. On the other hand, Taiwanese Americans also "other" themselves, thereby distancing themselves from the majority culture. By using terms such as "we Taiwanese (or Chinese)" and "they Americans," the informants create a distinction between "us" and "them," a distinction that consciously and continuously recognizes and highlights cultural differences and perpetuates their status as "the other."

In this study, the power of race (as well as culture) is more evident than gender in creating such two-way othering. As Chin (1997: 183) points out, "the issues of discrimination, identity, and alienation are closely interconnected and in many ways inseparable." In general, the commonly experienced "racial othering" frustrated, estranged, and alienated Taiwanese Americans in the workplace. In particular, the othering process produced not only gendered distress but also gendered strategies in claming agency. While significantly distressed, men adopted an accepting, acquiescent, or coalitional form of resistance by conforming to the role of "the other," thereby reinforcing their racial and cultural identification and maintaining the existing power relations. In contrast, although also distressed, women confronted structural inequalities in an assertive way by "de-othering" themselves.

CHAPTER 9

CONCLUSION – GENDERED TRANSNATIONAL STRUGGLES AND AGENCIES

As explained in Chapter Three, I utilized two frameworks in this study. The analytical framework illustrated my empirical concerns, investigating how immigration motives, familial relations, and work experiences affect mental health, and how these associations are related to the larger structure. The conceptual framework, in contrast, represented my theoretical concern, conceptualizing mental health from a structurative perspective. In this concluding chapter, therefore, I discuss the results and implications of this project in two different ways. I first summarize my major empirical findings according to the plan laid out in the analytical framework, and then discuss them from a structurative perspective. Following this discussion, I propose a "process model" to theorize Taiwanese Americans' mental distress. I conclude by addressing both the contributions and limitations of this study, and provide suggestions for future research.

A REVIEW OF MAJOR EMPIRICAL FINDINGS

My findings reveal that Taiwanese Americans' experience of distress is not only gendered but also transnational. They illustrate how gendered distress is experienced in a myriad of ways, and how transnational experiences intersect with gender in shaping Taiwanese Americans' emotional life.

First, within the whole sample, "education and migration" was the major pattern of immigration among Taiwanese Americans; the

249

majority of both men and women first came to the United States to study and then settled for job opportunities. When a comparison was made by gender, however, women were more likely than their male counterparts to migrate to unite families, and to settle for non-economic factors such as family reunion, children's education, political uncertainty in Taiwan, and a better living environment in the U.S. Moreover, middle-class and *benshengren* informants were more likely than their lower-class and *waishengren* counterparts, who relocated primarily for social reasons such as family reunion and children's education, to migrate for economic reasons, i.e., job opportunities.

"Men were pioneers, women followers" was the major pattern of decision making about immigration in the family, as most of the husbands made the decision to permanently relocate their families to the U.S. This tendency led to many women followers' regret that, although they had jobs, they did not have a career in the receiving society. Nevertheless, they enjoyed their work and were actively involved in social activities in the Taiwanese immigrant community. As a result, they tended to be both fatalistic and enthusiastic about their lives. On the one hand, Taiwanese women were willing to subordinate their wishes to those of their husbands, and believed that it was their "fate" and "duty" to follow their spouses wherever they moved, a tendency exemplifying a Chinese norm of appropriate womanhood. On the other hand, these women did not simply passively accept their "destiny," but rather, they passionately pursued alternative opportunities and created vibrant lives in their new homeland by going to graduate school, finding new jobs, or participating in social activities. Nevertheless, they continued to wonder if they might have had a "real career" had they remained in Taiwan.

Compared to their female counterparts, Taiwanese men experienced fewer emotional impacts from their choice to relocate in the U.S., mainly because most of them had been the decision-maker about immigration. Nevertheless, many men began to wonder if immigration had been the right decision when their children encountered problems with their self identity. Living in a society within which race is a significant factor that shapes inequality and discrimination, many second-generation Taiwanese went through a stage in which they struggled with their self-image and self-esteem. In contrast to the parental generation who retained their social circles in the Taiwanese immigrant community, second-generation children, from an early age, often directly suffered in dealing with their non-Asian peers. Despite the fact that the decision to migrate did not affect first-generation men psychologically in a significant way, because it produced an identity crisis in the next generation, the decision generated concern and worry about their children's ability to cope with their sense of self.

Second, in general, the gendered power structure in the Taiwanese American family took a patri-egalitarian form.[149] Although many couples jointly made important family decisions and shared domestic work, first-generation men sustained their dominant position in the family. Nuances existed, however, when the sample was compared across class and ethnicity. Middle-class couples were more egalitarian than their lower-class counterparts in all aspects (the decision to migrate, decisions about children's education, family finances, and the division of domestic labor). Among couples of different ethnic backgrounds, interracial (Taiwanese wife and Caucasian husband) families were the most egalitarian, while interethnic families were the most patriarchal.[150] *Waishengren* couples were more patriarchal than their *benshengren* counterparts in the decision to migrate, but more egalitarian in making decisions about children's education. These two types of family were similar in the way they divided household labor; both were patri-egalitarian.

---

[149] I analyzed the gendered power structure in the Taiwanese American family by examining how couples divided domestic labor and made decisions about immigration, finances, and children's education. The informants were fairly egalitarian concerning the decision about children's education, but patriarchal in the decision to migrate and division of household labor. Moreover, financial decisions in most Taiwanese American families were the responsibility of either a husband or a wife. I therefore used the term "patri-egalitarian" to describe this tendency (see Chapter Seven).

[150] Five of the eight interethnic couples in the sample were *waishengren* husbands and *benshengren* wives, and the other three were *benshengren* husbands and *waishengren* wives. When analyzing the gendered power structure between the couples, I did not find evident differences between these two forms of marriage.

Different aspects of the gendered power structure shaped various forms of spousal relationships and dynamics of family life, thereby producing different effects on men's and women's experience of distress. For instance, while women suffered from the tiredness associated with a "double-shift" because they were responsible for most domestic labor, men felt powerless to manage their children's education once they ceded authority for this matter to their wives.

In addition to the distress that directly resulted from the factors in my analytical framework (i.e., the division of domestic labor and decision-making power), I discovered other important issues that impaired Taiwanese Americans' mental health, especially women's, such as in-law relations and generational conflicts. In families within which mothers-in-law cohabited, first-generation Taiwanese American women were constrained by traditional Chinese norms that demand women adopt the roles of obedient wife and filial daughter-in-law. Such demands frequently caused women distress, no matter how "powerful" they were in their conjugal relations, how high their education was, how "Americanized" their social practices and values were, or how independent they were economically. Moreover, both generations of Taiwanese Americans, especially first-generation women, were concerned and bothered by inter-generational conflicts that were created by cultural differences. These conflicts can be illustrated by the differences in the two generations' values and behaviors concerning interracial marriage, education, and parent-child relationships. The unique "creolization" of Taiwanese Americans was produced by an on-going tug between Chinese and American cultures in everyday life, which, in turn, affected individuals' mental health.

Third, Taiwanese Americans' experiences of racial discrimination in the workplace engendered emotional strain more than did sexist treatment, and such work-induced mental distress was primarily a gendered experience. Racial discrimination in the workplace was broadly experienced among Taiwanese Americans, although the experience varied by social location. Men and first-generation were more likely than their female and second-generation counterparts to report the experience of racism, exclusion by co-workers, and report distress as a result of racial discrimination and segregation. In contrast, *waishengren* were more likely than *benshengren* to report being racially discriminated against, but were less likely to felt distressed as a result of racism.[151]

THEORIZING MENTAL DISTRESS: A STRUCTURATIVE PERSPECTIVE

As I discussed in Chapter Three, I approach mental distress from a structurative perspective and define it as a product of a situation in which *the confrontation between structure and individuals produces negative effects on individuals' psychological well-being*. The confrontation between structure and individuals is a sphere in which the dynamics of power is patent. It is also an ongoing and dialectic process within which various forms of agency are exercised. In individuals' social life, imposition of power (such as that which occurs within the context of social inequality shaped by gender, class, and race/ethnicity) that result in social inequality may, although not always, produce mental distress. When constrained by structure, individuals utilize available resources to negotiate, challenge, or resist the imposition of power. These acts of negotiation, contestation, or resistance are exhibitions of agency, signifying individuals as capable actors.

As a conceptual tool for theorizing mental health, this structurative perspective highlights the effects of socio-cultural structure, power relations, and agency on individuals' experience of distress. Using this framework, in Figure 9-1 I summarize the distress Taiwanese American men and women experienced and the contexts within which it was produced. Then, I elaborate on the material in the figure by discussing the contexts within which distress occurred ("Gendered Transnational Contexts"), cognitive responses to these contexts ("Gendered Emotional Transnationalism"), and Taiwanese Americans' agencies in the face of distress ("Gendered Agencies in Transnational Contexts and Struggles"). Finally, I propose a "process model" to theorize Taiwanese Americans' mental distress ("Process Model of Mental Distress – A Proposal Derived from the Case of Taiwanese Americans").

---

[151] As the privileged ethnic group in Taiwan, they were sensitive when encountering mistreatment. In contrast, perceiving racial inequality as a "norm" in American society, *waishengren* tended to accept their disadvantaged position and thus did not feel as distressed as their counterparts (see Chapter Eight).

Figure 9-1: Gendered Distress and Agencies in Different Socio-cultural Contexts

Contexts	Immigration		Family		Work	
Gender	Men	Women	Men	Women	Men	Women
Structure						
Social	1. general pattern: Education and migration	2. married couples: Men are pioneers, women followers	Patri-egalitarianism		Ethnicity, gender, and culture intersect in shaping inequalities	
Cultural	Chinese		Transnational		Transnational	
Individuals						
Distress	**Less,** Occurs when children face identity issues	**More,** Not having a career in the U.S.	**Less,** feel powerless about children's education	**Much more,** housework, conflicting cultural identification	**Much more,** racial discrimination, social exclusion	**Less,** racial discrimination, lack of role models
Power/Agency	Strategic	Redirective	Acquiescent	Situational	Acquiescent, Coalitional	Confrontational, Self-helping

Gendered Transnational Contexts

The social and cultural contexts within which Taiwanese Americans lived were transnational and gendered. Migrating to the U.S. from the island, Taiwanese Americans' social life was embedded in a transnational context, and deeply influenced by the social structures and cultural values of both the sending and receiving societies. The boundary between Taiwaneseness and Americaness was no longer clear. Socially, for example, American society has a much more significant hierarchical system of race than Taiwan. For Taiwanese immigrant men and women, therefore, the status of being "colored people" in the U.S. produces new life experiences, experiences that demands considerable social and psychological adaptation. As revealed in this study, Taiwanese immigrants' past ethnic relations on the island to some extent affected their attitudes and perceptions about their racially disadvantaged position in American society. For instance, *waishengren* and men, two privileged social groups in Taiwan, were more likely than their *benshengren* and their female counterparts to report experiences of racial discrimination, a product of "relative feelings of deprivation" that resulted from their shifting status from the advantaged (in Taiwan) to the disadvantaged (in the U.S.). In contrast, the status of being a visible minority for women did not cause as much burden because they were already disadvantaged before immigration.

Culturally, Taiwanese Americans were living in a transnational world that was built upon the interweaving of Chineseness and Americaness. This transnational cultural world provided a "miscellaneous pool" of values and norms, a repertoire from which individuals selected standards to guide and give meaning to their social practice. It also created varied contexts within which men and women produced, reproduced, and negotiated their cultural identification. The Chinese norm of *jia ji sui ji, jia gou sui gou* (married women should follow wherever their husbands move) played an important role in married women's decision to migrate. In the family and workplace, in contrast, both American and Chinese cultures affected Taiwanese Americans' social practices. Many couples practiced Western-styled egalitarianism in their spousal relations. First-generation women adopted an "American way" to manage unfair treatment in the workplace, but scrupulously abided by Chinese norms to behave as submissive daughters-in-law in the family. For many married women, the workplace was an "American world," while the family was a Chinese one. In contrast, first-generation men separated their family lives from work relations, a social practice that they considered "Americanized," but they maintained their public Chinese images as passive and quiet employees in the workplace. Because of their transnational background, Taiwanese Americans' cultural practices and identification were fluid, multiple, and sometimes contradictory within different contexts.

Gendered Emotional Transnationalism

Taiwanese American men and women experienced distinct emotional struggles. While work situations frustrated men, family life bothered women. For example, first-generation women encountered considerable emotional struggles within the family. They first faced the difficult decision to follow their husbands to live in a foreign country. At the outset, career women became homemakers and subordinated their well-being to that of their families. Although most women rebuilt their lives by going to graduate school or returning to the labor market after their children entered school, they continued to face various difficult situations that required considerable psychological adaptation. For instance, the burden of a double shift, the challenge of educating bi-cultural children, the ambivalence felt between behaving like a "good" Chinese daughter-in-law, and the impression management of acting "like an American" (rather than as a stereotypical Asian woman) in the workplace, in combination, created a complex context within which Taiwanese women experienced distress. Through these psychological struggles, first-generation women exhibited a fluid identification with their Chineseness and Americaness. When facing their "American children," Taiwanese immigrant women displayed anxiety and doubt that they were "sufficiently American." When facing their Caucasian colleagues, in contrast, they acted to contest social stereotypes about Asian women and to assert their Americanness when fighting for their own rights.

Within other contexts, these women struggled back and forth between American and Chinese social norms, looking for "appropriate" values and behavioral guidelines. For example, first-generation women suffered from the disturbance caused by their in-laws' "Chinese lifestyles" when they visited them, but were unable to manage this annoyance because they were expected (both by in-laws and by themselves) to meet the expectations of a "good woman" in Chinese norms, i.e., be caring, submissive, and tolerant. Although women tended to accept these Chinese norms, they did not want to. Such emotional conflicts, therefore, became a major source of women's distress in the family.

In contrast, Taiwanese American men's experiences of emotional transnationalism were mostly related to their work, especially in their perceptions of racial discrimination. Although Taiwanese American men recognized that their "Chineseness" was the primary factor that constrained work promotions, created racial segregation, and engendered psychological distress, they tended to adopt this label by "othering" themselves from the majority culture. Another example of first-generation men's emotional struggle can be illustrated by their worries about children's cultural identification, although this problem was much less serious than the distress engendered by their work.

Gendered Agencies in Transnational Contexts and Struggles

While Taiwanese American men and women were not too different in their psychological adaptation to the immigration decisions, they exhibited different styles of agency when encountering power. When dealing with the distress caused by the decision to settle, both men and women were fairly accommodating. Men adopted different strategies to help their children solve identity struggles, and women diverted their energy to work and social activities as a way to "compensate" for their regrets of not having a career. Because the distress associated with the decision to settle seemed minor, men and women appeared to manage well in their "journey of wondering." In contrast, as noted above, men and women experienced more evident emotional struggles in the family and workplace. They also took more diverse forms of agency in dealing with these struggles.

Men tended to adopt an acquiescent form of agency in both the family and workplace. Regardless of feeling powerless to make decisions about their children's educations, first-generation men usually did not take actions to change the power dynamics. Rather, they submitted to their wives' wishes, either to avoid potential arguments or simply because they considered the matter of children's education women's responsibility. In the workplace, although men felt enormously frustrated by racial inequality, they (both first and second generation) tended to normalize and justify their mistreatment and feeling of unfairness. Despite feeling excluded, they also tended to build their own social circle, excluding other racial groups from their orbit. Their acquiescence contributed to the maintenance of the status quo in the workplace, thereby reproducing the existing power structure. Chinese culture and men's role as the primary bread-winner in the family may contribute to their acquiescence in dealing with experiences of racial discrimination. While men may follow Confucian teaching that encourages the merits of hard work, tolerance, self-reservation, and silence, they also may not want to risk losing their jobs by fighting for equal treatment, especially in a "foreign" land where immigrants are disadvantaged in the labor market.

In contrast, the ways women exercised their agency was rather contextual. While redirective in dealing with distress associated with settlement decisions, their styles of exerting agency were situational in the family and confrontational in the workplace. Within the family, first-generation women were acquiescent, not bargaining for an equitable division of domestic labor. They were, however, assertive and insistent in terms of their children's education and courtship. While exhibiting authoritarian motherhood, these women tended to act as a submissive Chinese daughter-in-law despite the fact that such conformity contradicted their perceived Americaness and engendered enormous distress. In the workplace, by contrast, Taiwanese American women were aggressive and confrontational when encountering unfair treatment. They tended to challenge and change the existing power structure and relations when unfair treatment occurred. Probably women's (especially those who were married) flexibility in entering and leaving the labor market gave them more courage than men to confront conflicts in the workplace. Or, perhaps, women needed an "outlet" to release the distress resulting from their subjugation in the family. For women, the workplace appeared to be an "American arena" where they acted freely "like Americans," whereas the family was a "Chinese" sphere within which they were constrained by cultural tradition.

Process Model of Mental Distress –
A Proposal Derived from the Case of Taiwanese Americans

"Cases make no sense by themselves until they are linked to something more general" (Lazarsfeld and Rosenberg 1955: 388, quoted in Walton 1992: 124). After presenting findings of this study in two different ways, here I propose a model to theorize mental distress. My goal is to pursue what Walton (1992) states about the "generality" of a given case study, and what Haraway (1991) advocates as a production of "rational knowledge."[152]

As noted above, approaching mental distress from a structurative perspective systematizes my empirical findings in a way that highlights power relations between structures and individuals and their psychological impacts across contexts. By this approach I identify two key mechanisms, power and emotional transnationalism, that construct the context within which gendered distress is produced. In Figure 9-2 I present a model, what I call "the process model of Taiwanese Americans' mental distress," to illustrate the generality of this study in the view of a structurative perspective.

As noted above, within a power relation (e.g., conjugal, generational, in-law, co-worker), Taiwanese Americans search for behavioral guidance, meaning, and moral judgments from their "cultural toolkit" that contains both American and Chinese social norms. [153] This toolkit sometimes provides contradictory messages because it includes artifacts from two different cultural systems. These

---

[152] According to Walton (1992), although cases are situationally grounded, limited views of social life, they are not simply glimpses of the world or random instances of social activity. Cases always provide more or less sense of generality. Researchers therefore ought to make an argument about both the particular circumstance and the universe. Moreover, Haraway (1991) states that situated knowledges are about communities but not about isolated individuals. According to her, the only way to find larger vision is "to be somewhere in particular" in order to produce rational knowledge that preserves feminist objectivity (see Chapter Three).

[153] The concept of "toolkit" suggests the fluidity, spatiality, and interpretations of cultural meanings, as argued by Faist (2000b) and Swidler (1986). For more discussions, please see Chapters Three and Four.

conflicting messages engender psychological struggles – emotional transnationalism – about how one should behave in a given situation, thereby producing mental distress. To reduce such distress, individuals take different actions (e..g, to conform, acquiesce, or confront) that are exhibitions of personal agencies. These actions may transform or simply reproduce the power relation that was in place prior to the experience of emotional transnationalism and distress, thereby exerting different effects on individuals' psychological well-being (mitigating, sustaining, or exacerbating distress). In other words, individuals may or may not successfully reduce distress after transforming or reproducing power structures and relations, but exerting agency always empowers them.

As I demonstrated in Chapter Three, the encounter between individuals and structure are on-going and dialectic processes (Giddens 1979, 1984). Following this structurative viewpoint, the process of mental distress is not uni-directional. It does not end at the exertion of individual agencies. Rather, another process of distress may begin when the search for guidance and meaning provoked by the transformed or reproduced power relation once again creates ambivalent emotions, followed by personal actions of negotiation, contestation, or resistance. In this process of distress, socio-cultural structure (e.g., social systems, cultural norms, social locations of families and individuals) also affects how power relations are formed, if and how emotional transnationalism is engendered, and the ways individuals exert their agencies (see Figure 9-2).

Figure 9-2: Process Model of Taiwanese Americans' Mental Distress

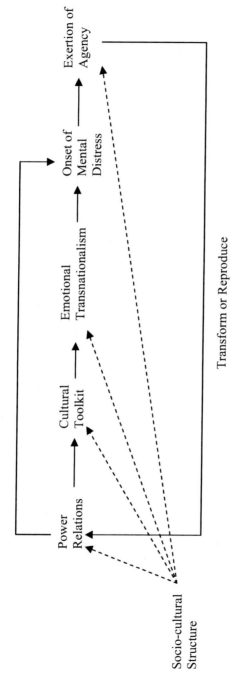

Power Relations → Cultural Toolkit → Emotional Transnationalism → Onset of Mental Distress → Exertion of Agency

Socio-cultural Structure

Transform or Reproduce

distress process

structural effects

Finally, the process in which mental distress is engendered may not always go through the whole path (power relations → cultural toolkit → emotional transnationalism → onset of mental distress → exertion of agency). In some circumstances, power relations directly produce distress without provoking emotional transnationalism (e.g., professional women's regrets about not having a career; men's feeling of powerless about children's education).[154] Yet, mental distress is most severe when it is engendered by the interweaving of power and emotional transnationalism (e.g., women's contradictory cultural identifications in the family; men's frustrations in the workplace).

CONTRIBUTIONS OF THIS RESEARCH

Findings in this study fill numerous gaps in existing knowledge about Asian Americans' experiences of distress. First and foremost, my study is one of the first qualitative studies to contextualize Asian Americans' emotional life. Previous studies that utilized clinical data or quantitative questionnaires ignored the social contexts within which distress is engendered. In contrast, by highlighting contexts, this research has enriched our understanding of mental distress among men and women. For instance, as this study has revealed, family was the most salient social institution within which women encountered enormous distress. In the family, women's inter-personal relationships with their husbands, children, mothers-in-law, and relatives created different interactive dynamics that produced varied experiences of distress. To explain this phenomenon, scholars who adopt a traditional quantitative approach may conclude that "familial relations" are a determinant force in women's distress. While such an approach answers the "what" question, the material I have documented in this book provides contextual illustrations responding to the questions of "how" and "why."

Second, sociologists have largely recognized that hierarchical social markers, such as gender, class, race or ethnicity, shape the

---

[154] It is also possible that individuals exert agency to resist imposition of power without experiencing emotional transnatinalism and distress. I do not include this direct connection between power relations and exertion of agency in my model, however, because this situation does not involve distress.

experience of people in different social locations. Adopting this standpoint perspective, this study highlights the heterogeneity of the sample and the effects of social location. This study further demonstrates how the influence of these structural positions on social and emotional lives varies across social settings and contexts. More specifically, this study takes immigrants' transnational background into consideration, examining informants' social locations across two societies. It therefore enhances our understanding about the complexity of structural (transnational, social, and cultural) effects on immigrants and their children.

Third, this research expands the concept of "emotional transnationalism," thereby enriching our understanding of the association between immigration and psychological well-being. In her study of Filipino youth, Wolf (1997) describes second-generation children's experience of emotional transnationalism. In this book I expand the notion of emotional transnationalism by giving it a clear definition and revealing its complex nature. I documented Taiwanese Americans' psychological struggles with the contradiction between their Chineseness and Americaness in the family and workplace, and how these struggles differed by social location (of both families and individuals) and varied under different circumstances. I also reveal how power interweaves with emotional transnationalism in shaping informants' experience of distress.

Fourth, my effort to theorize distress from a structurative perspective is an innovative attempt, pushing knowledge of mental health toward a new direction of theorization. By examining the dynamic and dialectic confrontation between structure and individuals and the way it affects mental health, this structurative approach highlights the importance of the contexts within which distress is produced. It also identifies two key mechanisms, power and emotional transnationalism, within the process of immigrants' experience of distress. Moreover, this study's approach to agency not only implicates the notion of structure into coping behavior, but it also empowers individuals as able social actors reacting to structural constraints. As I discussed in Chapter Two, one of the major gaps in the mental health literature is the neglect of social contexts. This structurative approach to theorization prioritizes the analyses of contextual factors of distress, thereby correcting this inadequacy. Its emphasis on the concept of agency also deters researchers from "othering" subjects.

LIMITATIONS OF THIS STUDY AND SUGGESTIONS FOR FUTURE RESEARCH

Every study is a work in progress, and therefore has its own limitations. Both the research methods I adopted and the nature of this research produced certain limitations in my findings. First, a substantial class bias exists in my sample. As detailed in Chapter Four, 89 percent of the informants I interviewed were middle-class. While this skewed distribution of social class may not deviate much from the general population of Taiwanese Americans because of the brain drain feature of their migration stream, it still led my investigation in a rather narrow direction and failed to reveal more about the social life of the lower-class. Conducting a study of lower-class Taiwanese Americans, however, may not be easy in practice. In addition to the fact that only a small portion of this population is lower class, Taiwanese Americans who work as laborers may not be "real" lower-class. Based on my observations and experiences in this project, many blue-collar workers own their own houses and luxury goods. Although lacking the skills and education necessary to find good jobs or to "assimilate" into the mainstream, they continue to have financial support from family that helps sustain well-off lifestyles in the U.S. This phenomenon may make the task of identifying lower-class individuals relatively difficult. Additionally, "real" lower-class Taiwanese Americans may not be easy to approach for interviews because most of them are already "burned out" by the effort to survive.[155] In spite of these difficulties, however, it is important and worthy of making efforts to understand the emotional life of lower-class Taiwanese Americans because social class itself is one of the key factors that produces inequalities in mental health.

Besides this sample bias, the dearth in knowledge about Asian Americans' and Taiwanese Americans' mental health essentially made

---

[155] Personal referrals through religious organizations would be helpful for recruiting lower-class informants because a variety of Taiwanese immigrants are involved in religious activities. Particularly those in need often obtain help, either spiritually or substantively, from religious groups.

this study an exploratory investigation. It was unable to investigate each subject of focus in detail, and often only explored issues at the surface level. For instance, the gender division of domestic labor, while serving only as one of the variables in the analytical framework, has had enormous scholarly discussion (see Presser 1994; Shelton 1996; Stafford 1977; Van Willigen and Drentea 2001). Factors such as the distribution of domestic chores (e.g., cleaning, cooking, doing laundry), feeling of fairness, employment status, number of children and their ages, perceptions of gender roles, social class, and race/ethnicity have all been examined to investigate how and why a couple make a certain arrangement. In this project, however, I did not examine each variable in detail, thereby leaving some gaps in my data that have constrained the depth of my interpretations.

Nevertheless, this deficiency, as noted above, builds the foundation for future work on distress issues facing Taiwanese Americans. For example, my study reveals that major sources of women's distress came from the family, especially their relations with in-laws and children. In contrast, men's distress was mainly caused by their experiences of racial discrimination in the workplace. These findings point out directions for future studies to pursue comprehensive examinations of women's familial relations and men's working experiences. In other words, by highlighting the structural contexts of mental distress, this study points out some issues that can be further refined. Below I provide specific suggestions for future research.

First, first-generation women's cultural identification within the family and workplace can be further examined. As revealed in this project, first-generation women frequently struggled with their identification as "American" or "Chinese" in their roles of mothers, daughters-in-law, and employees. Within which contexts do women identify themselves with the host or the sending counties and why? How effective are such identities in buffering distress? An investigation of women's cultural identification, its relation with transnational experiences, and its impact on mental health, would enrich sociological understanding of the subjects of gender and immigration as well as gender and mental health.

Second, religious (both Christian and Buddhist) organizations and large corporations that hire a great number of Asians could be important sources of information concerning the distress facing

Taiwanese Americans. Several informants in this study mentioned that they utilized the free counseling services their companies offered to help solve problems they encountered in the family and workplace. Collecting information from these firms, if possible, might be beneficial for understanding more about white-collar Taiwanese Americans' mental distress. Moreover, a diverse mixture of Taiwanese immigrants (both Christians and Buddhists) and their children (mostly Christians) are involved in religious organizations, from which they draw a sense of belongingness, ethnic identity, and assistance with adaptation. Why do Taiwanese Americans join a religious group? Is it related to their difficulties with adaptation and why? For which distress problems do Taiwanese Americans seek help from religion or religious groups? How effective is religion in buffering distress? Why do they choose a specific religious group (e.g., Buddhist, Christian, American, Chinese) to attend? Is this choice associated with their cultural or social identities? Why? Scholars have found the family to be an important resource on which Asian Americans rely for handling their distress (e.g., Rumbaut 1996; Sue et al. 1994; Wolf 1997; Uba 1994). Investigating the role of religion in Asian Americans' emotional life can highlight another social institution that serves similar functions with the family in buffering distress, yet has different characteristics and relations. Such an exploration would enrich sociological understanding of institutional effects on Asian Americans' mental health.

Third, interracial/interethnic courtships or marriages may be an interesting focus to explore the interplay of Taiwanese Americans' identification and perceptions of ethnic/racial and gender. As discovered in this study, second-generation Taiwanese Americans' courtships were one of the significant issues that engendered parent-child conflict in the family. In such a conflict, Taiwanese immigrants' conceptions about different racial and ethnic groups were exhibited and contested. These conceptions of the "other" also differed with respect to attitudes toward sons' and daughters' courtships. How do Taiwanese immigrant parents perceive the importance of race and ethnicity in their children's courtship or marriage? Do these perceptions differ in daughters' and sons' courtship or marriage? Why? How are these perceptions related to racial or ethnic prejudice in the larger society?

Courtships, therefore, could uncover the hierarchical intersection of racial/ethnic and gender perceptions.

Fourth, return migration can be studied to investigate the association between immigration motives and mental health from a transnational perspective. This subject, return migration, is particularly meaningful because it explores transnationalism from an Asia-centered perspective (Tseng and Jou 2000). International migration is one of the most drastic social actions, requiring considerable courage as well as social and psychological adaptation. As revealed in this research, the decision to migrate can cause mental distress, especially when the decision is not made by oneself. The decision to return, by the same token, is a radical move and may also engender psychological distress. How is the decision to return made in the family? Who is the primary decision-maker in the family about return migration? If and how does the decision-making process of return differ from that of emigration? What are the social and cultural factors that affect the decision to return? How do these factors differ from those of emigration? How does return affect individuals' psychological well-being? Are there any gender differences in this impact? What does return mean to men and women? How do the actions of emigration and return change the power relations of a couple and why? Investigating these issues would contribute to a comprehensive understanding of the immigration process as a transnational social action.

APPENDIX A:
OUTLINE OF INTERVIEW QUESTIONS

I. Social Demographic Backgrounds
1. gender
2. age
3. occupation(s)
4. education
5. year of migration
6. marital status
7. # of children (age, gender, etc.)
8. household situation
8-1. # of family members living in the household
8.2. geographic areas (e.g., suburban or Chinatown area)

II. Immigration Decisions and Mental Distress
1. major considerations or motivations to migrate to and settle in the U.S.?
2. whose decision to migrate?
3. whose decision to live in Chicago and why?
4. any psychological struggles because of immigration? How did you cope with these struggles?

III. Social Relations in the Family and Mental Distress
A. Gender division of domestic labor
1. who does domestic work at home? Do men share domestic work? Why or why not?
2. perceived contributions of domestic work to the family? overwhelmed by housework or double shift (both men and women)?
3. feel depressed or frustrated because of domestic work? How to deal with such emotions?

B. Family decision making
B-1. Financial decisions:
a. Who is in charge of finance for the family? Why?
b. Have you ever had any arguments with your spouse or parents about financial issues? How did you solve your disputes? Did you

feel stressed because of those arguments? If so, how did you deal
with the emotions caused by those arguments?

B-2. Children's education:

a.   Who decides children's educational issues in the family?
b.   Different expectations or rules for girls and boys? How and why?
c.   Any conflicts or arguments about children's education? How to
     deal with different opinions, if any, in the family?
d.   any conflicts or arguments between generations? Feel stressed?
     How to deal with these conflicts? How to deal with the consequent
     stress?

IV Social Relations at Workplace and Mental Distress

A. Racial and gender discrimination

1.   racial discrimination at work? How do you feel about it and deal
     with it?
2.   Does ethnicity constrain economic achievement at work? Do these
     constraints bother you? Feel frustrated? How to cope with
     frustrations?
3.   any sexist treatments at work? How do you feel and react?
4.   Does gender constrain your performance at work?
5.   Does race or gender affect you at work? Why? Which factor, race
     or gender, influences you more? Why?
6.   Do you feel frustrated or depressed because of racist or sexist
     treatment at work? How do you deal with such emotions? Do these
     experiences influence your motivation or interest for work? Why
     or why not?
7.   Who would you talk to about your problems at work?

B. Relationships with co-workers

1.   describe your relationships with your co-workers? (any good
     friends at work? Do you talk to them about your personal
     problems? Do you get together with them after work?) Please
     name three people at work you would talk to about your personal
     life and problems (white? Black? Asian?)
2.   feel depressed or frustrated because of not being included in the
     inner circle of social relations at workplace? How do you manage
     such frustration or depressive mood?
     perceived importance and social support from co-workers?

Appendix B:
Demographic Characteristics of the Sample

Age (N=54)

18-20	4 (7%)
21-30	14 (26%)
31-40	8 (15%)
41-50	13 (24%)
51-60	12 (22%)
61-70	2 (4%)
71 and over	1 (2%)

Gender (N=54)

Male	27 (50%)
Female	27 (50%)

Generation (N=54)

First generation	34 (63%)
Second generation*	20 (37%)

Class (N=54)

Middle class	48 (89%)
Lower class	6 (11%)

Ethnicity of Origin (N=54)

Benshengren	39 (72%)
Waishengren	15 (28%)

Marital Status (N=54)

Never married	21 (39%)
Married**	28 (52%)
Divorced	2 (4%)
Widowed	3 (5%)

* Includes two so-called one-point-five generation, who came to the U.S. at early age.

** Includes two women who were married to Caucasians, and one man who was in his third marriage. With the exception of the two women whose husbands were Caucasian, all informants' spouses were either first- or second-generation Taiwanese (including those who were divorced and widowed).

Appendix C: Coding Schemes

Broad Theme 1: Immigration and Mental Health (Chapter Six)
Subtheme #1: Decision maker or not
1. who made the decision to emigrate
   a. being the decision maker
   b. others made the decision
2. any gender/class/ethnicity of origin/immigration period differences?

Subtheme #2: The decision to migrate
1. motives for initial emigration
   a. family reunion
   b. job opportunities
   c. children's education
   d. better living environment
   e. political instability in Taiwan
   f. other considerations
2. motives for permanent settlement
   g. family reunion
   h. job opportunities
   i. children's education
   j. better living environment
   k. political instability in Taiwan
   l. other considerations
3. any gender/class/ethnicity of origin/immigration period differences?

Subtheme #3: Immigration-related distress
1. not being the decision-maker
2. regretting the decision to migrate
3. other factors
   a. adaptation difficulties
   b. feeling rootless
   c. job dissatisfaction
   d. homesickness
   e. feeling of self-sacrifice
   f. worry about the vanishing of Taiwanese heritage

4. any gender/class/ethnicity of origin/immigration period differences?

Broad Theme 2: Family and Mental Health (Chapter Seven)
Subtheme #1: Gender Division of Domestic Labor
1. how is domestic labor divided?
   a. the wife does all
   b. the wife does most of it
   c. fairly shared
   d. the husband does most of it
   e. the husband does it all
   f. hiring others to do it
2. any gender/class/ethnicity of origin differences?

Subtheme #2: Family Decision-Making
1. financial decisions
   a. the wife as the major decision-maker
   b. shared responsibility
   c. the husband as the major decision-maker
2. decisions concerning children's education
   a. the wife as the major decision-maker
   b. shared responsibility
   c. the husband as the major decision-maker
3. any gender/class/ethnicity of origin differences?

Subtheme #3: Family-related Distress
1. unequal division of domestic labor
2. powerless on family decision-making
3. other factors
   a. relatives
   b. mothers-in-law
   c. inter-racial and inter-ethnic marriages
   d. generational gaps
      (i) cultural differences
      (ii) values on achievement
      (iii) expressions of love
   e. religion
4. any gender/class/ethnicity of origin differences?

Broad Theme 3: Work and Mental Health (Chapter Eight)
Subtheme #1: Experiences of Discrimination
    1.   racial discrimination and the context
    2.   gender discrimination and the context
    3.   any gender/class/ethnicity of origin/generation differences?

Subtheme #2: Co-worker Relationships
    1.   close friends from work?
        a. what is(are) the friend(s)' race or ethnicity?
        b. activities after work
    2.   racial or ethnic segregation at work?

Subtheme #3: Work-related Distress
    1.   racial discrimination
    2.   gender discrimination
    3.   poor relationships with co-workers
    4.   other factors
        a.   job dissatisfaction
        b.   stereotypes about Asians
        c.   language barriers
        d.   glass ceiling
        e.   poor social skills
    5.   any gender/class/ethnicity of origin/generation differences?

BIBLIOGRAPHY

Agbayani-Siewert, Paulin, David T. Takeuchi, and Rosavinia W. Pangan. 1999. "Mental Illness in a Multicultural Context." Pp. 19-36 in *Handbook of the Sociology of Mental Health*, edited by Carol S. Aneshensel and Jo C. Phelan. New York: Kluwer Academic/Plenum Publishers.

Al-Ali, Nadje S. 2002. "Trans-or a-national? Bosnian Refugees in the UK and the Netherlands." Pp. 96-117 in *New Approaches to Migration? Transnational Communities and the Transformation of Home (Transnationalism)*, edited by Nadje Sadig Al-Ali and Khaid Koser. London: Routledge.

Alba, Richard D., and Victor Nee. 1997. "Rethinking Assimilation Theory for a New Era of Immigration." *International Migration Review* 31:826-874.

Allen, Elizabeth S., Donald H. Baucom, Charles K. Burnett, Norman Epstein, and Lynn A. Rankin-Esquer. 2001. "Decision-Making Power, Autonomy, and Communication in Remarried Spouses Compared with First-Married Spouses." *Family Relations* 50:326-334.

Aneshensel, Carol S. 1992. "Social Stress: Theory and Research." *Annual Review of Sociology* 18:15-38.

Aneshensel, Carol S., and Jo E. Phelan. 1999. "The Sociology of Mental Health: Surveying the Field." Pp. 3-18 in *Handbook of the Sociology of Mental Health*, edited by Jo E. Phelan. New York: Kluwer Academic.

Aneshensel, Carol S., Carolyn M. Rutter, and Peter A. Lachenbruch. 1991. "Social Structure, Stress, and Mental Health: Competing Conceptual and Analytic Models." *American Sociological Review* 56:166-178.

Astbury, Jill. 1996. *Crazy for You: The Making of Women's Madness.* Melbourne: Oxford University Press.

Baca Zinn, Maxine, and D. Stanley Eitzen. 1999. *Diversity in Families.* New York: Harper Collins College Publishers.

Bagley, Christopher R. 1993. "Mental Health and Social Adjustment of Elderly Chinese Immigrants in Canada." *Canada's Mental Health* 41:6-10.

Ball, Richard E., and Lynn Robbins. 1986. "Marital Status and Life Satisfaction among Black Americans." *Journal of Marriage and the Family* 48: 389-394.

Barbalet, J. M. 1985. "Power and Resistance." *The British Journal of Sociology* 36: 531-548.

Bartley, M., J. Popay, and J. Plewis. 1992. "Domestic Conditions, Paid Employment and Women's Experiences of Ill Health." *Sociology of Health and Illness* 14: 313-41.

Bebbington, P. 1996. "The Origins of Sex-Differences in Depressive Disorder - Bridging the Gap." *International Review of Psychiatry* 8: 295-332.

Becker, Gay, and Robert D. Nachtigall. 1992. "Eager for Medicalization: The Social Production of Infertility as a Disease." *Sociology of Health and Illness* 14: 456-471.

Bernard, Jessie. 1984. "Women's Mental Health in Times of Transition." in *Women and Mental Health Policy*, edited by Lenore E. Walker. Beverly Hills: Sage.

Bernal, G., J. Bonilla, and C. Bellido. 1995. "Ecological Validity and Cultural Sensitivity for the Cultural Adaptation and Development of Psychosocial Treatment with Hispanics." *Journal of Abnormal Child Psychology* 23: 67-82.

Barringer, Herbert R., Robert W. Gardner, and Michael J. Levin. 1993. *Asians and Pacific Islanders in the United States*. New York: Russell Sage Foundation.

Berry, John W., Uichol Kim, Thomas Minde, and Doris Mok. 1987. "Comparative Studies of Acculturative Stress." *International Migration Review* 21: 491-511.

Blair, S. L., and D. T. Lichter. 1991. "Measuring the Division of Household Labor: Gender Segregation of Housework among American couples." *Journal of Family Issues* 12: 91-113.

Bleier, Ruth (Ed.). 1986. *Feminist Approaches to Science*. New York: Pergamon Press.

Bloom, Shelah S., David Wypij, and Monica Das Gupta. 2001. "Dimensions of Women's Autonomy and the Influence on Maternal Health Care Utilization in a North Indian City." *Demography* 38: 67-78.

Brah, Avtar. 1994. "'Race' and 'Culture' in the Gendering of Labour Markets: South Asian Young Muslim Women and the Labour Market." Pp. 151-171 in *The Dynamics of 'Race' and Gender: Some Feminist Interventions*, edited by Haleh Afshar and Mary Maynard. London: Taylor and Francis.

Brettell, Carolin B., and James F. Hollifield. 2000. *Migration Theory: Talking across Disciplines*. New York: Routledge.

Brines, Julie 1993. "The Exchange Value of Housework." *Rationality and Society* 5: 302-340.

Broman, Clifford L. 1991. "Gender, Work-Family Roles, and Psychological Well-Being of Blacks." *Journal of Marriage and the Family* 53: 509-520.

Broverman, K. K., D. M. Broverman, F. E. Clarkson, P. S. Rosenkrantz, and S. R. Vogel. 1981. "Sex-Role Stereotypes and Clinical Judgments of Mental Health." Pp. 87-97 in *Women and Mental Health*, edited by E. Howell and M. Bayes. New York: Basic.

Brown, Tony N., Sherrill L. Sellers, Kendrick T. Brown, and James S. Jackson. 1999. "Race, Ethnicity and Culture in the Sociology of Mental Health." Pp. 167-182 in *Handbook of the Sociology of Mental Health*, edited by Carol S. Aneshensel and Jo C. Phelan. New York: Kluwer Academic.

Brown, T., K. Stein, K. Huang, and D. Harris. 1973. "Mental Illness and the Role of Mental Health Facilities in Chinatown." Pp. 212-231 in *Asian Americans: Psychological Perspectives*, edited by S. Sue and N. Wagner. Palo Alto: Science and Behavior Books.

Brubaker, Rogers, and Frederick Cooper. 2000. "Beyond Identity." *Theory and Society* 29:1-47.

Burawoy, M. (Ed.). 1991. *Ethnography Unbound*. Berkeley: University of California Press.

Burnam, M. Audrey, Richard L. Hough, Marvin Karno, Javier I. Escobar, and Cynthia A. Telles. 1987. "Acculturation and Lifetime Prevalence of Psychiatric Disorders among Mexican Americans in Los Angeles." *Journal of Health and Social Behavior* 28: 89-102.

Caldwell, R. A., J. L. Pearson, and R. J. Chin. 1987. "Stress Moderating Effects: Social Support in the Context of Gender and Locus of Control." *Personality and Social Psychology Bulletin* 13: 5-17.

Cavosora, Richard J. P. 2000. "San Francisco Guards Punished for Their Accents: Discrimination Spoken Here." Pp. 223-225 in *Asian Americans: Experiences and Perspectives*, edited by Timothy P. Fong and Larry H. Shinagawa. Upper Saddle River, NJ: Prentice Hall.

Centers for Disease Control and Prevention. 1999. *Health, United States*. U.S. Department of Health and Human Services.

Chang, Shirley L. 1992. "Causes of Brain Drain and Solutions: The Taiwan Experience." *Studies in Comparative International Development* 27: 27-43.

Chai, A. Y. 1987. "Freed from the Elders but Locked into Labor: Korean Immigrant Women in Hawaii." *Women's Studies* 13: 223-234.

Chakraborty, A. 1992. "Cultural Perspective in Indian Psychiatry." *Indian Journal of Psychiatry* 34: 1-2.

Chee, Maria W. L. 2005. *Taiwanese American Transnational Families: Women and Kin Work*. London: Routledge.

Chen, Hsiang-shui. 1992. *Chinatown No More: Taiwan Immigrants in Contemporary New York*. Ithaca: Cornell University Press.

Chen, Peter W. 1977. *Chinese-Americans View Their Mental Health*. San Francisco: R and E Research Associates.

Chen, Yu-Hua, Chin-Chun Yi, and Yu-Hsia Lu. 2000. "Women's Status in the Family: An Example of Family Decision Making." *Taiwanese Journal of Sociology* 24: 1-58. (in Chinese)

Chin, James W. 1997. "Asian Americans Still Face Significant Discrimination." Pp. 180-183 in *Asian Americans: Opposing Viewpoints*, edited by William Dudley. San Diego: Greenhaven.

China Post. 1990. "Emigration: The Third Choice Besides KMT and DPP." *China Post* January 9.

Cleary, Paul D., and David Mechanic. 1983. "Sex Differences in Psychological Distress Among Married People." *Journal of Health and Social Behavior* 24: 111-121.

Collins, Patricia Hill. 1986. "Learning from the Outsider Within: The Sociological Significance of Black Feminist Thought." *Social Problems* 33(6):14-32.

Collins, Patricia Hill. 1990. *Black Feminist Theory: Knowledge, Consciousness, and the Politics of Empowerment*. Boston: Unwin Hyman.

Conrad, Peter, and Joseph W. Schneider. 1992. *Deviance and Medicalization: From Badness to Sickness*. Philadelphia: Temple University Press.

Conzen, Kathleen Neils. 1991. "Mainstreams and Side Channels: The Localization of Immigrant Cultures." *Journal of American Ethnic History* 10: 5-20.

Davar, Bhargavi V. 1999. *Mental Health of Indian Women: A Feminist Agenda*. London: Sage.

Donnelly, Nancy D. 1994. *Changing Lives of Refugee Hmong Women*. Seattle: Washington University Press.

Dennerstein, Lorraine. 1995. "Mental Health, Work, and Gender." *International Journal of Health Services* 25: 503-9.

Dohrenwend, B. S., and B. P. Dohrenwend (Eds.). 1974. *Stressful Life Events: Their Nature and Effects*. New York: John Wiley.

Douglas, Many. 1975. *Implicit Meanings*. London: Routledge.

Doyal, Lesley. 1995. *What Makes Women Sick: Gender and the Political Economy of Health*. New Brunswick: Rutgers University Press.

Doyal, Lesley. 1979. *The Political Economy of Health*. London: Pluto Classic.

Eaton, William W., and Carles Muntaner. 1999. "Socioeconomic Stratification and Mental Disorder." Pp. 259-83 in *A Handbook for the Study of Mental Health: Social Contexts, Theories, and Systems*, edited by Teresa L. Scheid. Cambridge: Cambridge University Press.

Emerson, Richard M. 1962. "Power-Dependence Relations." *American Sociological Review* 27: 31-41.

Eitzen, D. Stanley, and Maxine Baca Zinn. 2000. *In Conflict and Order: Understanding Society* (Ninth Edition). Boston: Allyn and Bacon.

Espiritu, Yen Le. 2001. "All Men Are Not Created Equal: Asian Men in U.S. History." Pp. 33-41 in *Men's Lives*, edited by Michael S. Kimmel and Michael A. Messner. Boston: Allyn and Bacon.

Espiritu, Yen Le. 1997. *Asian American Women and Men*. London: Sage.

Fabrega Jr., Horacio. 1990. "Hispanic Mental Health Research: A Case for Cultural Psychiatry." *Hispanic Journal of Behavioral Sciences* 12: 339-365.

Fabrega Jr., Horacio. 1992. "The Role of Culture in a Theory of Psychiatric Illness." *Social Science and Medicine* 35: 91-103.

Faist, Thomas. 2000a. *The Volume and Dynamics of International Migration and Transnational Social Spaces*. Oxford: Clarendon Press.

Faist, Thomas. 2000b. "Transnationalization in International Migration: Implications for the Study of Citizenship and Culture." *Ethnic and Racial Studies* 23(2): 189-222.

Faris, R. E., and W. H. Dunham. 1939. *Mental Disorders in Urban Areas*. Chicago: University of Chicago Press.

Fee, Elizabeth (ed.). 1982. *Women and Health: The Politics of Sex in Medicine*. Farmingdale, NY: Baywood Pub. Co.

Flaskerud, Jacquelyn, and P. Y. Liu. 1990. "Influence of Therapist Ethnicity and Language on Therapy Outcomes of Southeast Asian Clients." *The International Journal of Social Psychiatry* 36: 18-19.

Foner, Nancy, Ruben G. Rumbaut, and Steven J. Gold (Eds.). 2000. *Immigration Research for a New Century: Multidisciplinary Perspectives*. New York: Russell Sage Foundation.

Foner, Nancy. 1997. "The Immigrant Family: Cultural Legacies and Cultural Changes." *International Migration Review* 31: 961-974.

Foucault, Michel. 1980. *Power/Knowledge: Selected Interviews and Other Writings 1972-1977.* Brighton: Harvester Press.

Foucault, Michel. 1965. *Madness and Civilization: A History of Insanity in the Age of Reason.* New York: Pantheon Books.

Freidson, Eliot. 1970. *The Profession of Medicine.* New York: Dodd Mead.

Fuchs, Stephan. 2001. "Beyond Agency." *Sociological Theory* 19: 24-40.

Gallin, Rita S. 2002. "The Politics of Resistance: Working-Class Women in Rural Taiwan." Pp. 61-78 in *Gender Politics in the Asia-Pacific Region*, edited by Brenda S. A. Yeoh, Peggy Teo, and Shirlena Huang. London: Routledge.

Gallin, Rita S. 1995. "Engendered Production in Rural Taiwan: Ideological Bonding of the Public and Private." Pp. 113-134 in *Engendering Wealth and Well-being,* edited by R. L. Blumberg, C. A. Rakowski, I. Tinker, and M. Monteon. Boulder, CO: Westview Press.

Gallin, Rita S. 1989. "Women and Work in Rural Taiwan: Building a Contextual Model Linking Employment and Health." *Journal of Health and Social Behavior* 30: 374-85.

Gans, Herbert J. 1992a. "Comment: Ethnic Invention and Acculturation: A Bumpy-Line Approach." *Journal of American Ethnic History* 11: 42-52.

Gans, Herbert J. 1992b. "Second Generation Decline: Scenarios for the Economic and Ethnic Futures of Post-1965 American Immigrants." *Ethnic and Racial Studies* 15: 173-192.

Garey, Anita Ilta, and Karen V. Hansen. 1998. "Introduction: Analyzing Families with a Feminist Sociological Imagination." Pp. xv-xxii in *Families in the U.S.: Kinship and Domestic Policies*, edited by Karen V. Hansen and Anita Ilta Garey. Philadelphia: Temple University Press.

Geertz, Clifford. 1983. *Local Knowledge.* New York: Basic Books.

Geertz, Clifford. 1973. *The Interpretation of Cultures.* New York: Basic Books.

Giddens, Anthony 1984. *The Constitution of Society: Outline of the Theory of Structuration.* Berkeley: University of California Press.

Giddens, Anthony. 1979. *Central Problems in Social Theory: Action, Structure and Contradiction in Social Analysis.* London: The MacMillan Press Ltd.

Gitlin, M. J., and R. O. Pasnau. 1989. "Psychiatric Syndromes Linked to Reproductive Function: A Review of Current Knowledge." *American Journal of Psychiatry* 146: 1413-1422.

Glass, Jennifer, and Tersushi Fujimoto. 1994. "Housework, Paidwork, and Depression among Husbands and Wives." *Journal of Health and Social Behavior* 35: 179-91.

Glazer, Nathan, and Daniel Patrick Moynihan. 1970. *Beyond the Melting Pot: The Negroes, Puerto Ricans, Jews, Italians, and Irish of New York City.* Cambridge: MIT Press.

Glenn, E. N. 1983. "Split Household, Small Producer, and Dual Wage Earner: An Analysis of Chinese-American Family Strategies." *Journal of Marriage and the Family* 45: 35-46.

Glick Schiller, Nina, Ninda Basch, and Christina Blanc-Szanton. 1992. "Transnationalism: A New Analytic Framework for Understanding Migration." Pp. 1-24 in *Towards a Transnational Perspective on Migration: Race, Class,Ethnicity, and Nationalism Reconsidered,* edited by Christina Blanc-Szanton. New York: New York Academy of Sciences.

Gold, Steven J. 1997. "Transnationalism and Vocabularies of Motive in International Migration: The Case of Israelis in the United States." *Sociological Perspectives* 40: 409-427.

Gold, Steven J. 2002. *The Israeli Diaspora.* London: Routledge.

Golding, J. M. 1990. "Division of Household Labor, Strain, and Depressive Symptoms among Mexican Americans and non-Hispanic Whites." *Psychology of Women Quarterly* 14: 103-117.

Goldring, Luin. 1996. "Blurring Borders: Constructing Transnational Community in the Process of Mexico-U.S. Migration." *Research in Community Sociology* 6: 69-104.

Good, B. 1977. "The Heart of What's the Matter: The Semantics of Illness in Iran." *Culture, Medicine and Psychiatry* 1: 25-28.

Gordon, Milton Myron. 1964. *Assimilation in American Life: The Role of Race, Religion, and National Origins.* New York: Oxford University Press.

Gore, Susan. 1992. "Social Psychological Foundations of Stress and Coping Research." Pp. 24-54 in *The Social Psychology of Mental Health: Basic Mechanisms and Applications,* edited by M. E. Oliveri. New York: The Guilford Press.

Gore, Susan L., and Thomas Mangione. 1983. "Social Roles, Sex Roles, and Psychological Distress: Additive and Interactive Models of Sex Differences." *Journal of Health and Social Behavior* 24: 300-312.

Gove, Walter R. 1987. "Mental Illness and Psychiatric Treatment among Women." Pp. 102-118 in *The Psychology of Women: Ongoing Debates,* edited by Mary Roth Walsh. New Haven: Yale University Press.

Gove, Walter R. 1972. "Sex Roles, Marital Roles, and Mental Illness." *Social Forces* 51: 34-44.

Gove, Walter R., and J. Tudor. 1973. "Adult Sex Roles and Mental Illness." *American Journal of Sociology* 77: 812-835.

Graham, H. 1990. "Behaving Well: Women's Health Behavior in Context." in *Women's Health Counts*, edited by Helen Roberts. London: Routledge.

Gu, Chien-Juh. 2000. "Asian Bodies in American Medical Settings: Taiwanese Immigrants' Medical Experiences in East Lansing." Paper presented at the 2000 American Sociological Association Annual Meeting. Washington, D.C.

Gu, Chien-Juh, and Rita S. Gallin. 2004. Taiwan. Pp. 848-857 in *The Encyclopedia of Sex and Gender: Men and Women in the World's Cultures,* edited by Carol R. Ember and Melvin Ember. New York: Kluwer Academic/Plenum Publishers.

Hall, Ellen. 1989. "Gender, Work Control, and Stress: A Theoretical Discussion and an Empirical Test." *International Journal of Health Services* 19: 725-45.

Handlin, Oscar. 1973. *The Uprooted.* Boston: Little, Brown, and Company.

Haraway, Donna J. 1988. "Situated Knowledges: The Science Question in Feminism and the Priviledge of Partial Perspecgtive." *Feminist Studies* 14: 575-599.

Haraway, Donna J. 1991. *Simians, Cyborgs, and Women: The Reinvention of Nature.* New York: Routledge.

Harding, Sandra. 1991. *Whose Science? Whose Knowledge?* Ithaca, NY: Cornell University Press.

Harding, Sandra. 1986. *The Science Question in Feminism.* Itaca, NY: Cornell University Press.

Harrell, S. and Huang, C. C. 1994. Introduction: Change and Contention in Taiwan's Cultural Scene. Pp. 1-18 in *Cultural Change in Postwar Taiwan,* edited by S. Harrell and C.C. Huang. Boulder: Westview Press.

Harper, Douglas. 1992. "Small N's and Community Case Studies." Pp. 139-158 in *What is a Case? Exploring the Foundation of Social Inquiry*, edited by Charles C. Ragin and Howard S. Becker. Cambridge: Cambridge University Press.

Hartsock, Nancy. 1983a. *Money, Sex, and Power.* New York: Longman.

Hartsock, Nancy C. M. 1983b. "The Feminist Standpoint: Developing the Ground for a Specific Feminist Historical Materialism." Pp. 283-310 in *Discovering Reality: Feminist Perspectives on Epistemology, Metaphysics,*

Methodology, and the Philosophy of Science, edited by Sandra Harding and Merrill Hintikka. Dordrecht: Reidel.

Hays, Sharon. 1994. "Structure and Agency and the Sticky Problem of Culture." *Sociological Theory* 12: 57-72.

Hekman, Susan. 1997. "Truth and Method: Feminist Standpoint Theory Revisited." *Signs: Journal of Women in Culture and Society* 22: 341-365.

Hing, Bill Ong. 1998. "Asian Immigrants: Social Forces Unleashed after 1965." Pp. 144-182 in *Immigration Reader: America in a Multidisciplinary Perspective*, edited by David Jacobson. Malden, MA: Blackwell.

Hing, Bill Ong. 1993. *Making and Remaking Asian America through Immigration Policy 1985-1990*. Stanford, CA: Stanford University Press.

Holli, Melvin G. and Peter d'A. Jones. 1995. "Introduction: Ethnic Life in Chicago." Pp. 1-14 in *Ethnic Chicago: A Multicultural Portrait*, edited by Melvin G. Holli and Peter d'A. Jones. Grand Rapid: William B. Eerdmans.

Horwitz, Allan V. 2002. *Social Control of Mental Illness*. Clinton Corners, N.Y.: Percheron Press.

Horwitz, Allan V., and Teresa L. Scheid. 1999. "Approaches to Mental Health and Illness: Conflicting Definitions and Emphases." Pp. 1-11 in *A Handbook for the Study of Mental Health: Social Contexts, Theories, and Systems*, edited by Teresa L. Scheid. Cambridge: Cambridge University Press.

Hossfeld, K. J. 1994. "Hiring Immigrant Women: Silicon Valley's 'Simple Formula'." Pp. 65-93 in *Women of Color in U.S. Society*, edited by M. Baca Zinn and B. T. Dill. Philadelphia: Temple University Press.

Houstoun, Marion F., Roger G. Kramer, and Joan Mackin Barrett. 1984. "Female Predominance in Immigration to the United States Since 1930: A First Look." *International Migration Review* 18:908-963.

Hsiao, Michael H. 1991. Immigration Issues. In *Report of General Taiwan SocialSurvey*. Taipei: Institute of Ethnology, Academia Sinica (in Chinese).

Hsu, F. 1985. "The Self in Cross-Cultural Perspective." Pp. 24-55 in *Culture and Self*, edited by A. J. Marsella, G. DeVos, and F. Hsu. London: Tavistock.

Huang, Hsin-Hui. 2000. "Taiwanese Men's Marriage Values and Participation in Domestic Labor." *Chinese Journal of Domesticity* 29: 59-80.(in Chinese)

Hubbard, Ruth. 1995. *Profitable Promises: Essays on Women, Science and Health*. Monroe: Common Courage Press.

Hune, Shirley. 2000. "Doing Gender with a Feminist Gaze: Toward a Historical Reconstruction of Asian America." Pp. 413-430 in *Contemporary Asian America: A Multidisciplinary Reader*, edited by Min Zhou and James V. Gatewood. New York: New York University Press.

Hurh, W. M., and K. C. Kim. 1988. *Uprooting and Adjustment: A Sociological Study of Korean Immigrants' Mental Health*. Final Report to National Institute of Mental Health. Macomb, IL: Department of Sociology and Anthropology. Western Illinois University.

Jabrega, Horacio Jr. 1990. "Hispanic Mental Health Research: A Case for Cultural Psychiatry." *Hispanic Journal of Behavioral Science* 12: 339-365.

Jayaratne, Toby Epstein, and Abigail Stewart. 1991. "Quantitative and Qualitative Methods in the Social Sciences: Current Feminist Issues and Practical Strategies." Pp. 85-105 in *Beyond Methodology: Feminist Scholarship As Lived Research*, edited by Mary Margaret and Judith Cook. Bloomington: Indiana University Press.

Jayasuriya, L. 1992. "The Problematic of Culture and Identity in Social Functioning." *Journal of Multicultural Social Work* 2: 37-58.

Kamo, Yoshinori. 1988. "Determinants of Household Division of Labor: Resources, Power, and Ideology." *Journal of Family Issues* 9(2): 177-200.

Kandel, D. B., M. Davies, and V. H. Raveis. 1985. "The Stressfulness of Daily Social Roles for Women: Marital, Occupational and Household Roles." *Journal of Health and Social Behavior* 26: 64-78.

Kandiyoti, Deniz. 1988. "Bargaining with Patriarchy." *Gender and Society* 2(3): 274-290.

Kanjanapan, Wilawan. 1995. "The Immigration of Asian Professionals to the United States: 1988-1990." *International Migration Review* 29: 7-31.

Kao, Grace, and Marta Tienda. 1995. "Optimism and Achievement: The Educational Performance of Immigrant Youth." *Social Science Quarterly* 76: 1-19.

Kaplan, Mark S., and Gary Marks. 1990. "Adverse Effects of Acculturation: Psychological Distress among Mexican American Young Adults." *Social Science and Medicine* 31: 1313-1319.

Kelly, M. Patricia F., and Richard Schauffler. 1996. "Divided Fates: Immigrant Children and the New Assimilation." Pp. 30-53 in *The New Second Generation*, edited by Alejandro Portes. New York: Russell Sage Foundation.

Kessler, R. C., and J. A. McRae. 1982. "The Effect of Wives' Employment on the Mental Health of Married Men and Women." *American Sociological Review* 47: 216-227.

Kibria, Nazli. 1990. "Power, Patriarchy, and Gender Conflict in the Vietnamese Immigrant Community." *Gender and Society* 4: 9-24.

Kibria, Nancy. 1993. *Family Tightrope: The Changing Lives of Vietnamese Americans.* Princeton, NJ: Princeton University Press.

Kim, Pan Suk, and Gregory B. Lewis. 2000. "Asian Americans in the Public Service: Success, Diversity, and Discrimination." Pp. 213-222 in *Asian Americans: Experiences and Perspectives,* edited by Timothy P. Fong and Larry H. Shinagawa. Upper Saddle River, NJ: Prentice Hall.

Kimmich, R. A. 1960. "Ethnic Aspects of Schizophrenia in Hawaii." *Psychiatry* 23: 97-102.

Kinzie, David J., and Wen-Shing Tseng. 1978. "Cultural Aspects of Psychiatric Clinic Utilization: A Cross-Cultural Study in Hawaii." *International Journal of Social Psychiatry* 24: 177-188.

Kitano, H. H. L. 1962. "Changing Achievement Patterns of the Japanese in the United States." Pp. 256-284 in *Changing Perspectives in Mental Illness,* edited by S. C. Plog and R. B. Edgerton. New York: Holt, Rinehart & Wilson.

Kitano, Harry H. L., and Roger Daniels. 1995. *Asian Americans: Emerging Minorities.* Englewood Cliffs, NJ: Prentice Hall.

Kivisto, Peter. 2001. "Theorizing Transnational Immigration: A Critical Review of Current Efforts." *Ethnic and Racial Studies* 24: 549-577.

Kleinman, Arthur. 1988. *Rethinking Psychiatry: From Cultural Category to Personal Experience.* New York: The Free Press.

Kleinman, Arthur, and Joan Kleinman. 1997. "The Appeal of Experience; The Dismay of Images: Cultural Appropriations of Suffering in Our Times." Pp. 1-24 in *SocialSuffering,* edited by Arthur Kleinman, Veena Das and Margaret Lock. Berkeley: University of California Press.

Krieger, Nancy, and Elizabeth Fee. 1996. "Man-made Medicine and Women's Health: The Biopolitics of Sex/Gender and Race/Ethnicity." Pp. 15-36 in *Women's Health, Politics, and Power,* edited by Kary L. Moss. Durham: Duke University Press.

Kuo, Chien-Lin, and Kathryn Hopkins Kavanagh. 1994. "Chinese Perspectives on Culture and Mental Health." *Issues in MentalHealth Nursing* 15: 551-567.

Kuo, W. H. 1984. "Prevalence of Depression among Asian Americans." *Journal of Nervous Mental Disease* 172: 449-457.

Kuo, W. H., and Y. Tsai. 1986. "Social Networking, Hardiness, and Immigrants' Mental Health." *Journal of Health and Social Behavior* 27: 133-149.

Kynaston, Chris. 1996. "The Everyday Exploitation of Women: Housework and the Patriarchal Mode of Production." *Women's Studies International Forum* 19: 221-37.

Landale, N. S., and R. S. Oropesa. 1995. "Immigrant Children and the Children of Immigrants: Inter- and Intra-Group Differences in the United States." Pp. 95-102. Research Paper. East Lansing: Michigan State University.

Lang, Olga. 1946. *Chinese Family and Society*. New Heaven, CT: Yale University Press.

Lai, Er-Jo, and Hsin-Hui Huang. 1996. "Married Men Participating in Domestic Labor." *Newsletter of Women and Gender Studies* 41: 10-18. (in Chinese)

Lazarsfeld, Paul F., and Morros Rosenberg. 1955. The Language of Social Research. New York: Free Press.

Lee, E. S. 1966. "A Theory of Migration." *Demography* 3: 47-57.

Lee, Jennifer, Annie Lei, and Stanley Sue. 2001. "The Current State of Mental Health Research on Asian Americans." *Journal of Human Behavior in the Social Environment* 3(3-4): 159-178.

Lee, M. L., Yang, Y. C., and Yi, C. C. (2000). The division of household labor: Employment reality or egalitarian ideology. *Taiwanese Journal of Sociology*, 24: 59-88. (in Chinese)

Lee, Yi-Ching. 1993. "Division of Household Labor in Double-income Families." *Domestic Education* 12: 49-56. (in Chinese)

Lefley, Harriet P. 1999. "Mental Health Systems in Cross-Cultural Context." Pp. 566-84 in *A Handbook for the Study of Mental Health: Social Contexts, Theories, and Systems,* edited by Allan V. Horwitz and Teresa L. Scheid. Cambridge: Cambridge University Press.

Lennon, Mary Clare. 1999. "Work and Unemployment as Stressors." Pp. 284-94 in *A Handbook for the Study of Mental Health: Social Contexts, Theories, and Systems,* edited by Teresa L. Scheid. Cambridge: Cambridge University Press.

Lennon, Mary Clare, and Sarah Rosenfield. 1992. "Women and Mental Health: The Interaction of Job and Family Conditions." *Journal of Health and Social Behavior* 33: 316-327.

Leung, Jin-Pang. 1998. "Emotions and Mental Health in Chinese People." *Journal of Child and Family Studies* 7: 115-128.

Levitt, Peggy. 2001. *The Transnational Villagers.* Berkeley: University of California Press.

Lin, C. 1990. Overcrowding Creates Taiwan Middle Class Exodus, *Free China Journal* October 5.

Lin, Chong-Cheng and Ho-Lin Lin. 1993. "Economic Differences among Ethnic Groups in Taiwan." Pp. 101-160 in *Ethnic Relations and National Identities.* Taipei: Institute for National Policy Research (in Chinese).

Lin, Holin. 1998. "Gender Culture as Economic Determinant: Household Resource Allocation Strategies among Ethnic Groups in Taiwan." *Journal of Social Sciences and Philosophy* 10: 611-659.

Lin, Holin, and Hsiang-Jie Lee. 1999. "Household Resource Allocation Strategies among Ethnic Groups in Taiwan." *Journal of Humanities and Social Sciences* 11: 475-528. (in Chinese)

Lin, Keh-Ming, and Freda Cheung. 1999. "Mental Health Issues for Asian Americans." *Psychiatric Services* 50: 774-780.

Lin, Nan, R. S. Simeone, W. M. Ensel, and W. Kuo. 1979. "Social Support, Stressful Life Events, and Illness: A Model and an Empirical Test." *Journal of Health and Social Behavior* 20: 108-119.

Loo, C., and P. Ong. 1982. "Slaying Demons with a Sewing Needle: Feminist Issues for Chinatown's Women." *Berkeley Journal of Sociology* 27: 77-88.

Loo, Chalsa, Ben Tong, and Reiko True. 1989. "A Bitter Bean: Mental Health Status and Attitudes in Chinatown." *Journal of Community Psychology* 17: 283-296.

Louie, Andrea. 2000. "Re-Territorializing Transnationalism: Chinese Americans and the Chinese Motherland." *American Ethnologist* 27: 645-669.

Louie, Andrea. 2004. *Chineseness across Borders: Renegotiating Chinese Identities in China and the United States.* Durham: Duke University Press.

Lowe, Lisa. 1996. *Immigrant Acts.* Durham, NC: Duke University Press.

Lowis, G.W., and P.G. McCaffery. 2004. "Sociological Factors Affecting the Medicalization of Midwifery." in *Midwifery and the Medicalization of Childbirth: Comparative Perspectives*, edited by E. van Teijlingen, G. Lowis, P. McCaffery, and M. Porter. New York: Nova Science.

Lu, Yu-Hsia. 1980. "Women's Attitudes toward Career Role and Family Role underthrough Taiwan's Social Change." *Bulletin of the Institute of Ethnology, Academia Sinica* 50: 25-66. Taipei. (in Chinese)

Lu, Yu-Hsia, and Chin-Chun Yi. 1996. "Evaluating the studies of family and
    women in Taiwan." in *The Development and Interflow of Sociological
    Studies in Taiwan, China, and Hong Kong*, edited by M. H. Hsiao and Y.
    H. Chang. Taipei: Taiwanese Sociological Association. (in Chinese).
Lum, Roger. 1985. "A Community-Based Mental Health Service to Southeast
    Asians Refugees." Pp. 283-306 in *Southeast Asian Mental Health:
    Treatment, Prevention, Services, Training, and Research*, edited by Tom
    Owan. Washington, DC: U.S. Department of Health and Human Services.
Lutz, C., and G. White. 1986. "The Anthropology of Emotions." *Annual
    Review of Anthropology* 15: 405-436.
Lutz, Helma. 1994. "The Tension between Ethnicity and Work: Immigrant
    Women in the Netherlands." Pp. 182-195 in *The Dynamics of 'Race' and
    Gender: Some Feminist Interventions*, edited by Haleh Afshar and Mary
    Maynard. London: Taylor and Francis.
Man, Guida. 2004. "Gender, Work, and Migration: Deskilling Chinese
    Immigrant Women in Canada." *Women's Studies International Forum*
    27(2): 135-148.
Marini, Margaret Mooney and Beth Ann Shelton. 1993. "Measuring Household
    Work: Recent Experience in the United States." *Social Science Research*
    22: 361-382.
Marsella, et al. 1985. "Cross-Cultural Studies of Depressive Disorders." Pp.
    299-324 in *Culture and Depression*, edited by B. Good. Berkeley:
    University of California Press.
Matsuoka, Jon K., Cynthia Breaux, and Donald H. Ryujin. 1997. "National
    Utilization of Mental Health Services by Asian Americans/Pacific
    Islanders." *Journal of Community Psychology* 25: 141-145.
Mazumdar, S. 1989. "General Introduction: A Women-Centered Perspective on
    Asian American History." Pp. 1-22 in *Making Waves: An Anthology by
    and about Asian American Women*, edited by Asian Women United of
    California. Boston: Beacon.
McCracken, Grant D. 1988. *The Long Interview*. Newbury Park, CA: Sage.
McGrath, E., G. P. Keita, B. R. Strickland, and N. F. Russo. 1990. *Women and
    Depression: Risk Factors and Treatment Issues*. Washington, D.C.:
    American Psychological Association.
McIntosh, Peggy. 2003. "White Privilege and Male Privilege." Pp. 70-80 in
    Reconstructing Gender, edited by Estelle Disch. Boston: McGraw Hill.

Meinhardt, Kenneth, Soleng Tom, Philip Tse, and Connie Young Yu. 1985. "Southeast Asian Refugees in the 'Silicon Valley': The Asian Health Assessment Project." *Amerasia* 12: 43-65.

Merton, Robert K., Marjorie Fiske, and Patricia L. Kendall. 1990. *The Focused Interview: A Manual of Problems and Procedures.* New York: Free Press.

Messias, Deanne K., Eun-Ok Im, Aroha Page, Hanna Regev, Judith Spiers, Laurie Yoder, and Afaf I. Meleis. 1997. "Defining and Redefining Work: Implications for Women's Health." *Gender and Society* 11(3): 296-323

Michels, R., and P. M. Marzuk. 1993. "Progress in Psychiatry: Part I." *New England Journal of Medicine* 329: 552-560.

Miles, A. 1988. *Women and Mental Health: The Social Context of Female Neurosis.* Brighton: Wheatsheaf Books.

Miller, J. 1976. *Toward a New Psychology of Women.* Boston: Beacon Press.

Mintz, Sidney W., and Richard Price. 1992. *The Birth of African-American Culture: An Anthropological Perspective.* Boston: Beacon Press.

Mirowsky, John, and Catherine E. Ross. 1986. "Social Patterns of Distress." *AnnualReview of Sociology* 12: 23-45.

Mirowsky, John, and Catherine E. Ross. 1986. "Social Patterns of Distress." *Annual Review of Sociology* 12: 23-45.

Mirowsky, John, and Catherine E. Ross. 1995. "Sex Differences in Distress: Real or Artifact?" *American Sociological Review* 60: 449-68.

Morawska, Ewa. 2003. "Disciplinary Agendas and Analytic Strategies of Research on Immigrant Transnationalism: Challenges of Interdisciplinary Knowledge." *International Migration Review* 37(3): 611-640.

Moritsugu, J., and S. Sue. 1983. "Minority Status as a Stressor." in *Preventive Psychology: Theory Research and Practice,* edited by R. Felner, L. Jason, J. Moritsugu, and S. Farber. New York: Pergamon Press.

Morokvasic, M. 1984. "Birds of Passage Are Also Women." *International Migration Review* 18: 886-907.

Morris, Lydia. 1990. *The Workings of the Household.* Cambridge: Polity Press.

Moy, Susan. 1995. "The Chinese in Chicago: The First One Hundred Years." Pp. 378-408 in *Ethnic Chicago: A Multicultural Portrait,* edited by Melvin G. Holli and Peter d'A. Jones. Grand Rapid: William B. Eeerdmans.

Newman, Joy P. 1986. "Gender, Life Strains and Depression." *Journal of Health and Social Behavior* 27: 161-178.

Ng, Franklin. 1998. *The Taiwanese Americans.* Westport, Connecticut: Greenwood Press.

Niles, F. Sushila. 1999. "Stress, Coping and Mental Health among Immigrants to Australia." Pp. 293-307 in *Merging Past, Present, and Future in Cross-Cultural Psychology: Select Papers from the Fourteenth International Congress of the International Association for Cross-Cultural Psychology*, edited by Walter J. Lonner and Dale L. Dinnel. Lisse, Netherlands: Swets & Zeitlinger.

Noh, Samuel, and William R. Avison. 1996. "Asian Immigrants and the Stress Process: A Study of Koreans in Canada." *Journal of Health and Social Behavior* 37: 192-206.

Nolen-Hoeksema, Susan. 1990. *Sex Differences in Depression*. Stanford: Stanford University Press.

O'Connor, Mary I. 1990. "Women's Networks and the Social Needs of Mexican Immigrants." *Urban Anthropology* 19: 81-98,

Olwig, Karen Fog. 2003. ""Transnational" Socio-Cultural Systems and Ethnographic Research: Views from an Extended Field Site." *International Migration Review* 37(3): 787-811.

Ong, Aihwa. 1999. *Flexible Citizenship: The Cultural Logic of Transnationality*. Durham, NC: Duke University Press.

Ong, Aihwa. 1996. "Cultural Citizenship as Subject-Making: Immigrants Negotiate Racial and Cultural Boundaries in the United States." *Current Anthropology* 37: 737-762.

Ong, Paul and E. Blumenberg. 1994. "Scientists and Engineers." Pp. 165-189 in *The State of Asian Pacific America: Economic Diversity, Issues, and Policies*, edited by Paul Ong. Los Angeles: LEAP Asian Pacific American Public Policy Institute and University of California at Los Angeles, Asian American Studies Center.

Ong, Paul and S. Hee. 1994. "Economic Diversity." Pp. 31-56 in *The State of Asian Pacific America: Economic Diversity, Issues, and Policies*, edited by Paul Ong. Los Angeles: LEAP Asian Pacific American Public Policy Institute and University of California at Los Angeles, Asian American Studies Center.

Ong, Paul, and John M. Liu. 1994. "U.S. Immigration Policies and Asian Migration." Pp. 45-73 in *The New Asian Immigration in Los Angeles and Global Restructuring*, edited by Paul Ong, Edna Bonacich, and Lucie Cheng. Phildelphia: Temple University Press.

Padilla, Amado M., Richard C. Cervantes, Margarita Maldonado, and Rosa E. Garcia. 1988. "Coping Responses to Psychosocial Stressors among Mexican and Central American Immigrants." *Journal of Community Psychology* 64:418-427.

Park, Jung-Sun. 1997. *Identity and Politics in a Transnational Community: A Case of Chicago Korean-Americans.* Doctoral Dissertation, Department of Anthropology, Northwestern University. Evanston, IL: Northwestern University.

Park, R. E. 1928. "Human Migration and the Marginal Man." *American Journal of Sociology* 33: 881-893.

Parker, G., G. Gladstone, and K. Tsee-Chee. 2001. "Depression int eh Planet's Largest Ethnic Group: The Chinese." *American Journal of Psychiatry* 158(6): 857-864.

Parrillo, Vincent N. 1991. "The Immigrant Family: Search the American Dream." *Journal of Comparative Family Studies* 22: 131-145.

Pearlin, Leonard I. 1999. "Stress and Mental Health: A Conceptual Overview." Pp. 161-75 in *A Handbook for the Study of Mental Health: Social Contexts, Theories, and Systems*, edited by Teresa Scheid. Cambridge: Cambridge University Press.

Pearlin, Leonard I. 1975. "Sex Roles and Depression." in *Life Span Developmental Psychology: Normative Life Crisis*, edited by L. H. Ginsberg. New York: Academic Press.

Perlmann, Joel, and Roger Waldinger. 1996. "Second Generation Decline? Children of Immigrants, Past and Present -- A Reconsideration." *International Migration Review* 31: 893-922.

Pessar, Patricia R., and Sarah J. Mahler. 2003. "Transnational Migration: Bringing Gender In." *International Migration Review* 37(3): 812-846.

Phelan, Jo C., and Bruce G. Link. 1999. "The Labeling Theory of Mental Disorder (I): The Role of Social Contingencies in the Application of Psychiatric Labels." Pp. 139-150 in *A Handbook for the Study of Mental Health: Social Contexts, Theories, and Systems*, edited by Teresa L. Scheid. Cambridge: Cambridge University Press.

Phizacklea, Annie. 1994. "A Single or Segregated Market? Gendered and Racialized Divisions." Pp. 172-181 in *The Dynamics of 'Race' and Gender: Some Feminist Interventions*, edited by Haleh Afshar and Mary Maynard. London: Taylor and Francis.

Portes, Alejandro. 2003. "Conclusion: Theoretical Convergencies and Empirical Evidence in the Study of Immigrant Transnationalism." *International Migration Review* 37(3): 847-892.

Portes, Alejandro. 1998. "Divergent Destinities: Immigration, the Second
   Generation, and the Rise of Transnational Communities." Pp. 33-57 in
   *Paths to Inclusion: The Integration of Migrants in the United States and
   Germany,* edited by Rainer Munz. New York: Berghahn Books.

Portes, Alejandro. 1996a. "Transnational Communities: Their Emergence and
   Significance in the Contemporary World-System." Pp. 151-168 in *Latin
   America in the World-Economy,* edited by William C. Smith. Westport,
   CT: Greenwood Press.

Portes, Alejandro, ed. 1996b. *The New Second Generation.* New York: Russel
   Sage Foundation.

Portes, Alejandro. 1984. "The Rise of Ethnicity." *American Sociological
   Review* 49: 383-397.

Portes, Alejandro, and Jozsef Borocz. 1989. "Contemporary Immigration:
   Theoretical Perspectives on Its Determinants and Modes of incorporation."
   International Migration Review 23: 606-630.

Portes, Alejandro, Luis E. Guarnizo, and Patricia Landolt. 1999. "The
   Study of Transnationalism: Pitfalls and Promise of an Emergent Research
   Field." *Ethnic and Racial Studies* 22: 217-237.

Portes, Alejandro, and Ruben G. Rumbaut. 2001. *Legacies: The Story of The
   Immigrant Second Generation.* Berkeley: University of California Press.

Portes, Alejandro, and Ruben G. Rumbaut. 1996. *Immigrant America:
   A Portrait.* Berkeley: University of California Press.

Portes, Pedro R., and Madelon F. Zady. 2002. "Self-Esteem in the Adaptation
   of Spanish-Speaking Adolescents: The Role of Immigration, Family
   Conflict, and Depression." *Hispanic Journal of Behavioral Science* 24:
   296-318.

Portes, Alejandro, and Min Zhou. 1993. "The New Second Generation:
   Segmented Assimilation and Its Variants among Post-1965 Immigrant
   Youth." *Annals of the American Academy of Political and Social Science*
   530: 74-98.

Presser, Harriet B. 1994. "Employment Schedules among Dual-earner Spouses
   and the Division of Household Labor by Gender." *American Sociological
   Review* 59: 348-364.

Pugliesi, Karen. 1992. "Women and Mental Health: Two Traditions of Feminist
   Research." *Women and Health* 19: 43-68.

Radloff, L. 1975. "Sex Differences in Depression: The Effects of
   Occupational and Marital Status." *Sex Roles* 1: 249-265.

Ragin, Charles C. 1992. "Introduction: Cases of "What is a case?"" Pp. 1-18 in
What is a Case? Exploring the Foundations of Social Inquiry, edited by
Charles C. Ragin and Howard S. Becker. Cambridge: Cambridge
University Press

Raijman, Rebeca, and Moshe Semyonov. 1997. "Gender, Ethnicity, and
Immigration: Double Disadvantage and Triple Disadvantage among
Recent Immigrant Women in the Israeli Labor Market." *Gender & Society*
11(1): 108-125.

Reskin, B. F., and S. Coverman. 1985. "Sex and Race in the Determinants of
Psychophysical Distress: A Reappraisal of the Sex-Role Hypothesis."
Social Forces 63: 1038-1059.

Robinson, J. P. 1988. "Who's Doing the Housework?" *American Demographics*
10: 24-63.

Rogler, L. H. 1989. "The Meaning of Culturally Sensitive Research in Mental
Health." *American Journal of Psychiatry* 146(3): 296-303.

Rosenfield, Sarah. 1999. "Gender and Mental Health: Do Women Have more
Psychopathology, Men More, or Both the Same (and Why?)." Pp. 348-60
in *A Handbook for the Study of Mental Health: Social Contexts, Theories,
and Systems*, edited by Teresa L. Scheid. Cambridge: Cambridge
University Press.

Rosenfield, Sarah. 1989. "The Effects of Women's Employment: Personal
Control and Sex Differences in Mental Health." *Journal of Health and
Social Behavior* 25: 14-23.

Rosewater, Lynne Bravo. 1985. "Schizophrenic, Borderline, or Battered?" in
Handbook of Feminist Therapy: Women's Issues in Psychotherapy, edited
by Lynne Bravo Rosewater and Lynore E. Walker. New York: Springer.

Ross, Catherine E. 1987. "The Division of Labor at Home." *Social Forces* 65:
816-833.

Ross, C. E., J. Mirowski, and J. Huber. 1983. "Dividing Work, Sharing Work
and in-between: Marriage Patterns and Depression." *American
Sociological Review* 48: 809-823.

Rubin, Herbert J., and Irene S. Rubin. 1995. *Qualitative Interviewing: The Art
of Hearing Data*. London: Sage.

Rumbaut, Ruben G. 1999a. "Assimilation and Its Discontents: Ironies and
Paradoxes." Pp. 172-195 in *The Handbook for International Migration:
The American Experience*, edited by Philip Kasinitz. New York: Russell
Sage Foundation.

Rumbaut, Ruben G. 1999b. "Passages to Adulthood: The Adaptation of
    Children of Immigrants in Southern California." Pp. 478-545 in
    Children of Immigrants: Health, Adjustment, and Public Assistance,
    edited by Donald J. Hern'Elndez. Washington, DC: National
    Academy Press.

Rumbaut, Ruben G. 1997. "Ties that Bind: Immigration and Immigrant
    Families in the United States." Pp. 3-46 in *Immigration and the Family:*
    Research and Policy on U.S. Immigrants, edited by Alan Booth, Ann C.
    Crouter, and Nancy Landale. Mahwah: Lawrence Erlbaum Associates

Rumbaut, Ruben G. 1996. "The Crucible Within: Ethnic Identity, Self-Esteem,
    and Segmented Assimilation among Children of Immigrants." Pp. 119-
    170 in *The New Second Generation,* edited by Alejandro Portes. New
    York: Russell Sage Foundation.

Rumbaut, Ruben G. 1989. "Portraits, Patterns, and Predictors of the Refugee
    Adaptation Process." Pp. 138-182 in *Refugees as Immigrants:*
    Cambodians, Laotians and Vietnamese in America, edited by David W.
    Haines. Totowa, N.J.: Rowman & Littlefield.

Rumbaut, Ruben G., and Kenji Ima. 1988. *The Adaptation of Southeast Asian*
    Refugee Youth: A Comparative Study. Washington, D.C.: U.S. Office of
    Refugee Resettlement.

Schilier, Nina Glick, Linda Basch, and Cristina Blac-Szanton. 1999.
    "Transnationalism: A New Analytic Framework for Understanding
    Migration." Pp. 26-49 in *Migration, Diasporas, and Transnationalism,*
    edited by Robin Cohen. Northampton, MA: Edward Elgar Publishing, Inc.

Schnittker, Jason. 2000. "Acculturation in Context: The Psychological Well-
    Being of Chinese Immigrants." Paper presented at the 2000 American
    Sociological Association Annual Meeting.

Sewell, Jr. William H. 1992. "A Theory of Structure: Duality, Agency, and
    Transformation." *The American Journal of Sociology* 98: 1-29.

Shelton, Beth Anne, and Daphne John. 1996. "The Division of Household
    Labor." *Annual Review of Sociology* 22: 299-322.

Shin, E. H., and K. S. Chang. 1988. "Peripheralization of Immigrant
    Professionals: Korean Physicians in the United States." *International*
    Migration Review 22: 609-626.

Shiva, Vandana (ed). 1994. *Close to Home: Women Reconnect Ecology,*
    Health and Development Worldwide. Philadelphia: New Society
    Publishers.

Showalter, Elaine. 1985. *The Female Malady: Women, Madness, and English Culture, 1830-1980.* New York: Pantheon.

Shu, Weider. 2001. Dissident Voices from Far Away. *Taiwan Historical Materials Studies* 17: 99-155 (in Chinese).

Simon, Robin W. 2002. "Revisiting the Relationships among Gender, Marital Status, and Mental Health." *American Journal of Sociology* 107(4): 1065-1096.

Simon, Robin W. 1995. "Gender, Multiple Roles, Role Meaning, and Mental Health." *Journal of Health and Social Behavior* 36: 182-94.

Smith, Dorothy. 1987a. *The Everyday World as Problematic: A Feminist Sociology.* Boston: Northeastern University Press.

Smith, Dorothy. 1987b. "Women's Perspective as a Radical Critique of Sociology." Pp. 84-96 in *Feminism and Methodology*, edited by Sandra Harding. Bloomington: Indiana University Press.

Smith, Raymond Thomas. 1988. *Kinshi and Class in the West Indies.* Cambridge: Cambridge University Press.

Snowden, Lonnie R. 1982. "Services to the Underserved: An Overview of Contemporary Issues." Pp. 9-20 in *Reaching the Underserved: Mental Health Needs of Neglected Populations*, edited by L. Snowden. Berverly Hills: Sage.

Srole, Leo, Thomas S. Langner, and Stanley Mitchell. 1962. *Mental Health in the Metropolis: The Midtown Manhattan Study.* New York: New York University Press.

Stafford, Rebeca, Elaine Backman, and Pamela Dibona. 1977. "The Division of Labor among Cohabiting and Married Couples." *Journal of Marriage and the Family* 39: 43-57.

Stonequist, Everett V. 1961. *The Marginal Man: A Study in Personality and Culture Conflict.* New York: Russell and Russell.

Stoppard, Janet M. 2000. *Understanding Depression: Feminist Social Constructionist Approaches.* London: Routledge.

Strauss, Anselm L. 1987. *Qualitative Analysis for Social Scientists.* Cambridge: Cambridge University Press.

Strober, H. Myra, and Agnes M. K. Chan. 1998. "Husbands, Wives, and Housework: Graduates of Stanford and Tokyo Universities." *Feminist Economics* 4: 97-127.

Suan, Lance, and John Tyler. 1990. "Mental Health Values and Preference for Mental Health Resources of Japanese-American and CaucAsian American Students." *Professional Psychology: Research and Practice* 21: 291-296.

Sue, Stanley, Daine Fujino, Li-tze Hu, David Takeuchi, and Nolan Zane. 1991. "Community Mental Health Services for Ethnic Minority Groups: A Test of the Cultural Responsiveness Hypothesis." *Journal of Consulting and Clinical Psychology* 59: 533-540.

Sue, Stanley, and Herman McKinney. 1975. "Asian Americans in the Community Mental Health Care System." *American Journal of Orthopsychiatry* 45: 111-118.

Sue, Stanley, and James Morishima. 1982. *The Mental Health of Asian Americans.* San Francisco: Jossey-Bass.

Sue, Stanley, Charles Y. Nakamura, Rita Chi-Ying Chung, and Cindy Yee-Bradbury. 1994. "Mental Health Research on Asian Americans." *Journal of Community Psychology* 22: 61-67.

Sue, S., and D. Sue. 1974. "MMPI Comparisons between Asian American and non-Asian Students Utilizing a Student Health Psychiatric Clinic." *Journal of Counseling Psychology* 21: 423-427.

Swindler, A. 1986. "Culture in Action: Symbols and Strategies." *American Sociological Review* 51: 273-286.

Takeuchi, David T., Edwin Uehara, and Gloria Maramba. 1999. "Cultural Diversity and Mental Health Treatment." Pp. 550-65 in *A Handbook for the Study of MentalHealth: Social Contexts, Theories, and Systems,* edited by Allan V. Horwitz and Teresa L. Scheid. Cambridge: Cambridge University Press.

Thoits, Peggy A. 1999. "Sociological Approaches to Mental Illness." Pp. 121-38 in *A Handbook for the Study of Mental Health: Social Contexts, Theories, and Systems,* edited by Teresa L. Scheid. Cambridge: Cambridge University Press.

Thoits, Peggy A. 1986. "Gender and Marital Status Differences in Control and Distress: Common Stress versus Unique Stress Explanations." *Journal of Health and Social Behavior* 28: 7-22.

Thoits, Peggy A. 1983. "Multiple Identities and Psychological Well-being." *American Sociological Review* 48: 174-187.

Thomas, Gail E. 1995. "Notes on Asian American Employment." Pp. 265-268 in *Race and Ethnicity in America: Meeting the Challenge in the 21st Century,* edited by Gail E. Thomas. Washington, D. C.: Taylor & Francis.

Thomas, William I., and Florian Znaniecki. 1984. *The Polish Peasant in Europe and America.* Urbana: University of Illinois Press.

Thomas, Veronica G. 1994. "Using Feminist and Social Structural Analysis to Focus on the Health of Poor Women." *Women and Health* 22: 1-15.

Triandis, H. 1993. "Collectivism and Individualism as Cultural Syndromes." *Cross-Cultural Research* 27: 155-180.

Tsai, Gloria Y. 1998. *Middle-Class Taiwanese Immigrants' Adaptation to American Society: The Interactive Effects of Gender, Culture, Race, and Class.* Doctoral Dissertation, Department of Sociology, University of Pennsylvania. Pennsylvania, PA: University of Pennsylvania.

Tsai, Shu-Ling. 1988. Social Status Attainment: A Comparison Study of Aborigines, Minnaren, Hakka, and Waishengren. Pp. 1-44 in *Taiwan Society in Change.* K. Yang and H. Chu (eds.). Taipei: Institute of Ethnology, Academic Sinica.

Tseng, Yen-Fen, and Sue-Ching Jou. 2000. "Transnational Taiwan-Taiwanese American Linkages: A Transnationalism Approach to Return Migration." Paper presented at the *American Sociological Association.* Washington D.C.

Tseng, Yen-Fen. 1995. "Beyond "Little Taipei": The Development of Taiwanese Immigrant Businesses in Los Angeles." *International Migration Review* 29: 33-58.

Tseng, W. S. 1973. "The Concept of Personality in Confucian Thought." *Psychiatry* 36: 191-201.

Tu, Weiming. 1994. "Cultural China: The Periphery as the Center." Pp. 1-34 in *The Living Tree: The Changing Meaning of Being Chinese Today*, edited by Weiming Tu. Stanford: Stanford University Press.

Tuan, Mia. 1998. *Forever Foreigners or Honorary Whites? The Asian Ethnic Experience Today.* New Brunswick, NJ: Rutgers University Press.

Turner, R. Jay, and Patricia Roszell. 1994. "Psychological Resources and Stress Process." Pp. 179-210 in *Stress and Mental Health: Contemporary Issues and Prospects for the Future*, edited by I. H. Gotlieb. New York: Plenum.

Turner, R. J., B. Wheaton, and D. A. Lloyd. 1995. "The Epidemiology of Social Stress." *American Sociological Review* 60: 104-125.

Tyree, Andrea, and Katharine M. Donato. 1986. "A Demographic Overview of the International Migration of Women." in *International Migration: The Female Experience*, edited by Rita J. Simon and Caroline B. Brettell. Totowa, NJ: Rowman & Allanheld.

Tzou, J. 1999, June 17. "First Blueprint on Policy for Women." *Free China Journal*: 4.

Uba, Laura. 1994. *Asian Americans: Personality Patterns, Identity, and Mental Health.* New York: The Guilford Press.

U.S. Bureau of the Census. 2003. *The Foreign-Born Population: 2000.* Washington, D.C.: U.S. Department of Commerce.

U.S. Bureau of the Census. 1993. *The Foreign-Born Population in the United States, 1990 Census of Population, CP-3-1.* Washington, D.C.: U.S. Department of Commerce.

U.S. Bureau of the Census. 2001. Census 2000 Summary File (SF 1) 100 Percent Data. Washington, D.C.: U.S. Department of Commerce.

U.S. Bureau of the Census. 2001. Census 2000 Supplementary Survey Summary Tables. Washington, D.C.: U.S. Department of Commerce.

U.S. Immigration and Naturalization Service (INS). 2001. 2000 *Statistical Yearbook.* Washington, D.C.: U.S. Government Printing Office.

U.S. Immigration and Naturalization Service (INS). 2000. *1999 Statistical Yearbook.* Washington, D.C.: U.S. Government Printing Office.

U.S. Immigration and Naturalization Service (INS). 1999. *1998 Statistical Yearbook.* Washington, D.C.: U.S. Government Printing Office.

U.S. Immigration and Naturalization Service (INS). 1998. *1997 Statistical Yearbook.* Washington, D.C.: U.S. Government Printing Office.

U.S. Immigration and Naturalization Service (INS). 1997. *1996 Statistical Yearbook.* Washington, D.C.: U.S. Government Printing Office.

U.S. Immigration and Naturalization Service (INS). 1996. *1995 Statistical Yearbook.* Washington, D.C.: U.S. Government Printing Office.

U.S. Immigration and Naturalization Service (INS). 1995. *1994 Statistical Yearbook.* Washington, D.C.: U.S. Government Printing Office.

U.S. Immigration and Naturalization Service (INS). 1994. *1993 Statistical Yearbook.* Washington, D.C.: U.S. Government Printing Office.

U.S. Immigration and Naturalization Service (INS). 1993. *1992 Statistical Yearbook.* Washington, D.C.: U.S. Government Printing Office.

U.S. Immigration and Naturalization Service (INS). 1992. *1991 Statistical Yearbook.* Washington, D.C.: U.S. Government Printing Office.

U.S. Immigration and Naturalization Service (INS). 1991. *1990 Statistical Yearbook.* Washington, D.C.: U.S. Government Printing Office.

Ussher, Jane W. 1991. *Women's Madness: Misogyny or Mental Illness?* Hemel Hempstead: Harvester Wheatsheaf.

Van Deusen, John. 1982. "Health/Mental Health Studies of Indochinese Refugees: A Critical Overview." *Medical Anthropology* 6: 231-252.

Van Willigen, Marieke, and Patricia Drentea. 2001. "Benefits of Equitable Relationships: The Impact of Sense of Fairness, Household Division of

Labor, and Decision Making Power on Perceived Social Support." *Sex Roles* 44: 571-597.

Vannoy, Dana. 2001. "Introduction: Gender and Power." Pp. 1-14 in *Gender Mosaics*, edited by Dana Vannoy. Los Angeles: Roxbury.

Vega, William A., and Ruben G. Rumbaut. 1991. "Ethnic Minorities and Mental Health." *Annual Review of Sociology* 17: 351-383.

Vega, William A., George J. Warheit, Joanne Buhl-Auth, and Kenneth Meinhardt. 1984. "The Prevalence of Depressive Symptoms among Mexican Americans and Anglos." *American Journal of Epidemiology* 120: 592-607.

Vilhjalmsson, R. 1993. "Life Stress, Social Support, and Clinical Depression: A Reanalysis of the Literature." *Social Science and Medicine* 37: 331-342.

Villarreal, Magdalena. 1992. "The Poverty of Practice: Power, Gender and Intervention from an Actor-Oriented Perspective." Pp. 247-267 in *Battlefields of Knowledge: The Interlocking of Theory and Practice in Social Research and Development*, edited by Norman Long and Ann Long. London: Routledge.

Villones, R. 1989. "Women in the Silicon Valley." Pp. 172-176 in *Making Waves: An Anthology of Writings by and about Asian American Women*, edited by Asian Women United of California. Boston: Beacon.

Waldinger, Roger, and David Fitzgerald. 2004. "Transnationalism in Question." *American Journal of Sociology* 109(5): 1177-1195.

Walters, Viviene. 1993. "Stress, Anxiety and Depression: Women's Accounts of Their Health Problems." *Social Science and Medicine* 36: 393-402.

Walton, John. 1992. "Making the Theoretical Case." Pp. 121-137 in *What is a Case*, edited by Charles C. Ragin and Howard S. Becker. Cambridge: Cambridge University Press.

Warner, W. Lloyd, and Leo Srole. 1945. *The Social Systems of American Ethnic Groups*. New Haven: Yale University Press.

Watts, S. J. 1983. "Marriage Migration, a Neglected Form of Long-term Mobility: A Case Study from Ilorin, Nigeria." *International Migration Review* 17: 682-98.

Weber, Max. 1978. *Economy and Society*. Berkeley: University of California Press.

Williams, M. 1989. "Ladies on the Line: Punjabi Cannery Workers in Central California." Pp. 148-159 in *Making Waves: An Anthology of Writings by and about Asian American Women*, edited by Asian Women United of California. Boston: Beacon.

Wolf, Diane L. 1997. "Family Secrets: Transnational Struggles among Children of Filipino Immigrants." *Sociological Perspectives* 40: 457-482.

Wolf, Diane L. 1992a. *Factory Daughters: Gender, Household Dynamics, and Rural Industrialization in Java.* Berkeley: University of California Press.

Wolf, Diane L. 1992b. "There's No Place Like "Home": Emotional Transnationalism and the Struggles of Second-Generation Filipinos." Pp. 255-294 in *The Changing Face of Home: The Transnational Lives of the Second Generation*, edited by Peggy Levitt and Mary C. Waters. New York: Russell Sage Foundation.

Wong, Bernard P. 1982. *Chinatown: Economic Adaptation and Ethnic Identity of the Chinese.* New York: Holt, Rinehart and Winston.

Wong, Herbert Z. 1982. "Asian and Pacific Americans." Pp. 185-204 in *Reaching the Underserved: Mental Health Needs of Neglected Populations*, edited by Lonnie R. Snowden. Beverly Hills, CA: Sage.

Wong, Morrison G. 1998. "Post-1965 Asian Immigrants: Where Do They Come From, Where Are They Now, and Where Are They Going?" Pp. 202-220 in *The History and Immigration of Asian Americans*, edited by Franklin Ng. New York: Garland.

Wong, Yuk-Lin Renita, and A. Ka Tat Tsang. 2004. "When Asian Immigrant Women Speak: From Mental Health to Strategies of Being." *American Journal of Orthopsychiatry* 74(4): 456-466.

Woo, Deborah. 2000. "The Inventing and Reinventing of 'Model Minorities': The Cultural Veil Obscuring Structural Sources of Inequality." Pp. 193-212 in *Asian Americans: Experiences and Perspectives*, edited by Timothy P. Fong and Larry H. Shinagawa. Upper Saddle River, NJ: Prentice Hall.

Wu, Nai-teh. 1993. Ethnic Consciousness, Political Support, and National Identity: An Exploratory Study of Ethnic Politics Theories in Taiwan. Pp. 27-51 in *Ethnic Relations and National Identities*. Taipei: Institute for National Policy Research (in Chinese).

Xieh, H. F. & Wang, L. R. (1995). *Taiwanese Women's Family Values, Needs, and Policy Implications.* Research project report, National Science Foundation. Taipei: R.O.C. Executive Yuan. (in Chinese)

Xue, Xiao-Hua. 1996. *Educational Movements in Taiwan: An analysis on the State and Society.* Taipei: Qian-Wei. (in Chinese).

Yanagisako, Sylvia Junko. 1985. *Transforming the Past: Tradition and Kinship among Japanese Americans.* Stanford: Stanford University Press.

Yamamoto, J., Q. C. James, and N. Palley. 1968. "Cultural Problems in Psychiatric Therapy." *Archives of General Psychiatry* 19: 45-49.

Yamanaka, K., and K. McClelland. 1994. "Earning the Model-Minority Image: Diverse Strategies of Economic Adaptation by Asian American women." *Ethnic and Racial Studies* 17:79-114.

Yeoh, Brenda S. A., Peggy Teo, and Shirlena Huang. 2002. "Introduction: Women's Agencies and Activisms in the Asia-Pacific Region." Pp. 1-16 in *Gender Politics in the Asia-Pacific Region*, edited by Brenda S. A. Yeoh, Peggy Teo, and Shirlena Huang. London: Routledge.

Ying. 1988. "Depressive Symptomatology among Chinese-Americans as Measured by the CES-D." *Journal of Chinese Psychology* 44: 739-746.

Yu, W. H. 2001. "Family Demands, Gender Attitudes, and Married Women's Labor Force Participation: Comparing Japan and Taiwan. Pp.70-95 in *Women's Working Lives in East Asia*, edited by M.C. Brinton. Stanford, CA: Stanford University Press.

Zhou, Min. 2003. "Negotiating Culture and Ethnicity: Intergenerational Relations in Chinese Immigrant Families in the United States." Paper presented at the annual meeting of the Committee on Family Research (RC06), International Sociological Association. Taipei, Taiwan.

Zhou, Min. 1997. "Segmented Assimilation: Issues, Controversies, and Recent Research on the New Second Generation." *International Migration Review* 31: 975-1008.

Zollar, Ann Creighton, and J. Sherwood Williams. 1987. "The Contribution of Marriage to the Life Satisfaction of Black Adults." *Journal of Marriage and the Family* 49: 87-92.

Zuckerman, Diana M. 1989. "Stress, Self-Esteem, and Mental Health: How Does Gender Make a Difference?" *Sex Roles* 20: 429-44.

INDEX